A Common Purpose

**The Residents of Brookhaven at Lexington
Remember WWII and the Decades That Followed**

By the residents of
Brookhaven at Lexington

Nancy Lansdon Hubert, Editor

 Linnaean Press
.com

Cambridge, Massachusetts

This book is prepared, published, and distributed by Linnaean Press in collaboration with Brookhaven at Lexington. Linnaean Press is an imprint of Bentley Publishers, 1734 Massachusetts Avenue, Cambridge, Massachusetts 02138 USA.

A Common Purpose: The Residents of Brookhaven at Lexington Remember WWII and the Decades That Followed, by the residents of Brookhaven at Lexington

ISBN 978-0-8376-1729-9
Linnaean/Bentley Stock No. 5WW2
Mfg. code: 5WW2-01-1406

Library of Congress Cataloging-in-Publication Data
A common purpose : the residents of Brookhaven at Lexington remember WWII and the decades that followed / by the residents of Brookhaven at Lexington ; Nancy Lansdon Hubert, editor.
    pages cm
"Brookhaven at Lexington, Lexington, Massachusetts."
Includes index.
ISBN 978-0-8376-1729-9 (alkaline paper) 1. World War, 1939-1945--Personal narratives, American. 2. World War, 1939-1945--Social aspects--United States. 3. United States--Social conditions--1933-1945. 4. Soldiers--United States--Biography. 5. World War, 1939-1945--Veterans--United States--Biography. 6. Civilians in war--United States--Biography. 7. Older people--Massachusetts--Lexington--Biography. 8. Brookhaven at Lexington (Nursing home)--Biography. I. Hubert, Nancy Lansdon, 1935- II. Brookhaven at Lexington (Nursing home)
    D811.A2C597 2014
    940.54'127309227444--dc23
                    2014021265

Design by Andrea Corbin, Linnaean Press.

The paper used in this publication is acid free and meets the requirements of the National Standard for Information Sciences-Permanence of Paper for Printed Library Materials. ♾

Manufactured in the United States of America.

Contents

Foreword

I AM SO PLEASED that we were able to collect and publish the stories of so many of our residents in their younger years. In the years to come the firsthand account of those days will be gone and it is so important that we collect the stories and share them.

I was so moved after reading the stories of the sacrifices that were made by everyone involved. These stories are not only a recount of battles, but also of what life was like for those not serving in the military. I have a much better appreciation for all that this group did for our country. I am so proud that they are part of the Brookhaven Community.

James M. Freehling
CEO/President
Brookhaven at Lexington

Publisher's Note

EACH OF THE contributors to this book began their individual journey through the events and geography of the twentieth century in a different situation. And each of the personal narratives here is rooted in a different way in the displacement and mobilization of World War Two and the decades that followed.

Taken together, however, these stories speak of a shared set of values and hopes, of the openness of American society, and of the educational and economic opportunities that made it possible for each of the authors to build a life here, and, eventually, come together and form a new community at Brookhaven at Lexington.

It's not surprising that such a resourceful and enterprising group would come up with the idea of a project to share their experiences and pass them to the next generation. Nor is it much of a surprise to those who know Joan Keenan and Kathryn McCarthy, that after putting together a team, they reached out with infinite charm to ask for "a little technical assistance on a new publishing project…"

And so it's been a privilege and a lot of fun to work with the residents and staff of Brookhaven at Lexington to prepare this book for publication.

Nancy Hubert quickly took on the role of editor, and has done a wonderful job pulling together and organizing manuscript, photographs, and biographical profiles—and has been enormously patient with round after round of editorial queries and requests for materials.

Broookhaven's professional leadership, guided by CEO Jim Freehling and supported by tremendous hands-on contributions by Sue Kirkpatrick and Laura Anderson, have played an absolutely essential role in supporting the residents and making this book possible. The Dana Home Foundation also contributed generously to help support some of the direct external costs of publication.

At the Linnaean Press, Janet Barnes has provided project guidance and Andrea Corbin has handled design and production editing.

Finally, I would like to personally thank Joan Keenan and Kathryn McCarthy for their many years of friendship and kindness, which is the basis for our contribution to this project—with the usual caveat that they should get only the credit and none of the blame.

Michael Bentley
Cambridge, June 2014

Preface

THIS BOOK IS a thoughtful and poignant reminder of war. They are the stories of men and women now living at Brookhaven at Lexington who were "there," their lives disrupted and changed by World War II. They are remarkable for their depth and variety and as a picture of what it was like living in a time of war. They inspire, even now, a sense of pride in realizing how Americans joined together, united in defending and defeating the threats to our way of life. In the abstract, war is a terrible thing; these stories are personal and remind us of the turmoil, sacrifices and dedication of a country at war on two fronts.

The attack on Pearl Harbor galvanized the country as a whole and moved individual citizens to unite for defense. What is often implied but left unsaid about the country during World War II, is the spirit of unity and determination demonstrated by the many American men and women who prepared for and went to war. Young men and women served in the armed forces; others found ways to support the war effort at home. They did essential work in the defense industry, volunteered for the Red Cross, or as plane spotters and air raid wardens, helped entertain soldiers and grew Victory Gardens. Even children had a role; they bought savings bond stamps, helped with scrap metal drives, collected cans and newspapers. This was everyone's war and everyone wanted to do whatever needed to be done. We were slow in getting started, and there were many glitches to be overcome, but once the country was organized it was a fearsome force. Has our country ever been so united in common cause as it was then? Times—and circumstances—change but I am still deeply moved by the stories of World War II and what they tell us about our country.

I think Tom Brokaw said it best; these people are of "The Greatest Generation." Our community is fortunate to have residents of that generation who later accomplished much throughout their lives—just scan a few of this book's biographies. Their wartime experiences were often a serious influence on their subsequent lives. One of the goals for this book, in addition to the histories, is that it serves as a reference guide for those who want to learn more about World War II and a country at war. Statistics and timelines provide the facts of war but they can't tell the human stories: the bravery of young men under fire; the intensity of essential defense work; the grief of a family when a cherished child is killed; the women left at home to manage families on their own as they waited for news of husbands, fathers or the special guy in their lives. These stories represent the basic values of our country and how fiercely we defended these values.

Our book was the brainchild of two wonderful women, Joan Keenan and Kathryn McCarthy, who realized there were many people at Brookhaven at Lexington who served in and lived during World War II and who had stories to be told. Without them, there wouldn't be a book.

Nancy L. Hubert, Editor

*Dedicated to the residents and staff
of Brookhaven at Lexington*

"IF WE ARE to heed the past to prepare for the future, we should listen to these quiet voices of a generation that speaks to us of duty and honor, sacrifice and accomplishment. I hope more of these stories will be preserved and cherished as reminders of all that we owe them and all that we can learn from them."

Tom Brokaw, *The Greatest Generation Speaks:
Letters and Reflections*
Random House, New York, NY 1999

Part One

War on the Horizon

THE UNITED STATES did not enter World War II until 1941 after Pearl Harbor was bombed, even though Hitler and the Germans had been capturing most of Europe during the previous two years. England, though heavily bombed, had managed to resist the Germans but lacked resources with which to fight. Refugees were fleeing from the Germans and the events of Kristallnacht were a warning of things to come for the Jews.

This first section of World War II remembrances begins before the United States was officially in the war and tells mainly the stories of fleeing refugees and their trials trying to escape from the Germans. Most war stories tell of battles; these stories remind us that war affects everyone, not just the men who fight but also those at home. There were many heroic deeds by citizens in Europe in World War II, and these are called to mind here.

Helen C. Aronson

Born 1927 · Berlin, Germany

Helen Chanee Aronson discussing geodes and crystals with colleagues at a mineral show in Tucson, Arizona, in the early 1990s. Helen loved incorporating minerals into her decorating business in New York City.

I was born Helen Fortgang in Berlin, Germany, in 1927. My family fled Germany in 1938 and we came to the United States in 1940. I was educated in New York City and started college at New York University in 1945. I married Marvin Aronson in 1948 and transferred to the University of Michigan where he was getting his PhD in psychology. After our education, we returned to New York and we had two children, David and Ruth. We lived in Mt. Vernon, New York, and my husband worked in Manhattan. After going to school, I worked part-time as an interior decorator. After he died in 2011, I moved to Brookhaven in 2012.

June 23, 1938—My War Begins

By Helen C. Aronson

Transcribed by: Deirdre Delaney

> "When the American officer told us again we couldn't make it, my father, who was usually a very mild-mannered man, had a real loud outburst… The head of the consulate came out and said, "What's going on here?" and my father said, "We have all the papers and every time we come here, your employee says that it's not good enough and it's not right. I think at this point it's just pure anti-Semitism and that he doesn't want us to go to America." The head of the consulate looked over our affidavits, our jewelry, and counted our money. Then he took out a stamp and next to our name it said accepted. We were thrilled that we would finally leave Portugal and go to America."

ON JUNE 23, 1938, I woke up to the noise of marching feet and singing and I realized that today my sister and I would be going to Belgium by train; I was scared. We had to leave our parents and school. The school I went to in Berlin, Germany, was a Jewish school because of an edict stating that Jewish children could not attend Gentile schools. That was an ordeal for me because the school was named after the Jewish Zionist Theodore Herzl, and it was located on Adolf Hitler Square, so just crossing that square, where the SS men were throwing stones and making fun of us, was a very scary thing for me. I didn't really like school. I wasn't looking forward to leaving, but my parents told my sister and me that we had to go by ourselves to my grandmother in Antwerp. The train would stop in Brussels and my aunt would come and meet us at the station.

When my aunt arrived with my uncle, we drove back to Antwerp, which was about an hour away, and we went to my grandmother's house, where we were going to stay until my parents came to be reunited with my sister and me. I was ten years old and my sister was twelve and since there was no adult supervision, my sister took over the role of making sure that I behaved well and that I did the right thing. She was very kind and I kept telling her, "I'm afraid, I'm afraid," and she would get annoyed and say, "Stop saying you're afraid, this is where we are and I don't want to hear it." I had an uncle who at the time was only nineteen and he would take me occasionally on his bicycle when my family went to the countryside, where we stayed for a couple of weeks during the summer.

After six to eight weeks in Antwerp, my parents finally arrived in Belgium. Even though they had the right papers to enter Belgium, they wanted to go illegally, so the Germans wouldn't know. They tried to cross the border between Switzerland and Germany and they were pushed back. The Swiss border patrol wouldn't let them come in, but there were people, who, for a certain amount of money, would smuggle you across isolated places where there were forests and where there were no border agents, and so my parents went to Holland, and then they came from Holland to Belgium.

When my parents came at least we were united and we were happy, because my grandmother, who was my father's mother, did not speak German, and we did not speak Flemish. She also spoke Yiddish, but we did not know Yiddish, so it was very difficult to communicate. She wasn't what you can think of as a loving grandma. I found out later that she was only 60, but my sister and I thought she was the most ancient thing we ever saw, so now at 84, I think it's very funny. My grandmother was very attached to my father and even though we were ready to go to Bolivia because we couldn't enter the United States, she kept saying, "Don't leave now, wait." We had reservations on a ship and my grandmother kept saying, "Take the next ship, stay." My father was very much under her influence and he kept postponing. We had papers from Bolivia that said that we were citizens of Bolivia. Those papers became very handy later in our journey, but at this time, we just figured that we would wait and take the next ship. Then of course it got too late, and on May 10, 1940, the Germans invaded Belgium and Holland. We had our first bombardment in Antwerp, very close to our hotel and left that day, realizing that we had to get out of Belgium, and that started our escape, leaving Belgium and entering France.

There were lots and lots of refugees walking, and the cars were bumper to bumper, so we had to abandon our car. With my parents, sister, and me were my grandmother, my uncle, his wife, and their six-week-old baby. We took as much as we could carry and started to walk, figuring the farther away we were from Belgium, the farther we were from the Germans. At night we took refuge by knocking on doors of private citizens and asking if we could sleep on the floor, in the basement, or the kitchen, just until sunrise, because we were going through France and we didn't want to travel at night.

Among the refugees, there was an open truck with a farmer driving, and his pregnant wife on the open truck bed who would periodically throw up. Nobody knew where to go, or how to do it, so my father asked the farmer, "Look, if we give you so much money, would you let us be next to your wife on the open truck because we've been walking and this way you have money in your pocket and we have a ride?" So that's how we got through a quarter of France. We took the southern route. I can't really explain what that is, because I'm not sure, but we avoided the Battle of Dunkirk when we went through. That battle took place about a day and a half after we left Dunkirk.

As children, we were very aware that it was touch and go. My sister was very stoic and I was always saying, "I'm afraid, I'm afraid." My mother tried to comfort us, because there were bombs falling near the truck. Some people got hit and died, so my mother said that not every bomb explodes or hits. That wasn't much of a comfort, but it was the only thing she could say to make us feel better. We were going in an open truck and maybe a mile away, the Germans rounded up a whole bunch of refugees and said that somebody had shot a German, and they were going to take hostages. They counted out five people to be shot. So you didn't know. You went to the right where they were or you went to the left. Everything was very uncertain and scary. And also, what happened then was the Luftwaffe, which was the German air force, would dive down and strafe. In other words, they were up high, and then they dove all the way down and shot people on the road and then they went back up. It was all very unpredictable.

There came a time when the farmer's wife was really feeling badly and the farmer was not Jewish. He said, "You know what, I think we'll stay here in this little town in France. My wife isn't feeling well and we can't just keep going. I don't know where we are going and we're not going any farther." And my father said to him, "Well look, when you don't go farther you won't need the truck. You're going to be settling in this little village, so would you consider selling me the truck?" And that's what happened. We bought the truck from him, he stayed. Now who was going to drive the truck? My uncle had a car, but he had never driven a truck before. We found ourselves in a part of the country with mountainous roads because we were crossing the Pyrenees, the mountains between France and Spain. In order to save gasoline, my uncle thought he would shut off the engine at the top of the hills and let us just roll down them, but to turn the engine off at the precise moment was difficult. At one point when he turned it off, we began slowly going backwards, and behind us were rows of cars, so my father grabbed the emergency brake, pulled it up, and called my uncle an idiot. Then they started the engine again and moved forward to avoid this disaster.

We were out of reach of the Germans marching into France. Maybe they took a different route, I don't know. We stopped at a place, Royan, that was in southern France, and we rented a house and were waiting for President Roosevelt to make an announcement about whether or not the Americans were going to help defend Paris, so that Paris would not fall and would stay French. It was not sure, and we all sat around the radio to hear what Roosevelt had to say and he said, in effect, "At this time we are going to let the French do their thing and we are not going to send help," and now we figured it was really serious because the French couldn't defend Paris alone. We knew that we couldn't stay in the south of France; we knew that we had to move towards Spain. When the French heard that the Americans were not going to help, they put out a new order that all refugees had to go back to their homes (some were French, some Belgian and some German), so whenever the refugees tried to move on, they were stopped.

My grandmother was listed as a refugee and my father said, "What should I do? If I take her with me and they say she must go back home, to Antwerp, then she'll go right back to the Germans." We had other family in southern France, a sister of my father with her husband and two children and another in-law, and my father said, "Look, you have another daughter with a husband and two children, and they're here too. My family is going to take a chance to go through because we have that letter from the Bolivian embassy." So very reluctantly we left my grandmother, two uncles and two aunts, two children and the baby, and continued alone on the truck.

Now the average policemen on the street were not usually very well educated and they couldn't read Spanish, so they didn't know what our letter from the Bolivian government said, but it started with "The Bolivian Embassy hereby," and when they read that far, they would say, "passe, excusez-moi," and we got through, all the way to Hendaye, which is a border town, to cross into Spain. We parked the truck somewhere and stayed in a church. It was really raining like crazy, and the border police from Spain sent us back a few times, but we had some money, some jewelry, which we showed them. We had also sewn in our shoulder pads and pockets more jewelry and diamonds, and we put stuff in the dirty diapers, which they didn't want to open up to see what we had, so we finally got through to Spain.

We went to San Sebastian. We thought we'd stay there, and take baths; we hadn't taken baths in months. My father was going to sell some of his diamonds to a local jeweler to have cash, but the local jeweler knew our position and offered us maybe a fifth of what they were worth; my father refused to sell them because they were worth much more.

My father told us to pack, and that we were going to try to go to Portugal, but that wasn't easy either because Portugal didn't have many trains running. We literally got on the last train. To get on it we were standing in line and it wasn't at all sure that we were going to get on it. There was a Polish officer whose white gloved hands came to push through, and my mother hit him with an umbrella and said, "Women and children come first." The man was in such shock. He was a big officer and we just went in and we never knew what happened to him. We got on the train. It's hard to know who else got on the train; it's a big blur, but in just a few hours, maybe five hours, we got to Portugal and we stopped in a little town called Curia. It was a resort town and the local people were glad for the business, so nobody stopped us and we stayed there for six months.

Periodically we went to the American consulate which was in a city called Porto. I would get hives that would swell up on my eyes and my lip, and we were afraid that the Americans would think that I had some strange disease. We would walk up and down the street and we would wait, hoping the swelling would go away, and it eventually did, and we went into the consulate. We were rejected twice, with excuses that we didn't have the right papers or that our affidavits weren't good. We did have affidavits from a very distant relative that my father knew and did business with between Germany and America. He had given us good papers, in addition to which we thought we had enough money with us, but we were rejected twice. When the American officer told us again we couldn't make it, my father, who was usually a very mild-mannered man, had a real loud outburst; today we would say he lost it. The head of the consulate came out and said, "What's going on here?" and my father said, "We have all the papers and every time we come here, your employee says that it's not good enough and it's not right. I think at this point it's just pure anti-Semitism and that he doesn't want us to go to America." The head of the consulate looked over our affidavits, our jewelry, and counted our money. Then he took out a stamp and next to our name it said accepted. We were thrilled that we would finally leave Portugal and go to America.

This brings us to December 1940. America did not enter the war until 1941, but I felt safe and relieved during the time before Pearl Harbor. My story wasn't really during the time when America went to war, but it certainly was my war, which started when Hitler told the Jewish children that they couldn't go to public schools.

Lilly Wolffers Szonyi

Born 1924 · St. Gallen, Switzerland

For Europeans the war is finally over. Lilly Szonyi got married, 1945, Zurich, Switzerland.

Lilly Wolffers Szonyi was born April 25, 1924, in St. Gallen, Switzerland, the youngest of three children (her brother Hans was nine years older, her brother Artur ten years older). Her family moved to Berlin in 1927 and thought about applying for German citizenship but because of her brother Artur's strenuous objections did not do so. On August 1, 1939, the family moved to Zurich. There Lilly worked for the Swiss Refugee Assistance organization and a number of other jobs in her late teens and early twenties. She met her husband, Geza Szonyi, a Hungarian-Jewish graduate student at the University of Zurich in 1942. They married in 1945 and had a daughter, Petra, and a son, David. In 1952 the family moved to Canada and came to the United States in 1953. After receiving an MSW from the University of Pennsylvania in 1960 she worked as a clinical social worker and later was in private practice. She moved with her husband Geza to Brookhaven in 2001. He died in 2009.

A Hanukkah Memory

By Lilly Wolffers Szonyi

> "It had become a symbol for all victims of Jewish persecutions, but also a symbol of hope and survival… May it reflect our faith in a more peaceful world."

I CAME HOME from school late afternoon and a little old man followed me up the three flights of stairs to our apartment. This was unusual because we rarely expected visitors at that time of the day. As I fumbled for my keys, he asked whether this was the Wolffers residence and whether Mr. Wolffers might be home. Yes, my father was home and without asking further questions I led him into the living room, where my dad was reading the paper. But now I was curious what this visit was all about.

It was in the spring of 1939 in Berlin, Germany. Strange and terrible things were happening all around us, and my father didn't seem uncomfortable with this man's visit. He simply asked him what he could do for him. The man, without actually introducing himself and giving his name, stated that he had heard that our family was Swiss and that we would be able to leave for Switzerland in the near future. Dad nodded and looked rather guilty for having been dealt such a fortunate fate of being a Swiss citizen. "I would like to ask you a very big favor," the little old man now said in a shaky voice and pulled out a small package he had kept hidden inside his jacket. "Please tell me what you have in mind," my father responded. Now, he opened the package and as I moved closer to see better I noticed his hands were trembling as he unwrapped a beautiful small Hanukkah Menorah in shining silver. "Lilly, look!" my father said with awe, "how extraordinary."

"It is," the man whispered—"it has been in our family for a very long time, and I want you to take it with you to Switzerland, to keep it safe. If I ever get out of Germany alive I'll reclaim it." My dad wondered how he would find us in Zurich, but the little man wasn't worried about that. He simply said, "I shall find you." He gripped my dad's hand in gratitude and almost kissed him. I don't know who was more shaken, my father or he. And then he left.

I have never forgotten this incident, although it happened more than 60 years ago. The Menorah traveled with us to Zurich in August 1939. World War II broke out on September 1 of the same year. Needless to say that we never heard from this "little old man" again. But we didn't give up hope for two or three years; then the hope faded and vanished altogether.

My mother polished the delicate silver Menorah each December when Hanukkah came around. We never talked about the incident or the Menorah because by now it had become a symbol for all victims of Jewish persecutions now and over the centuries, but also a symbol of hope and survival, like the story of the Menorah itself.

When Geza and I got married and moved to Canada in 1952 my parents gave us the Menorah. It was meant to be passed from one generation to another and it will survive us and our children. May it reflect our faith in a more peaceful world.

Heidi White

Born 1930 · Cologne, Germany

Heidi White, third grade, elementary school, Essen, Germany.

Heidi White was the daughter of Maria and Joseph Hofmann. She was born and raised in Cologne, Germany, and graduated from Aachen High School in Aachen, Germany, and St. Leonard's School. In 1954, while studying French language and literature at the University of Heidelberg, she met an American Fulbright student, Donald White, who became her husband. Married in 1954 in Aachen a few months later, she and her husband moved to New Haven, Connecticut. In 1957 they moved to Amherst, Massachusetts, where she worked at the Robert Frost Library. In 1986 Heidi and Donald moved to the Boston area where she worked at the Tufts College Library. Heidi published a book, *At the Edge of the Storm*, about her wartime experiences in 2003.

Cologne, Germany, 1942–1945

By Heidi White

> "For the next three years bombs were the nightly rain from the sky… I finally reached our street. It was now late afternoon. I cautiously stepped around a crater in front of our house, hoping that the dud, which my father had mentioned in his letter, had been defused and taken away. The building looked dead, with empty holes where windows had been. The heavy wooden front door was slightly ajar, but I had to struggle with all my strength to push it open."

IN 1942, THE AIR RAIDS on Cologne intensified, the piercing sound of the sirens rousing me from sleep every night. I was eleven years old at that time. Alongside my parents and my brothers I stumbled down the four flights of stairs to the cellar. Sometimes, through the cracks of the blackout shades, I could see the bright fingers of the searchlights moving across the dark sky, and hear the first shots of flak.

During the night of May 30 in 1942, a thousand British airplanes had flown over Cologne and had dropped their deadly cargo, 2,000 tons of bombs within 90 minutes. The Hochhaus, an office building 18 stories high only a few blocks from us, had turned into a giant flaming torch, still burning over the next few days. During another air raid attack a few incendiaries had torn through the roof and one had burst into flames in our apartment. Later that night I watched with horror as flames leapt out some windows of our neighboring house from floor to floor. Yet in the morning our house was still standing—the fire hadn't spread.

For the next three years bombs were the nightly rain from the sky. I stood huddled in the cellar, frightened yet praying for the

British and Americans to bring an end to the war as my parents had told me to do.

―――――――

At the end of the summer of 1944 my parents sent me to a Kinderheim in the Harz Mountains in the middle of Germany. It had been an orphanage at one time, but at the beginning of the war the nuns had opened their doors to refugees of all ages. I returned to Cologne in August of 1945. I had been able to get a ride on a truck that had brought salt from the Harz Mountains to Cologne. A woman my aunt knew, Frau Loehrer, was supposed to look after me during the long and dangerous travel. I knew that my parents were alive, but not where they were. In his last letter, which I received in February, my father mentioned that he, my mother and two of my older brothers would try to find shelter in a village near Cologne.

―――――――

Standing on an August day in 1945 next to the cathedral which seemed to be undamaged, I could see nothing but an immense field of ruins. Everything was flattened or crushed or blown to pieces, leaving here and there a torched brick wall, a blackened tree stump or twisted electrical wires. People scuttled amid the rubble, hushed and exhausted. An occasional rumble of an army truck punctuated a heavy silence that had settled over the entire city. Sentences from my father's last letter came to my mind: "When you hear the gospel of the end of the world, don't forget that the people in Cologne have suffered a temporary apocalypse." Standing next to Frau Loehrer, I was lost in thoughts about the Four Horsemen, about death and famine. Suddenly I heard her say that she would have to leave me there, that she needed to find a truck or car to get to Aachen.

Cologne, Germany, Cathedral in ruins. Struck by 14 Allied aerial bombs, part of the cathedral remained standing. These ruins supposedly were used by Allied aircraft as an easily recognized navigational landmark on their way deeper into Germany. Repairs on the Cathedral were completed in 1956 and it was named a UNESCO World Heritage Site in 1996.

"You know your way home, don't you? It's not very far and it's only afternoon. I hope you'll find your parents," she said.

I knew the names of the side streets, and tried to find them, but there were no more streets. A narrow path wound up and down over piles of rubble. I followed a couple of people, passing crosses made from birch branches. They marked graves; people still lay buried under the demolished houses.

I finally reached our street. It was now late afternoon. I cautiously stepped around a crater in front of our house, hoping that the dud, which my father had mentioned in his letter, had been defused and taken away. The building looked dead, with empty holes where windows had been. The heavy wooden front door was slightly ajar, but I had to struggle with all my strength to push it open. Gone were the red carpet and the flowerpots. Mortar and glass pieces covered the marble staircase. A sudden gust whirled gray dust around me and made my eyes well up. Our apartment door was dangling on a couple of hinges.

When I stepped into the apartment I heard a woman's voice. It was a colleague of my father. She told me that the Americans had appointed my father editor-in-chief of the first free German newspaper which was published in Aachen. He would only come to Cologne on weekends. My mother and my brothers were still in the village where they had found refuge. She didn't know when they would come back. She told me that she had to leave right away. "There's nobody in the whole building," she said. She then asked me if I had food. "There are some scraps, perhaps a little flour, left in the cupboard and a pail with water in the kitchen," she said. As she rushed out of the door, I said, trying to be courageous, "I'll be fine. I have some raspberries."

I wandered from room to room, staring at the desolation. Part of a wall leading to my room had crumbled. At the end of the hallway, in my parents' bedroom, I found a clean mattress. Some blankets were hidden under the bed. As the evening descended over the ruins of Cologne, I barricaded myself in my parents' bedroom and soon fell into a troubled sleep. In the middle of the night shots rang out. I heard screams, then more shots. "Please, God," I prayed as I lay shivering under the blanket, "don't let anybody come here. There isn't anything to steal anymore." The voices soon faded and I drifted off to sleep again. I dreamed of the four Horsemen of the Apocalypse still galloping over the city wielding the swords and spears.

I don't remember how long I had to fend for myself in the ruins of Cologne, perhaps for up to a week. I was overjoyed when I finally heard my mother's and my brother's voices as they entered the apartment. For the next months we still slept most nights in the village, but came back to our apartment to sweep glass shards and mortar pieces, to nail cardboard pieces or wooden planks to some of the windows. By the beginning of October we were able to install another potbelly stove—besides the one in the kitchen—in one of the rooms that served us as a family room. When my oldest brother was discharged from an American POW camp, and when my father was visiting us on a weekend, our family was finally together again. The war was over, but it still took three more years until we had enough food to eat.

These are mainly excerpts from my book *At the Edge of the Storm*.

―――――――

*Excerpts and photos from *At the Edge of the Storm: Memories of My German Childhood During World War II* by Heidi White. Published by the author, 2003.

Eva Gil

Born 1925 • Berlin, Germany

Eva Gil, approximately 2010, Lexington, Massachusetts.

Eva Gil was the daughter of Walter and Jenny Bresslauer. She was born in Berlin in 1925 and attended school there until she was nine, when her family moved to Palestine to escape the growing threat of Nazism. In Palestine she attended Hebrew schools and was active in sports, especially fencing. After leaving high school she worked as a secretary and then worked for the Youth Probation Service in Tel Aviv where she met her husband, David. They moved to the United States in 1957 with their twin sons. After they moved to Boston, Massachusetts, Eva attended Boston University and received a BA in psychology (Phi Beta Kappa) and an MA in counseling psychology also from Boston University. She then worked as a psychotherapist with a mental health agency. She studied Spanish and visited Mexico as a member of the Lexington-Dolores Hidalgo Sister organization for which she also served as treasurer. She moved to Brookhaven with her husband David in 2007.

My Life During World War II

By Eva Gil

"Early in the war, Tel Aviv was bombed on a summer afternoon, with a relatively large number of casualties. I remember the story of the hapless woman who was at the hairdresser and died while connected to a permanent-hair-wave machine. I was in a tailor shop in the neighborhood. When bits and pieces from the ceiling started to fall down, we dove under a table and then next to a retaining wall."

WORLD WAR II began in Europe in 1939. I then lived in Tel Aviv, Palestine, which was British. Our economy had crashed, partly due to the Arab uprising against the British and the then much smaller Jewish population, which predated the war. I was 15 years old and the most serious consequence for me was that I could no longer attend high school. An abbreviated business course prepared me for secretarial work. I was very much aware that it was my last chance at schooling.

Early in the war, Tel Aviv was bombed on a summer afternoon, with a relatively large number of casualties. I remember the story of the hapless woman who was at the hairdresser and died while connected to a permanent-hair-wave machine. I was in a tailor shop in the neighborhood. When bits and pieces from the ceiling started to fall down, we dove under a table and then next to a retaining wall. Through my sports club we were later trained to carry patients on stretchers. Fortunately, there was only one more minor air attack, but many air-raid warnings when we had to assemble.

The bulk of my war experience was actually my work at the Tel Aviv Services Club, which looked after service members on leave. I had an office job there but it was mainly a well-run and popular volunteer organization, sponsored by the municipality. I met a lot of interesting people of different ages and backgrounds. After work there were opportunities for dates and dances and sometimes good food at camp messes.

My sister joined the ATS—British Women's Army—when she was younger than 17. She served in Gaza and Cairo, mainly out of harm's way. After the war, she married an Australian air force officer whom she met in Cairo. She still lives in Australia. The war certainly changed her life.

Jacqueline Villars

Born 1928 · Neuchâtel, Switzerland

Jacqueline Villars at home in Switzerland at end of World War II, 1945.

I was born in 1928 in Neuchâtel, Switzerland. My father, Felix DuBois, was trained as an architect but, unable to find work at home in Switzerland, had gone to Paris where he worked as a graphic artist. There he met my mother Marie Trocmé, and after they were married they returned to Switzerland. My mother was French, of Huguenot descent. Growing up in Paris and with tuberculosis endemic in Europe, my mother wanted to be sure we got plenty of sunshine and fresh air. We lived in a little village above the Lake of Bienne; we got lots of fresh air but not much schooling. Later, my parents moved down the slope so we could attend better schools. My father was conscientious objector and was posted to the front as a paramedic. We learned at an early age not to divulge family matters anywhere, knowing that the German "Fifth Column" was everywhere as was the poster warning "the walls have ears." After the war I graduated from a school of graphic arts (1948) and married a theoretical nuclear physicist who couldn't find a job in his field in Switzerland. He received a fellowship in 1949 at the Institute for Advanced Study in Princeton, New Jersey, where Robert Oppenheimer had recently been named director, and we came to the United States. My husband was offered a position at MIT where he remained until retirement. We brought up our four children in Belmont, Massachusetts. I spent some time volunteering as a den mother, at MIT with foreign students, and worked on the side as a tapestry designer.

Sheltering Refugees

By Jacqueline Villars

"One morning the Gestapo arrived at the village of Chambon with buses, rounded up the 400 Jewish children and deported them to extermination camps (though it was not yet known that they were killing people at the camps). Daniel Trocmé, a young cousin of my uncle, was a teacher at the school and in charge of these children, some of whom were just eight years old. He felt that it would be too hard to let them go alone on such a long trip, so he decided to join them. He never came back."

MY SIBLINGS AND I were born in Switzerland to a Swiss father and a French mother. We spent the Second World War there. We were spared the German occupation but lived in constant fear that we could be invaded at anytime. All able-bodied men were called into service to protect the frontiers, as we were completely surrounded by the Germans in the west, north and east and Mussolini's army in the south.

My father, being a conscientious objector, was assigned to an army paramedic unit and was allocated a bedroom in order to have a place to care for the sick. Otherwise, most ordinary soldiers slept on straw in farms and barns where they were stationed because there were very few military camps. Men served for three months at a time, then were sent back to their civilian jobs for three months, then back again to the army—back and forth for the duration of the war. Boys were drafted at the age of 17; girls of the same age had to serve one month each year during the summer, living on a farm and working in the fields because manpower was scarce. For city girls like me it was tough. Blue jeans and sneakers did not exist. Women did not wear pants in those times except for skiing. We often had bloody arms and legs after collecting hay all day.

Mother was a descendant of French Huguenots (Protestants) who had been persecuted in the 16 and 17 centuries. They were a very small minority in France in 1940. After France surrendered to the Nazis, life became very hard for all French citizens and food was in short supply because the Germans confiscated all they could. Communications between occupied (northern) France and Switzerland were cut off and we had no way of getting news from family members who were still in France, except through the South where letters could be forwarded to the North. The Germans had cut France in half, letting Vichy France govern the South until 1942 when the rest of the country was invaded.

One of my maternal uncles, Andre Trocmé, was a Protestant and pacifist minister in a small village in the Cevennes, a mountainous area 100 miles west of Lyons, which at the time was in "Free France" (Vichy France). Many Jewish refugees escaping arrests in the North sought asylum in his village, Le Chambon-sur Lignon. All his parishioners, mostly farmers, housed and fed them at the risk of their lives, considering this a normal Christian duty. As the number of refugees increased, my uncle and an associate minister organized an underground railroad system to smuggle them across the Swiss border, 250 miles away. It was an arduous and risky enterprise getting through Vichy France and the pro-Nazi militia, but during the four years of war this small village of 5,000 inhabitants saved about 5,000 Jewish lives.

The American Quakers who had an office near Marseille asked my uncle to take 400 children they had saved when their parents had been arrested by the militia. They also gave financial help to feed, clothe and educate them because the villagers were very poor. In 1942 the Quakers had to flee as the Germans, fearing an invasion from the British and American forces who had just defeated Rommel's army in Africa, invaded southern France. By late 1943 the Nazis were also losing ground in Russia, consequently they became more and more aggressive in France, while guerilla fighters increased their attacks.

One morning the Gestapo arrived at the village of Chambon with buses, rounded up the 400 Jewish children and deported them to extermination camps (though it was not yet known that they were killing people at the camps). Daniel Trocmé, a young cousin of my uncle, was a teacher at the school and in charge of these children, some of whom were just eight years old. He felt that it would be too hard to let them go alone on such a long trip, so he decided to join them. He never came back.

Near the end of the war my uncle had to go into hiding for defying German laws. Shortly thereafter he was caught by the Gestapo, but miraculously escaped.

After the landing of Allied troops in Normandy in June 1944, the Germans retreated hastily, fighting and destroying everything they could. The "maquisards" (French resisters) pursued them from the South and Allied troops pursued them from the North. Fierce battles took place along the Swiss border and we could hear firing and bombing day and night. Schools were closed to prepare room to house foreign wounded soldiers. Straw and dry grass was spread on classroom floors because we had no other facilities to accommodate their large numbers. French, American, British, German and some Polish soldiers were all accommodated. High school male students, including my brother, were kept on hand to help or carry the wounded to military doctors. Many of the Germans were as young as 14. Most of these youngsters surrendered as refugees, but the Gestapo members were denied entrance, as they were considered war criminals. Once behind the Rhine, the Germans blew up their bridges and prepared their own resistance with fierce battles all the way to Berlin, until they surrendered.

All Europeans were deeply grateful to the Americans, who came to our rescue, who gave their lives to save ours from a fascist regime of five years. Without their sacrifices this part of the world would not have known its more than half a century of peace.

I say to them: "un grand MERCI."

The story of André Trocmé and Le Chambon was told in a book, *Lest Innocent Blood Be Shed, The Story of the Village of Le Chambon and How Goodness Happened There*, Philip Hallie, New York, N.Y., Harper Collins, orig. 1979, rev. 1994.

There was also a movie, *Weapons of the Spirit: The Astonishing Story of a Unique Conspiracy of Goodness* written, produced and directed by Pierre Sauvage, Pierre Sauvage Productions/Chambon Foundation, 1989.

Susan Haller

Born 1927 · Basel, Switzerland

Susan Haller, age 15, 1943.

I was born in Basel, Switzerland, to Alfred and Margaretha Weisskopf. We lived in a "green" suburb and there was no lack of playmates. After kindergarten and elementary school, I went to Girl's Latin School (Maedchengymnas) where I joined the Girl Scout movement. Later I spent a few months in war-torn Strasbourg, then returned to Basel to study at the University of Elementary and Secondary Education where I earned my diploma for teaching at elementary and secondary level and religious education. I began teaching in a public school in 1950. The university owned a chalet in the Alps where students could go during ski season. There I met my future husband, John (Hans) Haller, who was an expert in skiing and mountaineering, preparing himself for an extended stay in the Arctic where he planned to geologically map parts of the northeastern Greenland coast. We were married when he returned in 1952, He taught at the university and continued exploring as chief geologist of the Danish Lauge Expeditions. His biography was included in the book, *Toward New Horizons*. In 1964, he was asked to join the Harvard University faculty to teach structural geography and we moved with our two sons to Belmont, Massachusetts that year. There I taught Sunday School in the Belmont Methodist Church, later at Harvard Memorial Church. I also taught German at the German Saturday School in Boston. At home, I assisted my husband by editing and translating manuscripts for him. John died in 1984. I joined the Brookhaven community in August 2012.

War in a Neutral Country

By Susan Haller

"I realize that we Swiss people had the good fortune, undeservedly, to be spared the sufferings World War II had caused... I wish to express my gratitude to the Americans and British who had fought to liberate Europe from the plague of Nazi Germany."

Part 1: A Girl Scout's War Years

MY HOMETOWN OF Basel, Switzerland, shares its border with Germany and France. At the beginning of World War II, I was twelve years old and had just joined the Girl Scout movement. New tasks were added to our regular activities. Instead of heading for the Alps for summer camp, we pitched our tents in a village in the fertile region close to Lake Constance. Most of the able-bodied men had been drafted, so we became farmhands assisting overworked wives in various ways like picking red currants, shelling peas, mending socks...I loved it!

When the war was in its last phase I was given the opportunity to take part—just in a small way—in a Red Cross humanitarian mission. It was when the Allied forces had liberated Paris, but the regions closer to the Rhine were still under German occupation. Cities in the Alsace were heavily bombarded. Under the protection of the International Red Cross many thousands of children arrived in Basel by so called "Kinder trains." Here they had to transfer to a train headed for central Switzerland, away from the endangered border area. So it could happen that I got a phone call from my troop leader: "Tomorrow wear your uniform to school; you will be dismissed at ten A.M., then go directly to the Alsatian station [the French part of Basel's "Bahnhof"]." This I did, together with a few other Girl Scouts. I was waiting on the platform when the train from Mulhouse pulled in by steam engine locomotive. Out of each car door descended a nurse followed by many children. We lined them up, two by two, and led them into a dimly lit dining hall (the former French Station Restaurant). They sat down on long benches and we filled their plates with a thick soup. Quietly and subdued they began to eat it, but only nibbled at a piece of dark bread besides. We noticed that a few boys were taller than the rest of them. Were these perhaps 16-year-olds "smuggled in"—the limit had been set to 15-year-olds—to avoid being drafted into service by the German occupiers? Soon it was time for leading the sad "troopers" to the waiting train in the Swiss part of the "Bahnhof." On another day when another "shift" of Girl Scouts was on duty, they had to lead the children to Basel's Exhibition Hall, where they would have to stay overnight. That afternoon, they took them for a walk through the "Langen Erlen," a sparsely wooded area. The children seemed to enjoy it. But then, the roaring sound from an airplane (a Swiss one) cut through the air. Immediately the children ran off in all directions, seeking shelter at the foot of the trees. It would take quite a while to have them reassembled.

More "Kinder trains" arrived, some from Colmar or Belfort. One day we had to lead the boys and girls to an empty schoolhouse in "Kleinbasel" on the Rhine's riverbank. The next morning, they would be deloused, if necessary. In the evening, they were sitting or lying on thin mattresses on the floor of a small auditorium, away from home, on the way to an unfamiliar place, traumatized by their recent past. A girl had put her arm around her little brother trying to console the sobbing child. I could only hope that they would feel much better once they resided with their host family, and that V-E Day was not far away and they could reunite with their own.

Part 2: At Home When World War II Began

Susan Haller: My father, Alfred Weisskopf, a medic with the Switzerland forces, on furlough, WWII.

LIVING MY SHELTERED childhood, I did not grasp the danger that Germany's "Nationalsozialismus" could pose. I was amused by cartoons showing Hitler's face with his big mustache and also by those depicting British Prime Minister Chamberlain traveling with his umbrella negotiating with the "Führer." But then on September 1, 1939, I woke up to reality: the news was broadcasted that German troops had crossed the border into Poland. On my way to school I saw freshly mounted white posters with black lettering reading "2. Sept. Schweizer GENERALMOBILMACHUNG [mobilization]." When I returned home I saw that my father had changed from his business suit into his green-grey uniform bearing the insignias of a medic (or military orderly) in Border Protection-Battalion 250. He was kneeling on the floor rolling up his overcoat and meticulously fitting it around the square rigid backpack; the helmet came on top. He girded himself with a leather belt from which a saber-like utility tool ("Faschinen" knife) was dangling. He then bade us goodbye and left to join his comrades somewhere along the river Rhine. He served under the high command of Henry Guisan who had been elected general of the entire army by our Federal Assembly on August 31. The latter became my hero; I put a framed photo of him over my desk.

Months went by; then my mother and I could visit my father on Sundays. We took the train to Mumpf, a small town, and ate a meal with him at Restaurant "Zur Sonne." Afterwards we walked to a private home where a room had been converted into a small sick bay. There he would care for fellow troopers who had fallen ill. Back home, we regularly got postcards from him, sent by "field-post"; no stamp was needed. He weekly sent us a small canvas bag with dirty laundry in exchange for a clean set. There were times down the road when my father got dismissed for a certain period and could return to his civilian job. There in his capacity of personnel director, he made sure those employees who still were on active military duty would get their monthly "Soldaten paeckli," a box filled with goodies and a greeting with an uplifting poem.

Part 3: At School During the War Years

THERE WERE SIGNS of a new era all around. I saw traps for armed tanks being erected on the "Middle Rhine Bridge" and bunkers built on the banks and on surrounding hills. On rooftops of school buildings mushroom-shaped sirens were mounted. When they emitted their wailing sounds and I was in school, a six-story-high building, our teachers led us down into the basement where we sat in long narrow corridors. We heard the humming sounds of bomber planes accidentally flying over Swiss territory. The end alarm sounded and we went back upstairs. Several of our male teachers had been drafted and university students took their place. Ranks had changed; our principal served as a private while our custodian became his commanding officer! With time, we had become quite casual about the air alarms, even enjoyed the break when it occurred during a class we disliked. But this did change...on December 16, 1940, at nighttime the sirens began their wailing. Our little family went down into the innermost basement. I heard the usual engine noises from above, but then... a high-pitched sound, increasing whistling and a horrific boom! There were more...in the morning we learned that a few houses, mostly in the vicinity of the train station, had been hit. Basel, the darkened city, had erroneously been bombarded. I went to school at 7:00 and sat in class working on a test in Latin. One seat remained empty; Ruth arrived at 9:00, visibly shaken. A bomb had hit her neighbor's house and Mr. Zeller had been killed! That happened just half a kilometer over from my home!

Shortages in food and coal supplies became evident. Therefore, a huge can with soup, cooked in a military kitchen, was delivered daily to the school's basement. We went downstairs at the midmorning break, got our dishes filled and ate with good appetites. Several of Basel's school buildings were closed, so we had to share ours with a boys' high school. It meant longer morning sessions for us (and occasionally a message on a slip of paper from a "guest" who had used my desk in the afternoon). Toward spring our building was closed for a week; "coal vacation" was declared and we upper-class girls, led by our teachers, hiked up on a mountain in the Jura range. We were housed in a hostel and went skiing all day long. In summer, our principal assigned each of us to a farm in one of the villages in "Basel-Country." I lived for a month with a modest family in a small farmhouse, took care of the children and chickens, picked sweet cherries high up in a tree and helped

Susan Haller with two girl scout friends, "Sojo," "Gipsy," and "Loyos," taken on an outing in Switzerland in 1941.

The wires are cut. French women can cross the border into Swiss territory, May 8, 1945. Photo from Susan Haller.

make hay on a hillside above "Bennwil." At noon Frau Thommen, the farmer's wife, came up to us with a huge basket containing "homegrown" smoked bacon, bread she had baked in her wood-burning stove, plum pie with cream from their only cow—we sat down in the grass and I enjoyed these delicacies which I was no longer used to tasting!

At the end of summer, I headed back to school. V-E Day came next spring. On May 8, 1945, for 15 minutes all church bells in Switzerland were ringing. The next morning instead of heading directly to school, all teachers and students attended a service of thanksgiving at a nearby church. I realize that we Swiss people had the good fortune, undeservedly, to be spared the sufferings World War II had caused. In closing, I wish to express my gratitude to the Americans and British who had fought to liberate Europe from the plague of Nazi Germany.

Diana M. Bailey

Born 1943 · Bristol, England

Diana Bailey, 2010, associate professor, Tufts University, Medford, Massachusetts, 1990–2010.

I was born in Bristol, England, in 1943—in the middle of the war. My entire family, including an uncle in Burma, survived the war. I remained in England through my undergraduate years at St. Loyes in Exeter, then worked two years as an occupational therapist in a large psychiatric hospital outside of London in order to save the fare to emigrate. Between graduate degrees at Boston University and Northeastern University, I was a clinician and manager in psychiatric programs. I came to the United States in 1965 and have since lived in the Boston area and Colorado. I taught at Tufts University for 20 years until my retirement in 2010.

The Sound of Sirens

By Diana M. Bailey

> "I'm told a bomb dropped in our back garden, so close that it shifted the entire house an inch or so on its foundation.... The sound of sirens still makes the hair stand up on my neck....One might think a three-year-old child too young to remember such things, but the fear connected to that sound made its way into my brain and is still vivid today."

I WAS BORN and raised in Bristol, England, and although I was only three years old when the war ended, I have many memories of that time and the restrictions immediately afterwards. Bristol is a large aircraft-building city and a port, consequently it was heavily bombed and the entire city center was demolished. My father was in the RAF and was stationed at the aircraft factory, which shared space with the RAF base right in Bristol.

Though I was not aware of it, I'm told a bomb dropped in our back garden, so close that it shifted the entire house an inch or so on its foundation. I do know that the house had one course of bricks about an inch farther toward the street than the course below it.

My brother was three years older than me and was born when the war started in 1939. In the midst of the war, when he was three, he found a full-grown tortoise in the back garden. Though my parents tried very hard to find its owner, they never succeeded and Oswald became part of the family. He lived with us for 30 years until the day he didn't wake up at the end of his hibernation period. This, of course, means that he sailed through the war unscathed—in spite of the bomb in the back garden.

My brother and I were never happy being left with our elderly neighbors, Mr. and Mrs. Jeans, while my mother went to visit my father when he got a leave from the air force base. They were delightful people and always gave us a good tea, sharing their rations because they had no children of their own. But we dreaded the sirens going off when we were there because their cupboard-under-the-stairs, where we sheltered, was full of "creepy crawlies." We didn't mind spending time in our own cupboard-under-the-stairs because my mother kept it nice and clean and we took our books and a torch to read by. During the winter months, we would be sharing the cupboard with our tortoise and our cat. Oswald, the tortoise, spent his winter hibernating in a box of straw in said cupboard. He never woke even when jostled by us or surrounded by aircraft noise.

Of course, it took many years for things to get back to normal after the war and ration books for sweets were a reality for children for a long time. I remember the little sweet shop across the road as being dark with a bare unfinished, wood plank floor and rows and rows of large glass jars containing loose sweets, some wrapped and some not. Saturday mornings, my brother and I would watch impatiently as Mum used the kitchen scissors to carefully cut the

Bristol, England, 1945. Victory Day street party in Bristol, England. Diana Bailey (three years), her brother (seven years), her mother, grandmother and two cousins are in the crowded, bunting-covered street.

coupons from the ration book. Then came the mad dash across the road to meet our friends, all clutching two tiny squares of rough, heavy, grey paper less than 1 centimeter square. Each coupon was good for 1 ounce of sweets, together with two pennies. Our ration had to last the week but was almost always gone by the end of Sunday. We usually picked the smallest sweets possible, so we could get more for our money. For instance, you could get about ten of the small, red, hot ones but only two or three of the larger hard, multi-layered sweets. Occasionally, we would splurge one whole ounce coupon on one huge Gob Stopper.

We also used ration coupons for meat and sugar—and for other things my child's memory didn't register, such as nylon stockings. I remember my mother giving my brother and me her ration of meat "because we were still growing" and she didn't need it so much. And I remember the lady down the street giving me her ration of dried bananas each month because she didn't like them and she knew I loved them.

Another thing that lasted for several years after the war was the practice of using sunlamps in schools. I suppose because those of us living in cities that were bombed regularly spent so much time in shelters, out of daylight, it was thought that we should be given doses of artificial sunlight. While in school we would file to the gym, strip to the waist, don sunglasses and sit on long, low benches with sunlamps beaming on our backs. I don't remember how long we sat there but I do remember us all getting very fidgety because, for some unexplained reason, we weren't allowed to talk or read.

The sound of sirens still makes the hair stand up on my neck, and I can't bear to watch a movie that contains the wail of sirens. One might think a three-year-old child too young to remember such things, but the fear connected to that sound made its way into my brain and is still vivid today.

Hanna Friedenstein Chandler

Born 1917 · Vienna, Austria

Hanna Chandler, 1943. Trying to punt near Cambridge, England.

Johanna (Hanna) Friedenstein Chandler was born in Vienna, Austria, in 1917 to Paul and Gertrude Friedenstein. She grew up in Vienna and then, in 1938, she and her parents left Austria for England. There she graduated from the University College of London with a BSc. in chemistry. With her parents she immigrated to the United States in 1947. Later, she earned an MS in library science from Simmons College in Boston, Massachusetts. She became a U.S. citizen in 1953. During her working years she was active in the American Chemical Society and the Special Libraries Association. She also volunteered at the Boston Museum of Science. She was married at the age of 72 to Charles Chandler, whom she had known for several years. They met on the train as they commuted back and forth to their respective jobs.

D-Day

Thoughts on the 50th Anniversary

By Hanna Friedenstein Chandler

> "I shall always be grateful to those who fought in that war.
> I hope the time will never come when no one remembers
> what that war was about and why it had to be fought."

FOR AMERICANS OF our generation, the most memorable date of World War II is probably December 7, 1941. Most of us remember where we were when the news came that the Japanese had attacked Pearl Harbor. I was in England at the time (and not yet an American citizen), but I shall always remember listening to the BBC evening news on the "wireless"—and it must have been after 7 P.M., as Britain was on daylight saving time and thus eleven hours ahead of Hawaii. My reaction, and that of most people in Britain, I suspect, was "Thank God, now the Americans are in the war with us!"

By that time, we had been at war for more than two years. After Hitler's nonaggression pact with the Soviet Union in August, 1939 and the invasion of Poland on September 1, Britain and France declared war on Germany on Sunday, September 3. That's another date I am not likely to forget. I remember it as a beautiful sunny day—it seemed unbelievable that we were at war. I was both scared and glad. We would finally do something to stop Hitler.

As soon as Neville Chamberlain, the prime minister, had finished his brief announcement on the radio, the air-raid sirens went off. We found out later that it was only a test; but we thought we were being attacked already. We grabbed our gas masks and trooped down to our makeshift basement shelter. Then we heard a buzzing sound—could it be an enemy plane? It turned out to be a fly—and the "all clear" sounded soon afterwards.

The real airraids didn't start until 1940. Luckily, I didn't experience many, as I was at college in Wales during most of what became known as the Battle of Britain. But I came back to London during vacations and then for good after I graduated in 1941.

I don't remember when we began to see U.S. soldiers around London. One day a friend reported, with great amusement, that an American GI had approached her on the platform of the "Tube" (the London subway) and asked me, "Pardon me, do you speak English?" I guess he was a bit confused; but we were happy to know that the Yanks had indeed arrived.

It took another two-and-a-half years from Pearl Harbor to D-Day. Sometimes it seemed that it would never come, let alone the end of the war. We talked about "after the war" but couldn't imagine it really happening. But we never doubted that Hitler would eventually be defeated; it was inconceivable that we might lose the war. I only realized many years later how close we come to defeat.

I shall never forget D-Day. But what I remember most vividly is the evening before, when I stood on a hill in Hertfordshire and watched the planes heading for the Continent. There were hundreds of them; the sky was full of planes and the droning sound went on and on. They were huge planes, all with white stripes on their wings and bellies, so we knew they were "ours." We didn't know why they were there, but we knew something important must be happening. I only realized quite recently, when I watched a TV program about D-Day, that these were probably the planes transporting airborne troops to France to support the invasion from behind enemy lines.

The landing of Allied troops in Normandy on D-Day, June 6, 1944, did, of course, turn the tide and brought the liberation of Europe and, ultimately, the defeat of Nazi Germany. I shall always be grateful to those who fought in that war. I hope the time will never come when no one remembers what that war was about and why it had to be fought.

Part Two

Stranded Americans

THOUGH THE UNITED STATES did not enter the war right away, many American citizens were in potential danger and needed to escape. There are only two stories in this section but they remind us of what is was like to have a war raging in Europe and the need to get home.

Allen C. West

Born 1930 · Beirut, Lebanon

Alan West, age ten, feeding kangaroos at Koala Park, Australia, September 1941.

I was born in Beirut in 1930 and lived there until 1941 except for 1936–37 in Princeton, New Jersey. After wartime in Wellesley came Phillips Academy, Princeton, three-plus years in the Army and graduate work in chemistry at Cornell, 1955–60. I met Emily Mountz at Cornell and we married in 1958. We had three children. In 1966 we went from Williamstown, Massachusetts, to Appleton, Wisconsin. I started writing poetry in 1983 and taught chemistry at Lawrence University until 1994, when we came to Cambridge, Massachusetts. Emily died in 1999. I met Diane Kessler in 2006 and we moved to Brookhaven in 2007.

Evacuation, 1941

By Allen C. West

"If my narrative seems to have no fear or danger in it, that is because I never felt either of those emotions. I was old enough to relish all the new places we visited, the long ocean voyages, the unfamiliar experiences, but too young to understand the scary uncertainties that followed us from Beirut to Los Angeles. My mother had frightening and unhappy moments, but she never let us share them."

WESTERNERS IN THE Middle East have often been evacuated during turbulent times. In World War I, when Turkey joined the Central Powers, British and French citizens left or were interned. (After 1917, Americans were not, since Turkey and the United States never declared war on each other.) In 1940 the same situation arose in Lebanon and Syria after the fall of France, when a Vichy military government took control. In Beirut, I remember car headlights painted a translucent blue, part of the blackout regulations, and a sugar shortage that stopped Feisal's soda fountain from selling the yummy sundaes we called "chocolate muds," made with vanilla ice cream, chocolate sauce, malted milk and whipped cream.

I have used quotes from my mother's diary to give this memoir an alternate point of view. They are given exactly as they appear there—she must have often been hurried or under tension. It was obviously a difficult trip for her.

Americans were not affected by the Axis sympathies of the Vichy government, but in April 1941, Germany invaded Yugoslavia and Greece, landing planes on Syrian airfields to reach Iraq, whose government had declared war on Great Britain. (My mother's diary: *3 May, Sat. Iraq and Britain at war. Demonstration by students from Iraq + others. All foreign students sent home; 18 May, Sun. Tension increases—esp. Aleppo. Bill + I pack a trunk of silver + linen in eve.)* Everyone talked about German paratroops, and our suitcases were packed for weeks. (*May 19, Mon. word comes at noon that we are to leave tomorrow at 10 A.M. In P.M. Stu who has arranged cars says 7 A.M.)* On the 20th Germany's one paratroop division dropped on Crete. I now believe British intelligence knew that it was about to go into action, was afraid it would drop on Syria and told the American Legation in Beirut to get its people out, so the events of that day were not a coincidence.

(*20 May, Tues. Up at 5. Ready to leave at 7, Car comes at 8:30. Change cars in Haifa …Engine trouble Hot—change to good car at Nablus. Stop at Ramallah for drink. Soltaus send us to Bishop G. Brown's. Dodds get away at 10:00. They are attacked by bandits at 7 P.M. south of Nablus—passports, money, watches etc taken. In J. at 9 P.M.* [She added the following to her diary on Jan. 1, 1942:] *Reported to police + dogs put on scent. They go directly to village + find man + loot. Dodds rec, all back exc—few Pal. pounds.*) Five of us crammed into our taxi: my mother, father, sister Elisabeth (14), myself (10) and brother David (8). Inland from Haifa, the Plain of Esdraelon baked in the sun; the crowded taxi was very uncomfortable. It was an all-day trip, dark when we arrived in Jerusalem at the Anglican bishop's house. The families of most of our friends made the same trip.

My brother and I and some of our friends, but not our older sisters, were enrolled in the British Community School as boarders. I remember nothing about the classes, except that the work was sometimes bewildering. One night we all got up when the airraid siren went off and huddled in the hallways listening to the drone of one enemy plane above the city. The moon was full that night. (*6 June, Fri. no transportation yet for India or Australia; 7 June, Sat. 11th day for boys after exposure to chicken pox?*) On June 9 the headmaster told the school that "our troops" (which sounded very strange) had invaded Syria and Lebanon. We visited the Church of the Holy Sepulchre, the Dome of the Rock, the Mount of

Olives, Bethlehem's ornately decorated grotto. On the Dead Sea, we floated like corks. (*12 June, Thurs. in car to town to pick up Allen + David for A.M. at Dead Sea. Discover our two have chicken pox so return them to B.C.S.*) That was the end of all school work for us: with two English boys we shared an easy convalescence reading, playing games and watching the street below our balcony. (*17 June, Tues. ...Have tea with the "chicken poxes"—Allen, David, Ray Davis, Colin Pack. Read Sherlock Holmes to them. Itching over + spots drying up. David stopped counting at 180; 22 June, Sun. Germany declares war on Russia. Damascus falls to British.*)

On June 27 we went to Cairo. (*27 June, Fri . Boys out from B.C.S. in taxi by 7:30. Leave in car for Lydda at 8:25—arrive at 9:15. ... On train leave at 10:40 ....Arrive Kantara 6:15. Leave 8:15—Cairo 12:30. To Am. Girls' School.*) The train was hot and dirty, because open windows let in dust and soot as well as a breeze. The American Girls' School, where we stayed, was closed for the summer. There were often kites on the grounds out back, perhaps hunting for grasshoppers in the grass? One day three of us cooked them (grasshoppers) on a kid's stove. My cousin ate one, he says. I know I didn't! When bombers came over at night we crawled under our beds, listening to sirens and antiaircraft guns. We rode camels at Giza, climbed the Great Pyramid, went to see the step pyramid at Saqqara and often to the zoo, which had little boats we could paddle with our feet. (*9 July, Wed. Dentz has asked for an armistice in Syria. Wilson has asked that Beirut be "open city".*) Tutankhamen's treasures were underground, the museum closed. Remembering the color photos in *National Geographic*, I felt terribly disappointed.

To learn our travel arrangements, my father was summoned to a building in Cairo where a man unlocked the door of a small room with a finger to his lips, locked it behind them, sat down behind a desk, unlocked a drawer, took out a piece of paper, held it up so my father could read it, then locked it back in the drawer and let my father out. Not a word was said! And he never said a word about it until after the war. (*28 July, Mon. to Cooks for sign-*

The *Aquitania*, which was painted gray when the ship took us from Suez to Sydney, Australia, July 31, 1941–August 29, 1941. *(Wikipedia)*

ing ticket for Australia; <u>July 30, Wed.</u> Up at 5:30.... 2 special coaches to Suez. Arrive 11.—Thru passports and customs and on "Aquitania" at 2:30. Bill comes out with us. Sees our big cabin + bath + we say goodbye.) ["Bill" was our father. He returned to Beirut; we didn't see him for three years.] Our luggage was labeled *HMS Transport*, but we had crossed the Atlantic in 1937 on the *Aquitania* and to see its four stacks out in the harbor made it a comforting homecoming for me. She, the *Queen Mary* and the *Queen Elizabeth* were all busy carrying ANZAC troops from Sydney to Suez that summer, and German U-boats must have been looking for them. There was a ship burning in the harbor. It had been bombed the night before by German planes and hauled to shallow water so it could be salvaged.

(<u>31 July, Thurs.</u> Ports all closed for black out. Sleep on floor in hallway. Humidity awful. <u>1 Aug, Fri.</u> Children sleep in cabin. Out in hall after 3:30 sleep on floor. Making abt 21 knots. Have 1400 It. war prisoners aboard.) All down the Red Sea we were blacked out and one little electric fan did not cool us off at all. The Arabian Sea was fresher, brilliant blue water, flying fish, cool breezes. We had the run of the upper decks and lounges; there were very few passengers, about 30 of us from Beirut.

When the ship's siren signaled lifeboat drill, we gathered quietly at our station wearing our lifejackets, the only sounds the hull swishing through the water and the engine's rumble. The Italian prisoners of war being shipped to India were down below, and every day groups were aired on deck. One of the guards, an Englishman named Ginger, gave me some insignia including a tiny commando knife I still have. At Colombo, Ceylon (now Sri Lanka), the prisoners were taken off. We had two days in port, took a car up to the temple at Kandy, saw elephants carrying loads along the road in the jungle. (*7 Aug, Thurs. Colombo 7:00 off at 10:30. Leave for Kandy at 11:00. 72 miles up—3 hours. Perfectly beautiful all the way. Rice fields, cocoanut palms, rubber, coffee, tea, green-green. Stop at zoo, botanical garden, temple, tea factory. On boat at 8:00; 8 Aug, Fri. I take boys ashore. Rickshaw rides + window shop. Buy elephants…. No Matson sailings in Aug. not until Sept 19.*)

From Ceylon we sailed to Sydney, stopping at Fremantle (*16 Aug, Sat. Arrive at Fremantle early …."Queen Elizabeth" anchored near us.*) The weather was much colder, especially when the ship swung south of Tasmania to evade a submarine in the Bass Strait. (*19 Aug, Tues. Very cold. Get out fur coat.*) We kids spent hours in the lounge playing Monopoly and Battleship, bundled up because of the sudden change to winter. Out on deck we watched albatrosses soaring past. Our steward told us that the troops smashed all the china and glass on every trip. (Aussies were famous for their rowdiness in the Middle East during WWI). We arrived on August 23. (*Sat. In sight of land at 7 and "Queen E"…. Beautiful entrance to harbor.*).

Our home was a small hotel in Bondi Beach, a Sydney suburb on the coast south of the entrance to the harbor. There were slot machines in the lounge; 3 cherries or 3 lemons still conjure up cascades of coins. We went to Sydney for movies (*28 Aug, Thurs. All see "Fantasia" in P.M.*), and were told that there were sharks in the ocean. The lifeguard had lost a leg to one, but the water was too cold for us anyway, so we spent most days on the beach, which seemed to stretch for miles. (*3 Sept, Wed. Draw lots for cabins on Monterey… Thrilling to have letter from Bill from Beirut!*) We visited the harbor bridge and the zoo, where the sister of the MGM lion was the most exciting sight; fed kangaroos and saw koalas in a wild animal park. (*5 Sept, Fri...* *drive to Koala Pk via a most beautiful drive.... Kangaroos + koala bears perfectly fascinating. Delicious tea at kiosk—High spot of our stay.*) Took the train to Botany Bay to watch an aborigine throw a boomerang.

(*18 Sept, Thurs.* *Bkfst at 7:30. To dock at 8:30. Sail at 11:30, beautiful day, wonderful ship "Monterey"—Matson liner. Many Aust. airforce, who have use of cabin class, so we have run of ship. Australian govt taken over this boat. Cruiser near us all the time.*) (The airmen were on their way to England; rules of neutrality forbade American ships to carry troops of belligerent nations, so, under these circumstances, we were a legitimate target.) (my birthday: *21 Sept, Sun.* *Sight land and in Auckland's beautiful harbor all a.m. Dock about noon.*) While we were at Auckland we left the boat for a day to drive up into the New Zealand hills. I remember lots of sheep and how green it was. Quite a change from the dry Middle

"We sailed from Sydney to Los Angeles on Matson Line's *Monterey*, September 18, 1941–October 6, 1941." The *Monterey* was chartered by the U.S. Marine Corps in 1941 to carry 150 Chinese, Korean and Japanese missionaries along with stranded U.S. citizens to San Francisco. After reaching San Francisco, the *Monterey* was refitted and in December carried 3,349 fresh troops to Hawaii, returning to San Francisco with 800 casualties of the attack on Pearl Harbor. (*Wikipedia*)

East. (*25 Sept, 1st Thurs. Suva-Fiji Is. at 8. Sail at 5; 25 Sept (?), 2nd Thurs. Over International Date Line.*) 25 Sept (?) She should have said "*24 Sept, Wed*"! That's why a baby who was born on the ship on that day had, I thought, two birthdays, which seemed to be a wonderful thing!

We watched horse races in the lounge and one day a Joe Louis fight was broadcast. After Fiji the ship also stopped at Samoa (*26 Sept, Fri. Arrive Pago Pago at 8.... Boat in quarantine for measles and mumps among forces so no one can land. Gay dock + band plays + native dances.*) and Hawaii. (*1 Oct, Wed. Honolulu! Mrs. Huyler arranges for entertainment of our party for all day.... to Pali, Dole cannery, to Waikiki beach for lunch, to aquarium, aviaries, shop and on board for 4 P.M. sailing. Gay with paper streamers + leis.*) All the children thought that the sand on Waikiki was not nearly as nice as the Beirut beaches; too coarse and brown! My best friend and his family left the ship in Honolulu. They didn't reach the mainland until after Pearl Harbor. We landed at Los Angeles on Oct. 6.

If my narrative seems to have no fear or danger in it, that is because I never felt either of those emotions. I was old enough to relish all the new places we visited, the long ocean voyages, the unfamiliar experiences, but too young to understand the scary uncertainties that followed us from Beirut to Los Angeles. My mother had frightening and unhappy moments, but she never let us share them. The quotes from her diary reveal a little of those feelings. Only years later did it dawn on me that we were refugees. I always thought that being a refugee meant (as it did for many children) difficulty, uncertainty, danger and always fear. I remember that trip as a wonderful five-month vacation spent traveling around the world.

Marnie Wengren

Born 1916 · Springfield, Illinois

Margaret Lanphier with her first husband DeWitt, Newlyweds, summer 1939.

Margaret (Marnie) Wengren spent the first half of her adult life in the mining world. She was born Margaret Lanphier in 1916 in Springfield, Illinois. She graduated from the Master's School (Dobbs), Dobbs Ferry, New York, in 1934 and Vassar College, 1938. She then married DeWitt Smith, a mining engineer, and they moved to Bisbee, Arizona, where he was with the Copper Queen Mining Company for two years and then to Washington, D.C., where he was with the Board of Economic Warfare. Later they moved to Bonterre, Missouri, where he worked at the New York Zinc company and then to Boston. They had four children born in four different locations.

Later, Marnie married Dick Wengren in 1968. She moved to Lincoln, Massachusetts, in 1957 and became immersed in the Boston Museum of Fine Arts Gallery Instructor's program and in the De Cordova Museum, Lincoln, Massachusetts. At Brookhaven, she started the Art Committee and the collection of good pictures for Brookhaven walls.

A Ship Is Sunk at Sea

By Marnie Wengren

"Mrs. Smith and Jeanette were put in a lifeboat that got stuck on the davits and upended. Jeanette fell into the water, while Mrs. Smith was secured in the boat. It was the last she had seen of her daughter."

IN THE SUMMER between my husband's two graduate years in mining engineering, we were in Bisbee, Arizona, for copper mining experience. When we were ready to leave we went all the way to the West Coast briefly, then turned around to start the long drive east to Illinois.

We had known that my husband's father, Henry DeWitt Smith, an eminent mining engineer, who had inspired my husband's career, was planning his dream trip. He was taking his wife and daughter, Jeanette, to South Africa where he had spent much time opening up Tsumeb, an important copper mine. Mr. Smith had many associates and friends there whom he wanted his wife to meet and wanted her to see the famous Kruger National Park.

A cable had told us that the family party had gotten as far south as Lisbon when Mr. Smith's sense of unrest in Europe made him decide to return to England to find passage home. As my husband and I chugged east in our no-frills Chevy, which did boast a radio, we heard that a ship called the *Athenia* had been sunk.

When we reached my family's home in Illinois, we heard that my husband's family was on the *Athenia*. Mr. Smith had sent the news of their passage to an aunt in New Jersey who became our contact. For almost 48 hours we heard no further word of them.

It later emerged that the *Athenia* had indeed been sunk, presumably by a torpedo, but there was time to remove many of the passengers. Mrs. Smith and Jeanette were put in a lifeboat that got stuck on the davits and upended. Jeanette fell into the water, while Mrs. Smith was secured in the boat. It was the last she had seen of her daughter. Jeanette and her father were rescued separately by the yacht, *Southern Cross*, which had come to the aid of the *Athenia*.

Mrs. Smith had been picked up by a British naval vessel which had taken her to Glasgow, where she was admitted to a hospital. A wonderful coincidence occurred when Mrs. Smith glanced through the Sunday paper and read of the wedding of the daughter of a Smith classmate, who then housed Mrs. Smith while she waited for a convoy to take her home.

When at last we knew her expected arrival in Hoboken, my husband, his father, his sister and I were there to meet her. It was a weepy moment when Mrs. Smith looked down from the upper deck to see Jeanette standing there, because she did not believe it when people told her that her daughter had survived.

Mr. Smith was called several times to Washington for congressional investigations into the sinking of the *Athenia*. Some years later a German submarine captain corroborated the finding that it was a German torpedo that sank the ship. Of the 1,103 people aboard, 120 were lost. The sinking on September 3, 1939, marked the beginning of World War II in Europe.

Part Three

War in Europe

EVEN AS GERMANY rampaged across Europe and bombarded England, with thousands of refugees fleeing the conflict, the United States did not enter the war. Americans were vehemently opposed to war—memories of World War I were too close. Then the Japanese bombed Pearl Harbor; anger and outrage swept the country. It was, as President Franklin D. Roosevelt told Americans, "A date which will live in infamy." The United States declared war on Japan the day after Pearl Harbor; three days later the United States declared war on Germany, Italy and the other Axis powers. The United States was ready to fight—on two fronts—Japan and Europe.

One of the most immediate priorities was to build the armed forces. Between enlistments and the draft, the United States Army, Navy, Coast Guard and Marine Corps began preparing to fight. During World War II 16.1 million American servicemen served overseas, with 416,000 deaths. The average overseas time for a serviceman was 16 months. By the end of the war more than 61 countries were involved, with 72 million deaths worldwide. (Figures from www.statisticbrain.com.)

Most of the stories in this section were submitted by men who served in the U.S. armed forces in Europe. Their stories are reminders of the logistics, determination and small and large acts of heroism required by war. Most of these men were barely out of their teens with little or no experience of life, let alone war. They did the jobs they were asked to do.

Eleanor Lane

Born 1919 · Boston, Massachusetts

Eleanor and Philip Lane at the time of his retirement from
Stop & Shop, December 1978.

I was born in Boston, Massachusetts, during the influenza epidemic of
1919. My mother died when I was born. My grandmother cared for me
and my two sisters until my father remarried. We moved to Belmont,
Massachusetts and I attended Belmont schools. I especially enjoyed
my high school years and graduated from Belmont High School in
1936. I then went to Wheelock College to absorb some teaching
ability, graduating in 1939. I later taught for ten years at the Stratton
School in Arlington, Massachusetts. I married Philip Lane in 1941 and
he left for the war in 1943. My prayers were answered and he came
home safely from Europe in 1945.

It was wonderful to be together again in our home in Lexington. We
had two sons, Philip and Steven, who were an important part of the
happiness and laughter we had in our years together; they are now
parents and grandparents. I learned about Brookhaven when I was
a volunteer at Symmes Hospital in Arlington, Massachusetts and we
moved there. Since my husband's death six years ago, I appreciate
even more the caring and interesting lifestyle at Brookhaven.

The Departure for World War II

By Eleanor Lane

"The USS *Alexander* left port planing to join a huge convoy waiting outside the harbor.... the ship ran aground in the Brooklyn Narrows within sight of the city's skyline...."

WE WERE EXPECTING our first child when my husband, Philip Lane, received the government's undeniable "invitation" to join the war in 1943. After training at Ft. Benning, Georgia, he was assigned to the 10th Armored Division, nicknamed the Tiger Division, under General George Patton. After several months at Ft. Benning, the Division went to New York City, September 13, 1944. The night before they were due to depart, my husband's brother and his friends took my husband to dinner at the Princeton Club. The next morning he boarded the USS *Alexander* in New York City Harbor bound for an unknown destination. Because of security concerns, it was a common practice for the destinations of ships not to be announced.

Loading the ship with men and supplies was a long, slow process, but finally the ship was ready to sail. The USS *Alexander* left port planning to join a huge convoy waiting outside the harbor. Whenever possible ships crossing the Atlantic trav-

Philip Lane, 1943. Taken just before his unit left for Europe.

eled in convoys for as much protection as possible from enemy ships and submarines.

Unfortunately, the ship ran aground in the Brooklyn Narrows, within sight of the city's skyline. Whether due to overloading of the ship or missing a tidal change because of time spent loading the ship, the *Alexander* was aground.

The rest of the day was spent transferring supplies and men to hastily assembled ferryboats from the USS *Alexander* to the SS *Brazil*. The SS *Brazil* was a luxury liner converted for wartime use. Meanwhile, the convoy continued on ahead, leaving the 10th Division to catch up when it could.

Two days later, the *Brazil* left New York Harbor and sailed into a hurricane. When the huge fleet of the convoy was sighted there were welcome shouts from every man on the *Brazil*.

The 10th Armored Division reached their destination, Cherbourg, France, on September 23, 1944. They were the first American armored division to disembark on French soil directly from America. The Tiger Division posted 124 days of combat, defending

SS *Brazil* converted to a troop carrier in WWII. It carried troops originally on the USS *Alexander* after the Alexander ran aground in the Brooklyn Narrows. Troops and equipment were shifted from the Alexander to the SS *Brazil*, and the ship departed to join the convoy the Alexander was supposed to sail with. (*Bill Vinson and Ginger Casey*)

Bastogne and participating in
the Battle of the Bulge. Casualties numbered 8,381, which
was 78.5% of the Division's total operational strength.

Despite the difficult departure from New York City, Philip
Lane's return from World War
II went smoothly and he received a hearty welcome from

Philip Lane's insignia for his unit, the
U.S. 10th Armored Division

family and friends when he ar-
rived home to Lexington, Massachusetts, in December 1945.

While my husband was overseas, Philip, Jr., arrived. My sister,
whose husband was assigned to India, joined me in Lexington with
her two boys. Following the news of our husbands (mine in France
and Germany and hers in India) was of enormous importance. Our
three little boys helped us through those memorable years. The
best was when both men returned home safely. What a wonderful
reunion it was!!

Editor's Note: Philip Lane's nephew Jack Duffey has written
this account of his uncle's wartime experiences. *He [Philip Lane]
never spoke very much of this period…but I am sure he remembered
some remarkable events. Here is a brief synopsis of the 10th Armored
Division's activities.*

*The 10th Armored Division entered France through the port
of Cherbourg on 23 Sept. 1944 and put in a month of training at
Teurtheville, France, before entering combat. Leaving Teurtheville 25
Oct. the Division moved to Mars-la-Tour, where it entered combat
(1 Nov.) in support of the XX Corps, containing enemy troops in the
area. In mid-November it went on the offensive, crossed the Moselle
at Malling, and drove to the Saar River, north of Metz.*

*The Division was making preparations for the Third Army drive
to the Rhine when it was ordered north to stop the German winter
offensive, 17 Dec. The 10th held defensive positions against heavy
opposition near Bastogne, Noville, and Bras. Resting briefly in early*

1945. Philip Lane, third from the left, with members of the 10th Armored Division, on occupation in the Garmish-Partenkirchen area.

January, the 10th moved out again to defensive positions east of the Saar, south of the Maginot line. On 20 Feb. the Division returned to the attack, and took part in the clearing of the Saar-Moselle triangle, 15 March.

Driving through the Kaiserlautern, it advanced to the Rhine, crossing the river at Mannheim (28 March), turned south, captured Oehringen and Helibronn, crossed the Rems and Fils Rivers, and reached Kircheim, meeting waning resistance. The Division crossed the Danube on 23–25 April and took Oberammergau. On April 27, the 10th Armored Division, along with the 103rd Infantry Division liberated the Landsberg-Dachau concentration subcamp. In May the 10th drove into the famed "Redoubt" and had reached Innsbruck when the war in Europe ended (8 May 1945)....The Division posted 124 days in combat. Total casualties numbered 8381, which was 78.5% of total operational strength. Uncle Phil was never injured so far as I know. (Note from Eleanor Lane: Philip Lane and John Duffey [the father of Jack Duffey] were close friends for many years. John Duffey married Eleanor Lane's sister; she and Eleanor and their babies lived together while their husbands were overseas. The children of the Lanes and Duffeys grew up together and were very close.)

Albert D. Ullman

Born 1918 · Boston, Massachusetts

Albert Ullman, taken at Brookhaven, 2013.

Albert Daniel Ullman was born in Boston April 6, 1918, and grew up in Milton, Massachusetts. He graduated from Milton High School and Yale University, and began his doctoral studies in psychology at Harvard. After Pearl Harbor he enlisted in the Navy as an ensign. From 1942 through 1946 he captained four ships, first with North Atlantic convoys, then with the front ranks of the Normandy invasion at Gold Beach. After his naval service he was appointed a research assistant at Tufts University, Medford, Massachusetts. He then completed his PhD work in sociology at Harvard and became chair of the Tufts University Sociology Department in 1953. Subsequently, he served as dean of liberal arts at Tufts. From 1968 to 1973 he was provost of the university. The author of two books and numerous scholarly articles, Dr. Ullman was noted for his expertise in alcoholism, addiction and social psychology. Al married his high school sweetheart, Althea Hayes, June 17, 1941. They lived in Belmont, Massachusetts, where they raised five children: Stephen, Michael, Peter, Richard and Mary-Leslie.

A Casualty of D-Day, June 1944

By Albert D. Ullman

> "Our mascot... a cocker spaniel... was panicked by the destruction... and the blowing up of mines. She ran up and down the beach, in shock. She died on the way to the vet in Southampton.... [She was] the only casualty aboard the LCI."

I ENTERED ACTIVE duty as an ensign in the U.S. Navy on April 28, 1942, at Joint Army-Navy Operations in Boston. My first assignment was as a Navy plotter in a team that kept information on all ship, submarine and aircraft movements, which were posted on a large wall chart of the North Atlantic Ocean.

After a few months I applied for sea duty and was sent to Inshore Patrol School in Boston and then to Bar Harbor (Maine) section base. As the officer-in-charge of a converted yacht with a bad engine, we patrolled Bar Harbor and the Canadian border. We found no submarines and when our engines finally quit I was reassigned to Solomons Island, Maryland, for amphibious training. There I became a prospective commanding officer of a newly built LCI. After more training in Virginia, our group of LCIs were sent to Plymouth, England. There I experienced my first air raid.

Eventually our ship went to Southhampton where we stayed until the D-Day invasion in June 1944. On June 3, 1944, my LCI picked up 144 British soldiers from the 8th Durham Light Infantry as well as 60 others from New Docks, Southampton. Our LCI did not participate in the foray on June 5; we were aborted because of the weather. We crossed the channel during the night in the early hours of June 6. Our destination was the mine-swept channels north of the Seine Bay into what was called Gold Beach. We saw the coast of France at 8:55 A.M. that day.

Albert Ullman home on leave.

Under the continual noise of naval bombardment and much confusion, we went into the Jig Green sector of Gold Beach. One of the greatest difficulties with landing were beach obstructions and mines. We wanted to give the soldiers a dry landing but could not get to the beach. The LCI hit the lip of a bomb crater and we could go no further; the soldiers had to wade to shore through chest-high water. Small boats in the area were assigned to help ships unload. The troops had bikes and motorcycles to get ashore. The small boats wouldn't come when called, presumably because they were afraid of the mines and obstructions. There were a number of dead Royal Marines in the water and on the beach. A man with a boat hook tried to keep them out of the propellers.

The soldiers got off but we could not back the ship off; it didn't move. There were holes in an oil tank and numerous holes in the hull caused by shrapnel from exploding beach obstructions. The LCI was left high and dry, awaiting the tide. At noon our ship was asked to house about 100 German prisoners. They were, it turned out, Ukrainians with German officers. They stayed until about 8 P.M. Our LCI left the beach with the tide at around 10 P.M. Just after we departed, a German plane dropped a stick of bombs into the area where we had been stranded.

During that day, our mascot—a cocker spaniel named Buffy that I brought from home—was panicked by the destruction of obstacles and the blowing up of mines. She ran up and down the beach, in shock. She died on the way to the vet in Southampton. Reporters from the military newspaper, *Stars and Stripes*, heard about this from some crew members returning to England. Because our crew was among the first back from the invasion we were of interest to the reporters. One of their stories, about the death of our mascot, the only casualty aboard the LCI, commanded by Albert D. Ullman, appeared in the *Boston Globe*. When the story appeared, my wife Althea and my father learned I was okay, long before they would have heard otherwise.

One of my crew members was a black man named Phillip Buchanan. He was a steward's mate whose job was to care for the needs of the officers, particularly the commanding officer. Because Buchanan was the only member of the crew with actual gun experience (from a previous assignment on an LST), I made him the bow gunner. This placement was astonishing at that time in the segregated Navy of 1944.

In a letter to me Phillip Buchanan wrote: "There is one thing that I always wanted to thank you for. THANK YOU for assigning me as gunner on the #1 20-mm antiaircraft bow gun. Knowing how the Navy was in those days it showed me what a good captain you were. My experiences helped to mold within me a determination to get things done and to set the foundations for the rest of my life."

Buchanan and I met only once more and that was in Washington, D.C., at the dedication of the World War II memorial several years ago. Buchanan, who had a good career as a writer in the federal government, told me, his former commanding officer, "You changed my life."

Years later, in a letter to my son, I described my departure and return to Boston: "The train pulled out of South Station at 3 P.M., December 22, 1942. Your mother-to-be was on the platform wrapped in a camel hair coat. Two years later, I called her from New York on December 22, 1944, and arrived at South Station that night."

Charles B. Ketcham

Born 1926 · Oberlin, Ohio

Waiting for discharge, Fort Dix, New Jersey, 1946.

My parents were Charles and Lucille Ketch Ketcham. I was born in Oberlin, Ohio, in 1926 and grew up in various locations in Ohio since my father, a Methodist minister, was assigned to different churches in the state. I graduated from high school, Western Reserve Academy in Hudson, Ohio, in 1944 and entered the Army. I was sent to Camp Stewart, Georgia, to train as a meteorologist for antiaircraft defense. Actuarial tables for meteorologists soon ended that program, and we were sent to Camp Howze, Texas, for six weeks of advanced infantry training. Shipped to Metz, France, I became an infantry replacement in the 54th Armored Infantry Battalion, 10th Armored Division of the Third Army under General George Patton. At war's end, the 10th Armored Division was in Garmisch-Partenkirchen. I returned to the U.S. in August 1946 and went to Mt. Union College, Ohio, where I earned a degree in English. As a Fulbright scholar I studied philosophy for a year and theology for a second year at the University of Edinburgh in Scotland. I then studied theology for a semester at the University of Zurich in Switzerland. After I returned to the United States I attended Drew University, New Jersey, for a MDiv. Back to Scotland for a PhD at University of St Andrews. I returned to the United States in 1957. I spent two years as a minister at a church in Rockaway Valley, New Jersey, before becoming a professor of religion at Allegheny College in Meadville, Pennsylvania. Joyce Parker and I were married in 1950. We had one son. We retired to Conway, Massachusetts, in 1988 and I taught religion at Smith College, Northampton, Massachusetts, for nine years. We then moved to Newburyport, Massachusetts, and I taught various adult education classes for eleven years.

"Many of Us Who Are Here Carry Within Us Death"

—Chris Hedges, Veterans for Peace, October 7, 2012

By Charles B. Ketcham

> "With tears in my eyes, I rose; kicked his rifle farther into the woods; turned and walked away. I could not pull the trigger to end his suffering, nor have I ever been able to walk away from that lonely encounter in the woods."

"WE DO NOT speak of war. War is captured only in the long, vacant stares, in the silences, in the trembling fingers, in the memories most of us keep buried deep within us, in the tears." Chris Hedges spoke these words in his speech in New York on the eleventh anniversary of the war in Afghanistan, certainly a different war than World War II, but it applies to all wars, all veterans, all of us who were purveyors of death. It applies to me, and I can only witness.

In April 1945, Combat Command A of the 10th Armored Division, now east of the Rhine River, was under orders to advance behind the enemy front lines until we met serious resistance. We had been two nights without sleep—cold, hungry, fearful—under the continuous threat of an encounter with German armor or an ambush. Deadly confrontation was inevitable. Suddenly it happened. Our lead tank was disabled by a land mine so that the road into a small hill town was effectively blocked. Recurrent ambush experience told us that German artillery would already have this section of the road zeroed in; the scream of 88-mm shells would soon be shattering the terrain around us. Withdrawal was out of the question; part of any ambush plan is to cut off retreat, to isolate the enemy, to capture or annihilate them. But this day we thought one factor was in our favor. The hilly, wooded countryside suggested that the ambush was probably set up by German infantry, not a tank division. Hill country is not good terrain for tank warfare.

Our commanding colonel surveyed his terrain maps and swiftly made two decisions. The first was to get our tanks and armored halftracks off the road before they were destroyed by the German artillery. The second was to prepare to attack the town with our own armored infantry so that our armor could safely move in and secure the town. The ambush could be thwarted.

Just south of the town was a wooded area which bordered the town itself. It was configured like the letter H; the bottom half of the H was an open meadow, the sides and top half were woods leading into the town. We rapidly deployed our tanks and halftracks around the open area, and we who were infantry grabbed a bandolier of ammunition and our rifles and fanned out into the woods to advance on the town. There was instant resistance with sniper fire coming in from the sides and the front of the woods. Progress was perilously slow, and we were shooting and taking fire from an enemy we rarely saw. Our tactic was to overwhelm them with rifle power so that they would retreat before being exposed and killed. It soon became evident that one bandolier of extra ammunition apiece was not enough for such an operation, and I was sent back to the tanks and halftracks to get more.

When I returned to the meadow there was no evidence of soldiers or guard around the halftracks, and the tanks were all buttoned up. I soon discovered that the infantry guards were taking cover behind the armored plating of the halftracks and the tankers were inside their tanks. The answer to my shouts that I needed bandoliers was cryptic, "Hey man, you're crazy to be out there. There're snipers in those woods—a couple of guys have been shot already!" To which I could only reply, "Throw out the damned bandoliers. I'll keep moving." So I went from halftrack to halftrack begging for bandoliers and praying that if I kept moving I could escape the snipers' bullets. I could hear the sharp *snap* as the bullets whizzed around me. Finally I had twelve bandoliers, which was about all I could carry along with my M1 rifle, and headed back into the woods at the front of the meadow. Behind some trees I stopped to get my breath and noticed that a bullet had actually grazed my rifle which had been resting on my fore-arm as I walked. The adrenalin of battle blocked any celebration of my good luck.

I started through the woods to find my platoon so that I could distribute the bandoliers. I could hear the fighting going on just a hundred yards ahead of me. I heard someone cry out "Here!" not far to my left. I followed the cry expecting a GI needing ammuni-tion, but what I found was a wounded German soldier stretched out on the scrub bush of the woods, his stomach ripped open, his intestines exposed and protruding from his body. My mistake was immediately evident. He had cried out *"Hier!"* Auditorily the dis-tinction between *"hier"* and "here" was too negligible to detect. His rifle had fallen to one side, so I approached him....and our eyes locked—two blue-eyed boys in a black woods of chaos. Painfully he said to me, *"Schiessen Sie mich"* [Shoot me]. My high school German was good enough to know what he asked, but I feigned ignorance. I knew that he had to be in extreme pain; I knew that I would be the last person to see him, and should I leave him, he would surely die alone there in the woods; I knew that the unwrit-ten law of armored warfare was "never leave a wounded enemy behind you"…but I had looked into his eyes and had an encounter with a fellow human being. That had not happened to me before. With four months of combat behind me, I was one of the efficient killing machines that combat soldiers become, who turn other hu-man beings, the enemy, into objects, overcoats, virtual figures of evil power.

The boy had become none of those things, and I was not an efficient machine. With tears in my eyes, I rose; kicked his rifle far-ther into the woods; turned and walked away. I could not pull the trigger to end his suffering, nor have I ever been able to walk away from that lonely encounter in the woods. Decades have passed, and as I consider my own life experiences, my own attempts to find a meaningful existence, I think now I could pull that trigger. I think I could live more readily with the personal tragedy of such a decision than I have been able to do with the lingering guilt of my morally paralyzed indecision.

R. B. McAdoo

Born 1920 · Port Washington, Pennsylvania

Richard McAdoo, Fort Bragg, North Carolina, May 1942. A "buck private" in training for the field artillery.

I grew up in Port Washington, Pennsylvania, where I was born in 1920 to Henry and Margaret Nice McAdoo. I graduated from St. Paul's School in Concord New Hampshire, and from Harvard in 1942. I joined the Army in 1942 and was sent for three months' basic training at Ft. Bragg, North Carolina, then to Officer Candidate School at Ft. Sill, Oklahoma. A member of the 989th Field Artillery Battalion, we were sent to Europe in 1944. I was discharged as a captain. After the war I started working as an assistant editor at Harper & Brothers in New York, where I worked for 21 years and became vice president and general manager. In 1969 I moved to a new job with Houghton Mifflin Co. in Boston where I worked until retiring in 1982 as senior vice-president and a director of the general trade division. Mary Wigglesworth and I were married in 1948 and lived successively in Cold Spring Harbor, Long Island, New York; Cambridge, Massachusetts; and now Brookhaven. We treasure our three daughters and five grandchildren. After retirement Mary and I traveled the country in an RV. My book *Eccentric Circles* tells the story of our travels.

A Special Education

by R. B. McAdoo

"We were able to open the huge entrance doors, drive in and park by a big main building. On a platform beside this building long rows of bodies were stacked like cordwood waiting to be burned.... Wandering around inside the fences were a couple of hundred prisoners, still in striped uniforms and waiting for some arrangement to set them free.... As the noisy exchange was going on some of the prisoners at the rear of the crowd suddenly turned and started racing in the opposite direction. Across the field they had spotted two of their former guards who had donned prisoners' striped uniforms and were running desperately to escape. The inmates chasing them caught up with the two and beat them to death on the spot. No remorse."

WITH WAR AND the draft looming ahead in the fall of 1941, I managed to telescope my senior year of college into half the usual time, graduating in January, and enlisted in the Army in March of 1942. I was sent to Fort Bragg, North Carolina, for three months of basic training as a buck private in the field artillery, and from there to Officer Candidate School for another three months at Fort Sill, Oklahoma. By October I had been pummeled into the shape of a second lieutenant and was assigned to duty with the 989th Field Artillery Battalion at Camp Forrest, Tennessee.

The 989th Field Artillery was equipped with 155-mm guns—familiarly known as "Long Toms"—which could hurl a shell up to 13 miles. Because of the guns' long reach, our usual position in combat expected to be well back of the front lines, firing on the enemy's rear installations like bridges, ammunition dumps and railheads. The 989th was to be my outfit until the end of the war (and ever since, as its members have been gathering for annual reunions for over 60 years).

The battalion shipped out from New Jersey in the spring of 1944 with a convoy crossing the Atlantic and landed in Northern Ireland. There was no space for us in England, already packed with British, American, Canadian, Australian, New Zealand, South African, Free French and other troops readying for the invasion across the Channel. We followed across to Omaha Beach a month after D-Day, as part of General Patton's Third Army.

On the first of August the Allied forces, having won control of Normandy, launched the massive attack that started their race across France. Almost at once our battalion was engaged in the fighting that came to a climax in the great bowl anchored on the east by Falaise. The Third Army was soon engaged in forming the lower jaw of a pincer to reach around the retreating Germans from the south, while British and Canadians formed the upper jaw closing down from the north. The 989th found itself thrust up with front-line tanks and infantry in a rush to bring heavy artillery fire on the valley into which the Germans were being squeezed.

As S-2 on the battalion staff I was responsible for the setting up of observation posts—OPs—to follow movements of the enemy and spot targets for our guns. I was lucky enough to come upon an ideal high point beside an old farmhouse that commanded sweeping views of the great bowl through which the Germans were fleeing toward their homeland. Over the week that the rout continued, "my OP" became a focal point for much of the Allied brass to observe the decimation of German soldiers, horses, trucks, tanks, wagons, fleeing through the hail of bullets, shells, bombs.

About three days after the jaws finally closed I was able to drive down into this bloody cauldron of destruction. Ten years later, in an article for *Harper's Magazine* published under the title "The Guns at Falaise Gap," I remembered the scene this way:

"The floor of the valley looked much as it had before the haze closed over it the previous Saturday afternoon. The roads from the Foret de Gouffern to Chambois had been cleared again...by Allied troops moving through to the east—but from the ditches out across the bottom-lands the ground was still strewn with wreckage of equipment and human beings. Among these countless tortured images of defeat, the sight of the forsaken horses stung most sharply. The dead soldiers were past caring, the wounded had been borne away by the medical corps; all of them had at some point taken their individual chances with the cause that had brought them to this end. But the animals had no choice, and now they were left to limp about the remains of their masters they had dumbly served."

The collapse of resistance in western France might have led the Allied forces into Germany and a quick end to the war if they had been able to bring up supplies and ammunition fast enough to sustain the attack. But the halts needed for resupply allowed the Germans to organize new lines of defense along their border and continue fighting through the winter and spring of 1945. In those months our battalion suffered a number of casualties and had its share of tough engagements, though none as dramatic as the rout at Falaise. When the Nazis mounted their last desperate offensive in what became the Battle of the Bulge, our battalion held defensive positions along the border of Alsace.

Once inside Germany we pushed through scattered resistance into northern Bavaria. It was there, while on reconnaissance with a fellow officer, that I came on a scene that answered clearly any question of whether this war had been necessary. We found ourselves entering the town of Dachau, some twelve miles north of Munich, and site of the earliest of the notorious Nazi concentration camps. The street on which the camp was located ran through an area of comfortable homes—much like, say, Newton, Massachusetts—homes on one side of the street and the neat high walls of the camp on the other. Advance forces of American troops had pushed through the town two days earlier, and no one had yet figured out what to do about the camp.

We were able to open the huge entrance doors, drive in and park by a big main building. On a platform beside this building long rows of bodies were stacked like cordwood waiting to be burned. The other side of the building gave onto a flat terrain enclosed by strong, high wire fencing. Wandering around inside the fences were a couple of hundred prisoners, still in striped uniforms and waiting for some arrangement to set them free. They crowded excitedly to the barrier between us, and though we could not understand their mix of tongues, we could share in the jubilation of their rescue. As the noisy exchange was going on some of the prisoners at the rear of the crowd suddenly turned and started racing in the opposite direction. Across the field they had spotted two of their former guards who had donned prisoners' striped uniforms and were running desperately to escape. The inmates chasing them caught up with the two and beat them to death on the spot. No remorse.

The battalion marched through Bavaria to cross the Austrian border and come to a final halt in Salzburg. The 989th Field Artillery had then been in combat almost continuously from its first days of action in August until V-E Day in May.

Back home in November a promotion to the rank of major was approved for me, but I had no interest in staying in the military service. I left the Army with a captain's pay, after three and a half years of active duty. Enough of soldiering; but that service had been the most important education of my life.

Hamilton R. James

Born 1921 · Ft. Mitchell, Kentucky

Hamilton James, U.S. Army Air Force, before leaving for Europe in 1943.

Hamilton James grew up in Grosse Point, Michigan. His father, Hamilton David James, met his mother, Elizabeth (Liette) Renson, who was from the Grand Duchy of Luxembourg when he was there with the U.S. Army in World War I. His mother's family were Belgian but they had settled in Luxembourg. Ham spent his summers in Luxembourg and spoke fluent French. He graduated from Phillips Academy, Andover, Massachusetts, and went to Yale where he was in the ROTC. He graduated in 1943 and was posted to Fort Sill, Oklahoma, for training in field artillery and then to Camp Ritchie, Maryland, for training in intelligence. His intelligence group was then sent to England to await the invasion. He was a forward observer in the field artillery and liaison to the Free French. After the war he was with Great Lakes Steel and National Steel and in 1952 came East to join the Cambridge consulting firm Arthur D. Little, where he stayed until he retired. He married Waleska James in 1947; they had four sons and ten grandchildren.

Where Do I Find a Cavalry Horse?

By Hamilton R. James

"I got a call from SHAEF headquarters saying that General Patton had died the day before...and wanted to be buried with his troops in the American military cemetery at Hamm....They wanted...a cortege, a funeral procession, that would go through the city twice. They would bring 5,000 troops. It was in three days....The last request was to get all the troops' pants pressed the night before! (It had been raining and they thought they looked bedraggled.)....I got on the radio and asked the Luxembourg people for help. And the Luxembourgers really came through! They loved America, and they loved General Patton because he saved that country twice. When they first came through there Patton's 3rd Army liberated the country, and then in the Battle of the Bulge when the Germans got within ten miles of the city Patton stopped them again. Housewives called, volunteering to press the pants, and others to put up the officers. We got every flower in the country through somebody or other."

"WE LANDED AT Utah Beach, not Omaha. It was right next to Omaha but a different topography...so we could get inland a little faster than they could, but we got stalled because of the hedge-rows...several hundred years old, full of tangles and dirt, three feet thick and at least four or five feet high....You could be just ten feet from an enemy and not know anyone was there...so it took us a while to get established....Our division, the 79th (artillery), and two others were then sent to take Cherbourg because we needed a big port where we could bring in gasoline...and after that we went into Belgium."

Later. "We were next to the 2nd French armored division and I had the job of going over there and joining them and then reporting back to our division. I was with them in the Vosges Mountains when General Leclerc, knowing the Germans had mined the only pass and had artillery all set up, decided to go around the German defenses and took the entire armored division over the mountains at night off road on little paths....We could use no lights at all and many tanks were lost, but we came up behind the Germans! They were so demoralized that hundreds of them rushed to surrender."

Another night. "I don't know if we got lost or not (of course we didn't use lights) but our jeep ran into a German tank that was parked in the road and full of Germans sleeping. (It must have made a terrible noise in the tank.) Off we rolled into the ditch to hide. Fortunately by sheer luck we had jammed our jeep under the tank's gun so it wouldn't turn, and were able to crawl away."

"By the time the war was over in Europe we were down in Czechoslovakia and the guys in our division were going to go home. I signed up to go with the Allied military government to Luxembourg. (I had gone to Luxembourg each time I got leave to see my grandparents.) All the Allies had military representatives in Luxembourg, which had been an ally, even though the Germans claimed it was part of the greater German Reich. (Luxembourg got a little better rations during the war than the French or Belgians, but during the occupation they were under German law and could be forced to go into the German army or work in German factories.) They hated the Germans because of the First World War and the Second. Many of my friends there had been taken off to German prison camps and some never reappeared."

English, French, American and Russian officers governed Luxembourg together. "I was the senior officer in Luxembourg representing the American army. My boss was in Brussels, and I was to do whatever seemed necessary. We had some German prisoners and I used them to de-mine the Moselle, since they were the ones who had mined it."

"We had a lot of prisoners, German and some Russians the Germans had captured there and sent to the western front. The Russian chargé d'affaires wanted to send them back, but a lot of them weren't ethnic Russians and I knew they didn't want to go.

So I said, 'Let's have a lineup of all the troops,' and when they were all there I said, 'Those who want to return to Russia step forward,' and nobody stepped up. The Russian military were furious, but those prisoners stayed on in Luxembourg.

"One afternoon in the fall I got a call from SHAEF headquarters saying that General Patton had died the day before in an automobile accident and wanted to be buried with his troops in the American military cemetery at Hamm, about ten miles from Luxembourg City....They wanted to have a cortege, a funeral procession, that would go through the city twice. They would bring 5,000 troops. It was in three days.

"They wanted to know where to set up enough tents, and if some of the officers could be put up in local homes. They would bring food, and would tell me how many colonels could be put in a car, and bring the cars and the colonels. Then they called and said they'd like me to extend the runway at the airport because the Russian military would like to come in by plane.

"Next we had to deal with getting all the trains to stop so they wouldn't break up the procession. A lot of military big shots were coming using private railroad cars the Allies had liberated from the top Germans, and we needed room for them, and the French wanted to line up guns on a hill to fire a 21-gun salute. The last request was to get all the troops' pants pressed the night before! (It had been raining and they thought they looked bedraggled.)

"So I got on the radio and asked the Luxembourg people for help. And the Luxembourgers really came through! They loved America, and they loved General Patton because he saved that country twice. When they first came through there Patton's 3rd Army liberated the country, and then in the Battle of the Bulge when the Germans got within ten miles of the city Patton stopped them again. Housewives called, volunteering to press the pants, and others to put up the officers. We got every flower in the country through somebody or other.

"The horse was the hardest problem. Patton was a cavalry officer originally, so they wanted a cavalry horse so they could put empty boots in the stirrups and lead the horse in the procession. For the life of me I could not find a horse in Luxembourg that looked anything like a cavalry horse! So I got the lightest weight Percheron I could find and we cut off the hair at the bottom of the legs, down at the feet where it's thick. The Luxembourgers didn't notice the difference and I don't think the soldiers did either.

"The procession went through the town twice. Some of those command cars are pretty big and some of the streets are narrow, but they all got through twice and it went off without a hitch."

After his year in Luxembourg, Ham James left the army as a captain. The Belgian government made him a Chevalier de la Couronne de Chene for his part in liberating Belgium.

Charles Vivian

Born 1920 · Elizabeth, New Jersey

Charles H. Vivian, taken at Brookhaven, 2013.

Charles Vivian was born in Elizabeth, New Jersey. He graduated from Brown University and received a PhD from Harvard. During World War II he was an Army artillery captain. After the war he taught English at Southern Methodist University, then at Tufts University and at Bentley College. He was married to Mary Crowley and they had two daughters, Laura and Charlotte. After he was widowed, he married Elizabeth Parlato Bledsoe.

Shooting for Real

By Charles Vivian

> "We… crossed the Channel to France and began shooting for real."

EARLY IN 1942, after basic training at Fort Sill, Oklahoma, I went on to the Field Artillery School there, first as a student, and then for some months as a teacher of field artillery procedures. Next was assignment to a division which in a few weeks shipped off to Europe. We spent a few months of further training in England, then crossed the Channel to France and began shooting for real. Again, after some time we went into Belgium and Germany. Then we spent the rest of the war in support of the First Army.

I was assistant S-2 in the 142nd Field Artillery Group, and also an aerial observer, going up in light planes and conducting observed artillery fire. In my final rank as captain I received the Air Medal.

When World War II was winding down, partly because I knew some German, I was transferred into Military Government. Our function was to do some political work and supervise that of the Germans. From this last military assignment I was finally relieved and returned to the United States in 1945.

John R. Roberts, Jr.

Born 1922 · Philadelphia, Pennsylvania

Jack Roberts had a lifelong passion for golf. He was especially proud of playing for 80 years, after sinking a 35-foot putt at a father-son tournament when he was eight years old.

John "Jack" Roberts, Jr., was born in 1922 in Philadelphia, Pennsylvania, the son of John R. and Helen Paist Roberts. He grew up in Wyncote, Pennsylvania, and graduated from the Penn Charter School. He then attended the Wharton School at the University of Pennsylvania one year before entering the Army Air Force where he was trained to be a bombardier. Sent to Europe, he completed 30 missions over Germany before returning to the United States. He was planning to train as a pilot but the war ended and he left the service. He returned to the Wharton School at the University of Pennsylvania earning a degree in business management. He married Dene Parker in 1950. They had gone to nursery school together but had lost contact with each other, reconnecting after the war. Through his career, Jack and Dene lived in Boston, Massachusetts; Seneca Falls, New York; Indianapolis, and Crawfordsville, Indiana, where his company, Crawford Industries, is located.

Did Measles Change His Destiny?

By John R. Roberts, Jr.

"My new pilot was a steady family man, who neither smoked nor drank and whom I considered to be the safest possible leader for this duty. Because of his and his crew's high rating, this plane was the lead plane in large bombing missions, and as such, was especially vulnerable."

I ENLISTED INTO the Army Air Corps at the age of 19 when I was a sophomore at the University of Pennsylvania Wharton School.

I trained as a bombardier and in 1944 was assigned to a B-17 crew of nine men: pilot, copilot, navigator, bombardier, four gunners and one radioman. Assigned crew members work together throughout their entire service. I learned to use the Norden bombsight, a breakthrough invention. So that it would not fall into enemy hands, we were taught how to destroy it in case the plane was badly damaged in enemy territory.

Just about the time we were to leave for our final training in England, I came down with measles. As this was considered dangerously contagious, I was sent to a special hospital for isolation.

When I was released from the hospital, I was assigned to a new crew. My new pilot was a steady family man, who neither smoked nor drank and whom I considered to be the safest possible leader for this duty. Because of his and his crew's high rating, this plane was the lead plane in large bombing missions, and as such, was especially vulnerable. Our 398th Bombardment Group flew thirty missions, mostly over Germany, before returning to the United States, five missions fewer than usual because of the increased danger to the lead plane in a squadron. The main danger was from the Luftwaffe fighter planes rather than from the ground.

A true leader, my pilot kept in touch with his crew for the rest of his life and visited my family in Indiana and the other crew members through the years. I always wondered how the bombardier in the crew of my first assignment had fared. I tried for years to find out the man's name and life, because that other bombardier's assignment would have been my destiny.

After my tour of duty ended, I intended to reenlist for pilot training and was on my way from California to Stewart Field, when V-J Day came. And happily for all, this changed my plans. I left the service and returned to college.

Officers of Jack Roberts' WWII plane: from left to right: Joe Buehler, navigator;
Roger Weum, copilot; Jack Roberts, bombardier; Ray Armour, pilot. Photo taken
in London, England; note "Big Ben" in the background. Roger Weum, the copilot,
later piloted his own B-17 but was shot down over Merseburg, Germany. He was
the only member of the original crew who did not return home.

Sam Berman

Born 1923 · Marathon, New York

Samuel Berman, U.S. Army Air Corps, 1944.

Samuel Berman was born in Marathon, New York, in 1923 and grew up in Binghamton, New York. His parents were Isaac and Sarah Berman. The family then moved to Roxbury, Massachusetts, and he graduated from Roxbury Memorial High School. He spent one year at the University of Wisconsin, then entered the service. He went to radio school at Sheppard Field, Texas, and gunnery school in Florida. He was discharged as a sergeant and returned to the University of Wisconsin, subsequently going into the family business in Boston. He married Vivian Matchnick in 1951 and they had four children. During his service career, Sam was awarded the Air Medal seven times and the Distinguished Flying Cross for his efforts when his plane was hit by enemy fire and the pilot was temporarily unconscious. He revived the pilot and as the navigator for the plane, he was able to direct the plane (which had lost its route) back to safety.

The Plane Was Diving Straight for the Ground

By Sam Berman

"A fragment of an antiaircraft bomb had shattered their Plexiglas window and they were both stunned. Their faces had so many cuts they looked as though they had been skinned. I shook the copilot and pointed to show him we were diving toward the ground."

MY WIFE AND I have friends in France with whom we often travel. Our friend was a cartoonist and a former rugby player. Former rugby players are a friendly group and we met many of these wonderfully funny guys in many places throughout France. One of the players we met was from Corsica and he and his wife were building a vacation home there. I told him I had been stationed in Corsica during World War II and had always wanted to go back. They immediately invited us and our good friends to visit them in May 1989. Their house was built in the mountains overlooking an area that had once been an airfield during the war. It was a very nostalgic trip for me.

Corsica was important to me because of my time there during the war. I joined the U.S. Army in December of 1942 hoping to become a pilot. Unfortunately I did not pass the eye exam and was sent to radio and gunnery school instead. In July 1944 I was sent overseas and eventually to Corsica to fly B-25 combat missions over southern France and northern Italy. My unit was in the 12th Air Force and the 321st Bombardment Group.

A shortage of bombardiers developed in September 1944. B-25 air crew regulations required that the bombardier also be

The Distinguished Flying Cross Is a military decoration awarded to any officer or enlisted member of the United States Armed Forces who distinguishes himself or herself in support of operations by "heroism or extraordinary achievement... in an aerial flight, subsequent to November 11, 1918." (*Wikipedia*)

trained as a navigator. I was very quickly trained to be a navigator and a bombardier.

On November 10, 1944, I was assigned to a crew that would fly a mission to knock out a railroad station in Ostiglia, Italy, in the Po Valley. We were attacked by a heavy barrage of antiaircraft weapons. The plane was severely damaged; we lost one of our two engines, and several crew members were injured. After we dropped our bombs, the plane was in a nose dive toward the ground. I decided it was time to get out so I went to the hatch with a parachute and was about to jump when I realized no one else was bailing out. I checked the pilot's compartment and saw both pilots were slumped over. A fragment of an antiaircraft bomb had shattered their Plexiglas window and they were both stunned. Their faces had so many cuts they looked as though they had been skinned. I shook the co-pilot and pointed to show him we were diving toward the ground. He smiled, tested the controls and the plane responded. He then shook the pilot who also seemed uninjured except for the many cuts on his face. They asked me to fix a course out of Italy that avoided further antiaircraft weapons. I looked at my charts which showed known antiaircraft installations in Italy and picked a course I hoped would be okay. Luckily it was good enough to get us back to Corsica. (Editor's note: Berman was awarded the Distinguished Flying Cross for his actions during this mission.)

Corsica in 1989 was much the same as I remembered it, but there was no sign of our airfields. They had been restored to

Samuel Berman in a B-25 airplane. Taken by the Army for hometown newspaper.

farmland. We asked a farmer if he knew exactly where our airfield had been. He pointed out the location of the former airfield and told us he had been a small child at that time and he and others had counted our planes going and coming back to assure themselves we all survived each flight. I was moved by that because we thought the locals were indifferent and only tolerated our presence there. After all, they didn't need us to liberate them; they had driven the Germans out before we got there. Even now, as I write about that time, I relive it.

Franklin A. Lindsay

Born 1916 · Pasadena, California

Frank A. Lindsay at a British training camp in Palestine before parachuting into Yugoslavia, May 1944.

Frank Lindsay was born in 1916 in Pasadena, California, where he grew up. He graduated from Stanford in 1938. He entered the service in 1941; his first assignment was to deliver military equipment to Iran. He then joined the Office of Strategic Services. He parachuted into Yugoslavia to join the Yugoslav Partisans in 1944 and worked with them to blow up the rail lines in southern Austria. Later, he was head of the military mission to Tito. He was awarded Slovenia's highest decoration, the Gold Medal. He wrote a book about his wartime experiences, *Beacons in the Night.** After the war, he was involved in a wide range of activities: he was a member of the U.S. Atomic Energy Commission; he helped set up the European side of the Marshall Plan; and helped fellow OSSer Frank Wisner establish OPC, the precursor of the CIA. In the private sector he spent time at the Ford Foundation and McKinsey & Co. and was head of ITEK Corp., a high-tech company whose products included the cameras for scouting the moon. He also served on the U.S. Senate Intelligence Advisory Committee; chaired the Committee for Economic Development's program and policy committee; and chaired the board of the National Bureau of Economic Research. After retirement he started a seven-year stint helping Ukraine's International Management Institute turn its curriculum toward a market economy. While in Kiev, he also worked with Ukraine's National Security Council and helped develop a program for Ukraine's military officers. This program continues in an expanded form to include not only participants from Ukraine but also from the other countries surrounding the Black Sea. He married Margot Coffin and they had three children and three granddaughters.

Behind Enemy Lines

From *Beacons in the Night: With the OSS and Tito's Partisans in Wartime Yugoslavia*

By Franklin A. Lindsay

> "The OSS had taken me on because I was an engineer who was expected to know something about blowing up bridges and railroads, because I had inflated my claims to fluency in Germany and Russian, and because I had volunteered."

OUR DROP INTO Slovenia was scheduled for April in 1944, but our first two attempts to find the reception party on the ground had failed and so we missed the end of the April moon. This was now already mid-May, and our third try.

Our mission was to disrupt communications in the northern part of Yugoslavia and southern Austria. The OSS had taken me on because I was an engineer who was expected to know something about blowing up bridges and railroads, because I had inflated my claims to fluency in German and Russian, and because I had volunteered.

We had been four hours in the air. In our flight plan the TOT, time over target, was 23:45. It was now midnight. The dispatcher, a Royal Air Force sergeant, came aft from the cockpit. He removed a wooden cover from a hole, about four feet in diameter, in the floor of the bomb bay. The sides of the hole were about three feet deep, enough to allow a man to sit on the edge and still keep his feet from the plane's rushing slipstream below. Through the hole there was only the black of a moonless night.

Alongside the hole Lt. Gordon Bush, Lt. Schraeder and I, sweating out our parachute drop, watched the flight dispatcher as he went about his business. Corporal James Fisher, my radio operator, slept as soundly as he had during most of the flight. The navigator had brought the Halifax long range bomber to the area in which, if his navigation was accurate, the aircraft commander should be able to see the reception signals on the ground. After several wide, searching turns, he spotted a fire. As he flew closer a flashlight winked the prearranged Morse code recognition signal. It was the letter D, the right one for that night. We were set to jump.

As the plane turned, the dispatcher moved the cargo containers with our two radios, the batteries for the radios, our packs, and the medical supplies for the Partisans to the edge of the hole. He then attached the ends of strong web lines—static lines—to rings on the parachutes of each container. The opposite ends were already attached to rings on the inside of the aircraft. When the lines were pulled tight as the containers fell from the plane the chutes would be pulled open automatically. As a precaution the dispatcher wore a body harness that tied him to the plane so that he could not fall through the hole as he wrestled the containers to the end.

A red warning light in the top of the bomb bay over the hole came on as the pilot started his second pass. When the green light went on, the sergeant quickly pushed out each of the containers. The static lines, having pulled open their chutes as they fell away from the plane, rattled dryly against the underside of the aircraft. I was acutely aware that we ourselves would go out in the same way.

The sergeant pulled the lines in quickly as the plane circled again. It was our turn. I shouted above the roar of the engines to wake Fisher as we got ready for the jump. I was not as calm as he about what lay ahead. Shraeder and I now hooked our own static lines to the rings on the sides of the fuselage while the dispatcher hooked the other ends to the parachutes strapped to our backs. We then took our positions sitting on the edge of the hole across from each other.

My training jumps had all been from a standing position in the door of a plane. For reasons I don't understand even today, the thought of passively dropping through a hole into the night was infinitely more disagreeable than jumping through an open door. Now I sat at the edge of the hole looking down at absolute black nothing.

Being sure I was hooked up at both ends totally consumed those last few minutes. I knew that a replacement radio operator had been killed in a drop to the same area a month earlier. Both he and the dispatcher had been in such a funk immediately before the drop that neither had remembered to hook up his line to open the chute. In British operations, such as this, unlike American, a reserve chute was not provided and there was no way the main chute could be opened once one had dropped through that hole. I pulled first on the end attached to the plane until I was sure it, and not some other line, had been firmly attached. Then I reached over my shoulder to feel if the other end was attached to the parachute on my back, and then with my hand I ran the length of the line at my side to be sure it was the same one that was attached to the chute. I must have repeated this instinctive bit of reassurance four or five times.

By now the red light indicating we were again approaching the drop area was on. I put my hands on the edge of the hole ready to shove off. The dispatcher was standing across from me. As the green light went on, he gave the thumbs-up sign and shouted to me over the roar of the engines, "It's a piece of cake!"

Out I went.

———

By nightfall we were completely surrounded. The Partisan chief of staff passed word to me that as soon as it was dark we would start moving. One of the brigades would cover our breakout.

The moon had not yet risen. It was a black night and the heavy forests shut out the starlight that normally provides enough light to see by on moonless nights. Those of us with watches tied them on string around our necks and hung the watches on our backs so that the man behind could follow the luminous dial on the man ahead. We attempted to make as little noise as possible but I thought we must have sounded like a herd of elephants as we slipped on rocky slopes and tangled with heavy branches. We moved all night long, only stopping from time to time to listen for possible German movements.

As we worked our way out of the SS encirclement, we saw, toward morning, a large fire burning in the valley below. Partisans had slipped undetected to the German barracks and set it afire. In the early days of the war Tito told the Partisans to meet an enemy offensive both by withdrawing from an unequal battle with a superior force and by slipping behind them to destroy their bases. By dawn we were out of the encirclement and on a nearby mountain. We had been led all night by a peasant boy who had grown up on the Pohorje and who knew every ridge and ravine, every path. It was another lesson in the importance of winning the support of the local population to provide safety, protection and support, without which no armed group could have survived.

We stopped long enough to make radio contact with Caserta and received a message asking us to "give explanation why 5 planes failed to find your signal last night." We replied: "Yesterday afternoon and evening 2,000 SS attacked drop area. Impossible to receive planes. Still moving."

The next day we passed by one of the underground hospitals. As the war progressed, the Partisans had constructed hidden hospitals high in the mountains where it was unlikely that German troops would come. This eased the terrible burden for the fighting brigades of carrying their wounded: on the march four able Partisans were required to carry one wounded man plus all their weapons. These hospitals were often underground, with hidden entrances carefully camouflaged. A wounded man would be brought within a mile or two of the hospital and left alone at a prearranged spot, the location of which was often changed. Hospital couriers would then arrive to pick him up and take him the rest of the way, thus ensuring that only the hospital's staff knew of its location. If German patrols did come into the area, the hospital personnel would leave water and food for the patients, and then leave after covering the entrance completely with sod and leaves. Only disguised air vents remained open. The wounded would be left alone, hidden, for as long as a week if necessary.

Elaborate precautions were taken not to leave a trail from the pickup locations to the hospitals themselves. Parts of the path were routed across rocky ledges or flowing streams. Moss-covered stones were turned upside down for people to step on, then returned to their undisturbed mossy sides. The Germans often used dogs to follow human scents. To throw them off, an arm or leg that had been amputated in hospital was dragged along false trails.

When the patients were well enough to leave, they were blindfolded and led out of the hidden area so that they could never tell under German torture the location of the hospital they had been in. Most of the hospitals escaped detection, although a few were discovered. In those cases the wounded were murdered in their bunks and the hospitals burned on top of them.

In Stajerska we were never able to arrange a landing strip, so the wounded who could walk made the long march south to the clandestine airstrip in Dolenjska. The others had to be carried to the nearest hidden hospital, often miles away through the thick forests to the top of the mountains.

---

*From *Beacons in the Night: With the OSS and Tito's Partisans in Wartime Yugoslavia*, Franklin Lindsay. Stanford University Press: Stanford, CA, 1993.

Nancy Sweezy

Born 1921 · New Hampshire

Nancy Sweezy at Brookhaven.

Nancy Sweezy was born October 14, 1921, in New Hampshire. She grew up in New Hampshire, and was educated at the Boston Museum School of Fine Arts and the Smart School. She joined the war effort in 1940 and worked for the OSS first in Washington and then in Europe. After the war she and her husband Paul M. Sweezy and their three children lived in Wilton, New Hampshire, and then Cambridge, Massachusetts. She was a leading folklorist in the United States and was known to a generation of musicians for her role as president of the board of directors of the Club 47, an important player in the folk music revival of the 1960s and early 1970s. In the mid-1960s, she moved to North Carolina to revive the famed Jugtown Pottery. She helped inspire a revival of the traditional pottery community and watched it grow from 7 potteries in the area to more than 115 today. Always an advocate for human rights and a believer in the magic of music, dance and handmade objects to preserve the soul of culture and its community, she was an intrepid author, teacher and mentor. In 2006, the National Endowment for the Arts celebrated Nancy's leadership in the field of folk arts by declaring her a National Living Treasure and presenting her with the Bess Lomax Hawes National Heritage Fellowship at the Library of Congress. The National Heritage Fellowship presentation also acknowledged her work with Ralph Rinzler, director of the Smithsonian Institution's annual Folklife Festival on the Mall in Washington, D.C. She founded the Refugee Arts Project which collaborated with the Cambodian, Hmong and other Southeast Asian communities in the preservation of the traditional crafts and performing arts. She was the author of a seminal book, *Raised in Clay*, on the Southern pottery tradition, published by the Smithsonian Press. Her book *Armenian Folk Arts, Culture, and Identity*, was published when she was in her 70's.

★ *Biography continued on page 109*

How I Stumbled into the OSS

By Nancy Sweezy

"What didn't I know? I didn't know we had changed enemies....I was shocked. All intelligence was now to put
a high beam on the USSR, which had just broken Germany's
strength in the heart of Russia, thereby shortening the war
considerably."

I WENT TO a cocktail party in Washington in 1942 and stumbled
into a job when a fellow guest said come to my office tomorrow.
I passed muster and took the job after promising to never reveal
where I worked. Five days later I was in the Research and Analysis
Branch (R & A) of the Office of Strategic Services (OSS). I worked
two years in the Washington office and the following year in London, Paris and Germany.

R & A was assessing and updating changes in Germany's
capacity to fight the war. This new intelligence agency used its
sweeping powers to pluck the brightest and best scholars from
universities, government, wherever they were. The scholars ana-
lyzed information they found in foreign newspapers, magazines
and other publicly available sources about the state of the German
economy and war effort.

I began reading pages of mimeographed excerpts of letters
from Germany that held bits of information like, "There's no bread
in the stores," which I took to the relevant section. But I soon figured out what might be more interesting and useful. Our director,
Chandler Morse, visited each of the seven sections once a week
to find out what they were discovering and periodically, he sent
their findings to U.S. military leaders and diplomats overseas.
My suggestion was to send an interim report so they would know
what was in the pipeline. Chan liked the idea, so I joined him on

his visits, took notes and wrote up what I thought they had said. Sometimes I had it wrong, but I soon caught on to the ideas and material of their research and Chan sent the updates once a month to England, North Africa and Italy—wherever the activity was. The response was positive.

When part of R & A was moving to London, I asked to go too. Finally Chan said, "Okay, come along, you always find something useful that no one else has noticed." I crossed the Atlantic on a bitterly rough trip in November of 1944 in a convoy of blacked-out troopships shielded by U.S. destroyers that zigzagged to prevent German submarines from getting a straight shot for their torpedoes. I was on an old cruise ship manned by the British navy. Just the smell of their kippered herring breakfast sent me out of the line and back to my hammock where I swung for a good many days as the ship tossed about. We finally arrived in the quiet waters of Glasgow harbor.

Gil Winant, our ambassador to Great Britain, invited me to stay at the Embassy until I found an apartment. His daughter had been my best friend in school and I had lived with the family for two years. Gil took me to see Parliament in action and we ran into Churchill coming off the floor, who looked at me so intently, I thought he had taken in every thought I ever had in one long glance. He nodded, grunted, spoke to Gil and went out the door.

I had arrived when the last of the Germans' air attacks, the V-2 missiles, were falling on London. They were terrifying as well as hugely destructive. You could hear one coming, getting closer and closer. When the sound cut off you held your breath until it hit the ground and exploded and you realized you were still alive. If you were at home, you rolled under the bed to avoid flying glass. If you were on a cot in the fire duty house already dressed, you just grabbed your jacket and helmet before going onto the street with blankets and water and a white kerchief used to signal a medic that you were beside a wounded person. Gil and his staff were always on the street until everyone was taken care of and fires were out. The Brits naturally loved him for his active concern for them.

Once settled in for work at the 40 Berkeley Square office, I reversed the report process and sent back to Washington what the London team was discovering. We were working next to the EOU (Enemy Objectives Unit), which selected bombing targets. I sorted captured German small arms by serial number to assess their production for EOU.

When we moved onto the continent, I wore a WAC's uniform with second lieutenant bars, memorized a serial number, and had a quick lesson in how to gouge out an enemy's eyes. Fortunately, I only met the enemy later in Germany when the war was over and many were pleading they were forced to join the Nazi party in order to have a ration card.

We had moved to Paris before V-E Day and its wild night of celebration. The city was brightly lit from the top of the Eiffel Tower to the humblest houses, and filled with music, dancing and wine that the French offered to all Americans. I started out the evening with friends and soon lost them in the swirl of the crowd. But I never felt alone. The crowd was one organism that danced and walked the night away absorbed by the heady atmosphere of French joy until dawn, when the magic dissipated and I found my way back to our hotel to stand in line for a shot, supposed to help with hangovers.

I must have done some work in Paris but I can't remember what it was. I do recall finding Errol Flynn sitting at my desk one day making a model ship. He was in Paris only because Madeleine Carroll was there for some job and wanted him along. The movie star used my office off and on for a week before he and Madeleine departed. I never did see her and I was glad to have my own space again. We were still in Paris when FDR died and had priority to enter Notre Dame for his service. The crowd outside the cathedral parted to let Charles de Gaulle pass. He was tall with such a rigid posture, you thought he might fall over backwards. The service was a moment of shared grief for Americans and French alike.

We moved to Wiesbaden in Germany as the U.S. Army was moving rapidly, trying to get to Berlin before the Russians could.

The Russians won this race, thereby dividing east from west for decades. My job in the Wiesbaden office was to look at how the "Morgenthau" plan to deindustrialize and denazify Germany was being carried out. I knew what was supposed to happen from studying the Joint Chiefs of Staff 1067 paper. It was a tough plan aimed at making Germany a pastoral nation. I looked in corners where other things were going on and was immediately called in to see Allen Dulles, head of OSS in Europe. He put his arm around my shoulder patronizingly and said, "Well dear. It's all right, you just didn't know, but don't do that again."

What didn't I know? I didn't know we had changed enemies.

I was shocked. All intelligence was now to put a high beam on the USSR, which had just broken Germany's strength in the heart of Russia, thereby shortening the war considerably. A revised more lenient plan came out from Washington, basically aiming to prevent Germany from failing into the Soviet orbit, which indeed they might have done if they were treated too harshly. The new plan was for the lower-level Nazis to continue running the country; Hitler's atomic scientists were to be taken to America to help our scientists get the atom bomb before the Russians did; and the most egregious war criminals were to be held for trial at Nuremberg.

Most people in this R & A group were politically liberal or even radical, and agreed it was time to go home. Chan sent me to Vienna to take word of what was going on to the R & A staff there. I signed Eisenhower's name to a travel permit so I could get going, everything was pretty loose by then. I stayed a few days in Vienna and returned to Wiesbaden snuggled up to Paul Sweezy, chief writer of R & A reports, because it was very cold in the open jeep and because it felt good.

Back in Wiesbaden, I was invited to go to Berlin in the Russian Zone by an American diplomat stationed there, who was courting me. I went, of course, and promptly sold my watch to a Russian soldier for $45. I was late to that market; the week before an American watch brought $1,200. With that business done, we walked a few steps to a low door that led down into Hitler's underground bunker and backed down a ladder, his stairway directly into their tiny, squalid, two-room apartment where Hitler and his new wife, Eva Braun, had killed themselves. Their bodies were taken up into the garden and burned when the Russian army was literally one block away. Without a second thought, I helped myself to a page or two of Hitler's schedule still placed on a small table in a hall by the bathroom and snagged a smidgeon of flowered fabric from the couch on which Hitler had died.

The Russians did not allow us to go through the large formal part of the underground building. But we did explore what was left of the heavily bombed Kanzleides Führers (the Reich Chancellery), next to the bunker, where there were hundreds and hundreds of saucers—no cups—on huge wide stairs that led to nowhere. I took two saucers and, after a while of puzzling, realized the Russians could fasten cups to their belts, as Civil War soldiers did here, but had no use for saucers. Shortly after this visit, the Russians blew up the bunker and I gracefully turned down the diplomat's proposal of marriage.

We returned to London from Wiesbaden in a rattletrap B-27, signed all our exit papers, bade each other farewell and, at that moment, Paul and I decided to marry. He flew back, while I, now with the rank of first lieutenant and an annual salary of $3,000, recrossed a calm Atlantic on a troopship full of GI's, who, at the sight of the Statue of Liberty, blew up hundreds of condoms into balloons and set them flying over New York Harbor.

<hr />

 ★ *Biography continued from page 104*
She compiled the book after numerous trips to Armenia (during a time of danger and unrest there) with her son, the photographer Sam Sweezy. In 2004, at the age of 83, she cocurated, with potter Mark Hewitt, for the North Carolina Museum of Art, "The Potter's Eye: Art and Tradition in North Carolina," and collaborated with Mr. Hewitt on her last book, a companion to the exhibit with the same title.

Robert Solow

Born 1924 · Brooklyn, New York

Robert Solow, from the mid-1990s.

I was born in Brooklyn, New York, on August 23, 1924, and raised there in Flatbush. My father was a furrier, and he once gave me some occupational advice: "You can grow up to be anything you want, but if you go into the fur business I'll kill you." I went to neighborhood schools: P.S. 197, Seth Low Junior High School (that was a nickel bus ride away) and James Madison High School. From there I went to Harvard College, finishing up after the war and going on to a PhD in economics. I met Barbara Lewis in class in October 1942, we had a couple of dates, and that did it. We were married a couple of days after I got off the boat in August 1945. She didn't think her father could manage seeing his daughter marrying a guy she had known for a couple of months and then hadn't seen for three years. But he did.

My first and last job was at MIT, starting in 1949; I retired in 1995. Of course I had occasional leaves: at the Council of Economic Advisers during the Kennedy administration, a year at Cambridge and another at Oxford. I got the Nobel Prize in economics in 1987 and the National Medal of Science in the 1990s, but the thing I'm proudest of is that, together with my friend Paul Samuelson, we built the MIT economics department from practically nothing to the best department in the country. We came to Brookhaven in 2010.

In Real Time:
Decoding—Translating—Recoding

By Robert Solow

"We managed. We survived Cassino, we did Rome, we survived the Gothic Line between Florence and Bologna. It took two years, all uphill."

I TURNED 18 on August 23, 1942, started my junior year at Harvard in September and decided pretty quickly that beating Hitler was a lot more important than sitting around in classes. So I went downtown and enlisted in the Army, and was told to report to Fort Devens in November. At Devens, the Army classification system, which was famous for stuffing square pegs in round holes, actually did an excellent job with me. I had two accidental skills: I knew German and I knew Morse code. So I was assigned to the Signal Corps, basic training at Camp Edison, New Jersey, and signal intelligence training at Vint Hill Farms Station, Warrenton, Virginia. The training was pretty poor, but by early 1943 I was shipped off to England and shortly thereafter sent to Algeria with a handful of others to join a short-range radio intercept company that had (barely) survived the battle of Kasserine Pass. That company was my home for the next two years. We fought the war in Italy from the very beginning (in Reggio di Calabria across the Strait of Messina) until the German surrender on May 5, 1945, when we had reached Feltre, a small town near Trento in the north of Italy.

We had absolutely nothing in common with the famous intellectuals at Bletchley Park in England who cracked high-level German codes over a long period of time. We were part of U.S. II Corps, and we intercepted low-level tactical messages from German units at the front. Our traffic was between platoon and company or between company and battalion or sometimes between battalion and regimental headquarters, never anything grander than a regiment. I would guess about two-thirds of the messages we copied were in code, and one-third in plain language. The codes in use were pretty simple. They had to be; the guys coding the message had to work fast, in real time and often under fire. And of course we had to break the code equally fast, in real time and sometimes under fire, because the intelligence would otherwise be useless. If a battalion of the 15th Panzer Grenadier Division radioed to one of its companies that there would be a delivery of rifle, machine gun and mortar ammunition at such and such a place on the map at such and such a time, we had to be able to read the message and get the word to II Corps soon enough so that the delivery could be greeted by a couple of fighter-bombers or, more likely, some artillery fire. We were pretty good at that and apparently the Germans had no idea that this was going on.

We worked out of the backs of three built-up 2½-ton trucks. Two of these were occupied by radios and radio operators, six to eight per truck. The third truck was for those of us, like me, who read the plain language messages, broke the coded ones if we could, translated them into English, tried to identify the German units that had sent and received them, located things on maps, and so on. Some days nothing much happened, some days were very hairy.

This was of course long before the transistor. Those radios needed electricity, provided by a gasoline-powered generator (operated by a guy named Drinkwater, who was known to drink anything and everything except water). This meant that we could only do our job when we were stationary. By itself this was not a major problem, because in Italy the front only moved sporadically. The real problem was that the radio transmitters on which we were eavesdropping were low-power and high-frequency, so that the transmission was line-of-sight. It was almost true that if you couldn't see it you couldn't hear it. We had to get as close to those transmitters as we could, but we could not afford to be visible or we and our equipment would be sitting ducks for those German 88s. Fortunately we didn't have to worry about being spotted by airplanes because we owned the air over Italy. But German artillery observers, who almost always had the high ground, were watching. Finding a place to hide where an antenna could still "see" was a big deal.

We managed. We survived Cassino, we did Rome, we survived the Gothic Line between Florence and Bologna. It took two years, all uphill. I'll tell one anecdote and then provide a brag for our small company.

We may have contributed to the Allied decision to bomb the Benedictine Abbey at Montecassino. The question always was whether the Germans were actually using the Abbey. One day we picked up a message—in plain language, actually—that read "Ist Abt oben im Schloss?" In context this was completely ambiguous. "Abt" is German for "Abbot" so the question might have been whether the Abbot was up there in the castle (Abbey). However, among the paratroopers who were then defending Cassino the word used for battalion was "Abteilung" always abbreviated as "Abt" without a period. So the message could just as well be read as asking if the battalion headquarters was up there in the Abbey. The answer was, "Yes, since last Wednesday."

This information was transmitted to II Corps with a full explanation that there was nothing in the message to suggest which was the intended meaning. I think we did point out that if it was a reference to the Abbot, it was the first time he had been mentioned in the hundreds of messages we had intercepted in the course of time. Today the general opinion is that it was a mistake to destroy the Abbey, but I have to admit that we were glad, after all those months, to see the B-17s.

Now for the brag. You will remember the Battle of the Bulge in the winter of 1944–45: the Germans managed in total secrecy to concentrate several divisions near the Ardennes Forest in northern France and southern Belgium, and they were able to launch a large surprise attack. They very nearly broke through the Allied lines—hence the Bulge—but were eventually stopped. If they had succeeded, it would have been a very important event.

We were told by a participant that, on hearing the news, General Keyes (commanding II Corps) convened a meeting of his senior staff officers. At one point he asked: "Could this happen to us?" After a moment, his chief of intelligence replied, "No." General Keyes: "Why not?" Answer: "The Germans could not move that many new troops into the line without Faison's people finding out." We were Faison's people; Jack Faison was our CO. It was probably so: they could not have laid wire everywhere, would have had to resort to radio, and we would have heard all these strangers.

Our war ended on May 5. (By the way, we heard it first from the Germans!) We were sent back to a lovely spot, Riva at the head of Lago di Garda, and billeted in an empty school until August, when we convoyed down to Naples, boarded the SS *Cristobal*, bound for Norfolk, Virginia, and, we thought, eventually Japan. Somewhere in the Atlantic Ocean the ship's PA system announced the dropping of the Hiroshima bomb. We cheered.

Anne M. Smiddy

Born 1929 · Doorwerth, Netherlands

Anne Smiddy, taken in the early 1960s.

I was born, Anne Marie Jose van Zanten Jut, in 1929 in a small place called Doorwerth about five miles west of the city of Arnhem in the Netherlands. With my parents and younger sister, we lived a sheltered and comfortable life until the outbreak of World War II for us on May 10, 1940. After the death of my father we moved to Oosterbeeck, a suburb of Arnhem. We survived the Battle of Arnhem in 1944. After the war I went back to high school in another part of the country. Our home had been destroyed and we lost most of our possessions. After high school I went to the school for social work in Amsterdam and got my certificate. I worked three and a half years as a social worker in Landsmeer, a small town north of Amsterdam. At age 27, I married Michael Smiddy, an English physicist. We immigrated to the United States in 1958. From 1961 onward we lived in Lexington, Massachusetts. My husband passed away in 2010. I have two married sons and five grandchildren.

An Unusual Meeting

By Anne M. Smiddy

"What had they left behind? Was it right what they had done, leaving those civilians in their cellar? What chance would these people have to come out alive? What could they have done differently? What a disaster! The inside pain went on and on."

Introduction

THE FOLLOWING STORY, "An Unusual Meeting," takes place during the Battle of Arnhem, September 17–25, 1944 in the Netherlands, occupied by the Germans in World War II.

The First British Airborne Division landed about two miles from where I lived, at Oosterbeek, west of Arnhem. Their mission was to secure the bridge over the Rhine at Arnhem. They made their headquarters in Hotel Hartenstein, right opposite the lane where we lived, and they also made part of headquarters in our house. We lived in a duplex house (two houses under one roof). Germans occupied our house in 1943 and they had made a door opening between the two half houses. My mother, sister and I took shelter in our neighbor's cellar. I was 15 years old.

He rushed down the staircase into the cellar where mother, Hanneke and I were sitting on a mattress on the floor against an inside wall. We were with our next-door neighbors, Mr. and Mrs. Rosman, a middle-aged couple, and two other ladies from our neighborhood who had fled from their home and found shelter with us. They were seated on kitchen chairs away from the underground glassless window. The cellar was small, only about 14 by 18 feet, just large enough to accommodate us. The date was September 21, 1944, during the battle of Arnhem.

"You are a bit on top of the war, aren't you?" he said and sat down at the bottom of the stairs. His lighthearted remark was slightly off-beat but he wanted to ease the situation, feeling badly about what was happening to us. He was not an ordinary English Airborne soldier. For one thing he wore a red beret instead of a helmet. Furthermore, out of his jacket peeked a white collar. He was a chaplain. He had heard of our existence and wanted to know how we were making out after the last shelling attack. He was delighted to hear my mother speak fluent English and asked her how that came about. She told him that she went to a ladies college at Cheltenham when she was 17 years old. "What a coincidence, our regiment was stationed quite near there; you must be a lot younger than I am." "I don't think so; I am a lot older than you are." It turned out that mother was a few months older. Both were 36 years old.

He asked her then about the neighbors in the big house on the other side of the field next to our house. An elderly lady and a young woman were living there. The young woman had given birth a couple of days earlier. Did mother know anything about her? "Oh, don't be concerned about her. They are traitors.

The west side of our home in Oosterbeek, summer 1945.

The son of the old lady is a Dutch SSer." During the British landing a wagon with a red cross appeared and picked the son up. He was in civilian clothes with a fake bandage around his head. "The coward! Don't pity them," mother continued.

Summer 1945. Our garden in Oosterbeek. Aurora lost her knee, which hit the Rev. W. R. Chignell in the back during shelling in Oosterbeek.

Later, the chaplain remembered her vehemence and thought how he himself, a minister, in the heat of the fight, had been encouraging his men to do some good shooting. He remembered too how he had been swearing—speaking words he had not used since before his ordination. This battle was his very first experience, finding out the gruesome reality of war. In the first assault he kept standing up, instead of dropping down flat on the ground, until his assistant quipped, "Padre knows for sure where he is going!"

His visit was short. As the days of fighting became more desperate he came to visit a few more times. Once he came to ask for sheets so he could bury the dead. On Sunday, the 24th of September, he gave a short service in our home cellar. Mother had asked to attend a service but it was too dangerous so he did not allow her. In the afternoon he was busy transporting a badly wounded man to the same cellar, when a mortar shell exploded four yards away. It wounded his helper and something hit his back too. It was a piece of the marble sculpture in our garden; the knee of Aurora had been blown off by the shell. A moment later he was helping another wounded soldier on a stretcher with four others into our home cellar when a shell hit the roof, with the result that four more men were wounded. That cellar was not safe to use anymore and we were asked if we could make some room for them in ours.

"My bedroom after the battle of Arnhem (summer 1945) in Oosterbeek, The Netherlands."

They stayed with us for an hour or so, and then were transported to the Red Cross post in town. With my field hockey stick as a pole, a white sheet and the red part of our Dutch flag fastened to it with safety pins making a Red Cross flag, they made it on foot under the most dangerous circumstances. It was a miracle that our friend came back. He was exhausted and slept for half an hour next to me. The next day he called from upstairs for my mother and told her to put a sign on the cellar door saying "Dutch Civilians." Nothing more was said. It was obvious that something ominous was going to happen that night. A matter of life and death. Nobody knew. What happened to him then I only learned from his diary much later.

The Escape

REV. W. R. CHIGNELL, as we later got to know him, was going to leave that night. Word had come of a new plan from headquarters right across the main road at Hotel Hartenstein. The mission to keep the bridge at Arnhem had failed. The German armor proved to be overwhelming against the Allies' limited firepower. We witnessed with horror airlifts of new supplies, intended for our troops, but dropped in the enemy zone. The only course for the Allied troops now was to reach their last stronghold. This meant crossing the Rhine to the south. The Dorset battalion on the other side of the river Rhine was going to assist in the escape of the Airbornes.

In the afternoon Chignell had gone into the battlefield with Lt. Martin Culverwell after a violent shell attack. This quiet spell was a good time to find the wounded. The Germans did the same. How surprised Chignell was when a German helped him with a better aid for the wound he was treating for the English soldier. When the half dozen wounded were brought behind their own lines, the fighting resumed. Now Chignell knew how near the Germans were. Any moment they could be overrun. Casualties were coming in all the time and medical supplies were getting very short.

Chignell opened his emergency rations and decided to eat it all. He drank a little foul water. He needed all the strength he could get, for what lay ahead of him was not promising. There was no time to fear being killed. It did not matter anymore, one way or the other. He was in God's hands and that was good. Just do what he had to do. He cut off the sleeves of his smock and pulled them over his boots to make less noise, and he blackened his face to be less visible.

With John Hooper, a senior officer, he made up a party of wounded and helpers and set off for the Hotel Hartenstein. It was a frightful trip. Never did he feel more naked going over that field in front of the house. But they all made it to headquarters, through the only entrance, and were seen by no German snipers.

The hotel was crowded with men. In the cellars were the wounded. Those who could walk were placed in groups of 20 to set off for the Rhine, a distance of one and a half to two miles, leaving at intervals of a few minutes. The escape route was only about 200 hundred yards wide and in some places not clear of Germans.

Chignell asked permission from General Urquhart, who was with his staff in one of the cellars, to say prayers. As many as could get into the cellar joined in and they said the Lord's Prayer together. Then Chignell gave them the blessing and left.

After a nerve-wracking wait, Chignell's group finally left at 10:15 P.M. The night was pitch dark, and a heavy rain came down. Each man held on to the tail of the smock of the man in front of him to find his way in the dark. They crawled through bushes, over fallen trees and branches and around craters; an indescribable mess! The shooting from snipers came from everywhere. There were tracers and flares. They came to a road where the machine gun firing came from both ends. Once they found themselves in a crater, the shells exploding all around them. The Rev. Chignell thought he would never be able to get out of there. It lasted five or ten minutes but to him it was an eternity. The going was ever so slow; they skirted around two or three fields. In one they stopped because of a bright star shell. There were also red tracer bullets being fired regularly in two lines over their heads from south of the river. Someone behind Chignell whispered, "Where the bloody hell do you think we are?" An unexpected voice from behind the hedge said, "You keep between the red lights, chum, and you will be all right." It was one of the Dorset men covering their escape.

They went on, wading through a ditch and crossing a railroad track and finally came to the open meadowlands near the river where dead cows were scattered about and small bushes at the edges provided the only cover. Reaching the river Chignell began to wonder how he would get across. He could not swim. The Rhine is 150 to 200 yards wide and the water flows very swiftly. Lt. Peter Jackson decided to swim and some followed him. The others stayed with Chignell hoping to find a boat. In the dark they heard some splashing in the water. Chignell had the nerve to call out. How exceptionally lucky they were. The answer was in English. Dorset men had found a large tub like a rowing boat and were helping the Airbornes to get across. They arrived safely.

A white tape led them to a barn where they received a mug of delicious hot tea. Then, being totally exhausted, Chignell dropped onto the floor and slept. He did not waken, even when a fire broke out in the barn. The Dorset men managed to extinguish it without disturbing all the sleeping men. The next morning everybody had to go towards Nijmegen, in liberated territory. Chignell was walking in a daze, not quite comprehending what had happened. It was like somebody else was walking instead of him, putting one foot in front of the other. Next to him was John Place, who had also been in our house. They moved on in silence along the dike, each with his own thoughts trying to make sense out of the whole situation.

What had they left behind? Was it right what they had done, leaving those civilians in their cellar? What chance would these people have to come out alive? Could they have done things differently? What a disaster! The inside pain went on and on. Then

Monument erected by people of Gelderland, which reads:

"50 years ago British and Polish airborne soldiers fought here against overwhelming odds to open the way into Germany and bring the war to an early end. Instead we brought death and destruction for which you never have blamed us. This stone marks our admiration for your great courage remembering especially the woman who tended our wounded. In the long winter that followed your families risked death by hiding allied soldiers and airmen while members of the resistance helped many to safety. You took us then into your homes as fugitives and friends. We took you forever in our hearts. This strong bond will continue long after we are all gone. September, 1994."

Chignell made a suggestion to Place, "There is one thing we can do and that is to pray to God." Both men knelt down on the side of the dike and prayed for us and all people.

After a few days of travelling through the south of the Netherlands and Louvain in Belgium, they flew from Brussels in American Dakotas back to England. Rev. Chignell's chief job then was to write or visit the relatives of men killed or missing. Only one man in five came home.

Shortly after our liberation in May 1945, Rev. W. R. Chignell came back to Oosterbeeck to help with the identification of dead soldiers and also to find out what happened to us. We had survived the ordeal. We met; it was joyous. We became friends for life.

In 1993, on our last visit, he gave me his diary. We have shared what life is about. On the first of January 1994, Rev. W. R. Chignell passed away peacefully at 84.

Chankey Touart

Born 1919 · Mobile, Alabama

Chankey Touart, 1942, U.S. Army Weather Service.

Chankey Touart was the only son of Colonel Clarence and Hellene Barnes Touart of Mobile, Alabama. He grew up in Mobile and graduated from the University of Chicago as a Phi Beta Kappa majoring in physics. He joined the U.S. Army hoping to be trained as a pilot but instead was trained as a meteorologist and then was sent to England in charge of a group of meteorologists. In England he was a part of the U.S. Army weather service. He was awarded the Bronze Star and returned home as a lieutenant colonel. After the war, he became the director of the Atmospheric Science Division of the Geophysics Research Directorate Meteorology Lab at Hanscom Field in Bedford, Massachusetts. He was married to the former Mary Louise Chorley and they had three children, Ellen Touart-Grob, Katherine Touart Wilson and Douglas Barnes Touart, as well as five granddaughters, Anabel, Erika and Caroline Grob and Eliza and Susannah Wilson.

Winning the Bronze Star

By Chankey Touart,
Submitted by Mary Lou Touart

> "(In 1942 the) U.S. Army Air Corps weather personnel were assigned to southern England (and from there)...helped direct bombing missions over Germany...often...on duty 24 to 26 hours a day."

CHANKEY N. TOUART was a native of the South and began the University of Chicago when he was 16, graduating Phi Beta Kappa with a degree in physics and mathematics. He had a yen to be a pilot and would have made it, except the Air Corps decided to send him overseas after he had learned to fly as a cadet. He took the original cadre of U.S. Army Air Corps weather personnel overseas to be under the command of the 8th Air Force. This was in 1942. They were assigned to southern England and at one time lived in lavish scale at the home of an English earl. The group helped direct bombing missions over Germany. Often he and the men under his command were on duty 24 to 36 hours a day. When he returned to the United States he brought with him the Bronze Star he had been awarded by the Air Force.

Chankey Touart's memories of his assignment

"THE B-17 AND the B-24 were the heavy bombers flown over Europe in World War II by the U.S. 8th Air Force. Since the two types differed markedly in operational characteristics, they were seldom teamed in a joint mission and when they were, a distinctive operation order had to be written for each type.

"The 1st Bombardment Wing of the VIII Bomber Command flew only B-17s, while the 2nd Wing flew only B-24s. The supply channel decreed that both types would be provided to the third and last wing. In view of the added difficulties of operating a hybrid force, Washington assigned as commander of the 3rd Wing a seasoned, iron-assed colonel by the name of Curtis E. LeMay.

"The first groups to join the 3rd Wing were B-17s. They went operational in 1943 without notable difficulty. Not so for the first B-24 group. Its initial mission never got off the ground. One eager-beaver bombardier checked his bombs before takeoff and found that their fuses had not been armed. Other aircraft in the group reported the same fatal flaw, so the mission was scrubbed.

"The second B-24 mission of the 3rd Wing did get airborne on schedule. The assignment was relatively simple: to attack a railroad marshalling yard north of Brussels. The bomb run was to the north, across the city. In those days, it was OK to bomb a military target in occupied territory, but it was a strict no-no to spill bombs over into civilian areas.

"The 8th Air Force bombers flew their missions in a mathematically optimized formation. At the point was the lead aircraft, which did all of the independent navigating and targeting for the entire formation. When the lead bombardier toggled his bombs, the other aircraft immediately followed suit.

"Flying higher in the formation and behind the lead aircraft was the deputy lead, whose function was to take over both the navigating and the targeting if the lead aircraft was disabled.

"On the particular Brussels mission, the deputy lead bombardier, flying his very first combat mission, had foreseen a problem. On the bomb run, he had to be continuously sighting on the target so as to be prepared to take over.

But with one eye glued to the bombsight, he would be hard-pressed to see the bomb-release by the lead bombardier. So he struck a deal with his navigator, who shared the cramped nose section of the B-24: 'I'll concentrate on the Norden; you watch for the lead bomb-drop. When that happens, you tap me on the shoulder, and I'll toggle our bombs.'

"So, at last they started the bomb run. Our earnest young bombardier began really sweating. 'Where the hell is the target?' He was frantically scanning up and down and all around when he felt a solid thump on his shoulder. He toggled his bombs, and half the formation behind him did likewise.

"Back at Wing Operations, a flash intelligence report came in and the word was sickening; the formation had sprinkled bombs across Brussels itself. The atmosphere became ponderous as the Wing staff awaited the detailed debriefing reports after the formation landed.

"LeMay himself took the eventual call from the group commander. With jaw hard-set, he listened for several minutes without a word. He then rocked back in his chair and let out a mighty roar of laughter. LeMay was a dead-serious war-fighter, not given to laughing on duty. What had broken his composure on this occasion was the disclosure of what had caused the sorry mishap; it was not the navigator who had tapped our bombardier on his shoulder; no, it was the astrodome that had fallen out of its mounting above the bombsight."

ALTHOUGH CHAN WAS generally safe, the tensions were always there. He spent three and a half years in England, finally returning home as a lieutenant colonel. It was his plan to be assigned in the Pacific, as his father was a colonel commanding troops there with the final intention of invading Japan. But the war ended with

The Bronze Star Medal is the fourth-highest individual military award and the ninth-highest by order of precedence in the U.S. military. It may be awarded for acts of heroism, acts of merit or meritorious service in a combat zone. (*Wikipedia*)

the atomic bomb and both men returned home. Chan continued as a reserve status in the Air Corps and would have retired as a lieutenant general but he gave it up after graduate school at New York University. There he met his future wife, Mary Lou. He was hired to be director of the Atmospheric Science Division of the Geophysics Research Directorate Meteorology Lab at Hanscom Field in Bedford, Massachusetts. Upon his retirement in 1976, he was awarded the U.S. Air Force Decoration for Exceptional Civilian Service, the service's highest civilian honor, for weather support to the Advanced Ballistic Reentry Systems Program and further cited for outstanding research achievements and managerial abilities.

Al Quinzani

Born 1919 · Boston, Massachusetts

December 1943. Al Quinzani home on leave before shipping out for Europe.

Albert G. Quinzani was born in Boston, December 14, 1919. He graduated from an Arlington, Massachusetts, high school in 1938. During weekends and summer vacations he worked in the family bakery business learning all the operations necessary for a thriving and successful business. After high school he attended Boston University majoring in business but left after completing his junior year to attend the American Institute of Baking in Chicago from August to December of 1941. He returned to Boston University and received his diploma in August 1942. After serving in the European theater, he was discharged in June 1946. He began working in the family business, Quinzani's Bakery, in September 1946. At the bakery, he expanded the facilities, creating a fully automatic plant. Albert met Vivian Kietzman while in Illinois in 1943; they married in 1947. They lived with their two children, Joan and Larry, for almost 50 years before moving to Brookhaven.

War with the Quartermaster Corps

By Al Quinzani

> "I...was (a) company commander of a small American company charged with overseeing about 200 Italian prisoners of war who had been transported to England from Africa on empty cargo ships. Selected prisoners were allowed to become "co-operators," which was allowed by the Geneva Convention, but they could only work in hospitals and medical depots."

IN 1941, FEARING we would soon be at war, I postponed my senior year at Boston University to attend the American Institute of Baking's technical and management course in Chicago, Illinois. I then finished at Boston University in the summer of 1942 and entered the service. I completed basic training and was admitted to Officer Candidate School. Because my family was in the bakery business and I had extra education in baking, I was assigned as a second lieutenant to the Quartermaster Corps. I was assigned to a bakery battalion in Illinois where we trained recruits—first to be soldiers and then to be bakers.

Soon we were in England where I was made company commander of a bakery company where we trained on new *mobile* English bakery equipment which could bake thousands of loaves of bread daily and could change locations quickly.

The European invasion in June 1944 was successful and within a few months the Allied forces swept across France, liberating Paris. Paris was then declared an Open City. The Allies expected millions of refugees. Although these numbers did not materialize, the Allies had made plans to feed the incoming refugees as well as all Allied personnel.

As conditions changed, several bakery companies were de-clared surplus, including ours. We were all reassigned. I spoke some Italian so was made company commander of a small Ameri-can company charged with overseeing about 200 Italian prisoners of war who had been transported to England from Africa on empty cargo ships. Selected prisoners were allowed to become "co-op-erators," which was allowed by the Geneva Convention, but they could only work in hospitals and medical depots.

The English government had provided us with the grounds and buildings of a castle just outside the city of Burton-on-Trent. The castle and other buildings had been cleared, but with numer-ous tents, the accommodations were fine. We had the responsibil-ity of providing food, housing, clothes, medical needs and security for the Italian prisoners. There were no fences or MPs but we had no problems, as the Italians knew they would be returned to the POW camp if they violated the rules.

The work at the medical depot was demanding—unloading freight cars, breaking down the large containers of medical sup-plies and equipment, stocking shelves, filling and packing orders from hospitals. In March of 1945, the medical depot was moved to Liege, Belgium, and we followed, working there until the war in Europe ended.

All the POWs were soon repatriated. The Quartermaster Corps had the huge task of dealing with all the food, clothing, vehicles and munitions that were left over when the war end-ed. Most of these materials were headed to the Pacific war, but when that ended everything had to be returned to the United States, sold or given away. Many, many soldiers and officers with the higher "points" were soon on their way home. I had very few points since I was not involved in the actual fighting of the war. I spent the next year in several battalion headquarters supervising Quartermaster Corps companies as they carried out their mission. I was promoted to captain and finally set sail for the United States and discharged on June 15, 1946. It was an honorable three and three-quarters years of service but free of the dangers and unholy conditions endured by so many.

June Odbert Smith

Born 1918 · Sturgeon Bay, Wisconsin

June 1943. June Odbert, Women's barracks at Ft.Custer, Michigan. New army attire as a second lieutenant in the Army Nurse Corps.

June Irene Odbert was born and raised in Sturgeon Bay, Wisconsin. Her parents were Eugene (a civil engineer) and Edna Kelly Odbert.

I graduated from high school in Sturgeon Bay and went on to the University of Wisconsin at Madison, receiving a certificate of nursing and a BS in science. I served in the Army Nurse Corps, from 1943 to 1945, when I returned to the United States and accepted a position as an instructor of student nurses at a hospital in Memphis, Tennessee. In 1947, I was persuaded by a friend, who had been a Navy nurse, to join her in going to Venezuela to teach. Standard Oil of New Jersey was building a new oil refinery which included a new hospital and needed nursing instructors. This is where I met my husband, Robert Louis Smith, who was an engineer on the project. We decided to be married in Venezuela where we had many friends. We arranged to have a civil service by inviting the mayor of a local town to marry us. We were married under old Spanish law. This old law stated that all I owned now belonged to my husband, that I had to ask his permission before leaving the house and that I would walk behind while he rode the burro. We had a small religious service a day later at a friend's house. A Mormon friend offered to conduct the service; my maid of honor supplied the marriage vows of her Lutheran faith. Bob was raised a Presbyterian, I attended the Congregational church. We had a true ecumenical wedding. After a two-week honeymoon we were back

★ *Biography continued on page 139*

A World War II "MASH" Unit

By June Odbert Smith

"We were in Phalsbourg, casualties were very heavy and the surgical teams were operating at full capacity. Suddenly, on the morning of January 4, we nurses were alerted and told to pack for an emergency departure as we were too near the front lines. We collected our personal belongings, threw them into our bedrolls and climbed onto trucks and were driven back to Épinal…"

AFTER THREE YEARS at the University of Wisconsin, I entered the University School of Nursing to become a registered nurse. After graduation in 1943, I joined the Army Nurse Corps and became a proud second lieutenant stationed at Fort Custer in Michigan. In 1944, I volunteered for overseas service and in early fall I found myself at Fort Bragg, North Carolina, with a newly formed 117th Evacuation Hospital. We were sent overseas, landing at Marseille, France, and traveled north by train to join another Evacuation Group in Épinal, France.

The army had what I called layers of service. There were field hospitals and, as such, were designated to be among the "forward" hospitals—those hospitals closest to the fighting troops, including battalion and aid stations, division collecting and clearing stations and evacuation hospitals. At the rear were general hospitals, which were designed to be completely immobile. Each type of hospital was designated to perform a different function in an evacuation chain that would be set up to get the wounded off the battlefields and into medical care as quickly and as efficiently as possible.

Our 117th Evacuation Hospital was a 400-bed semi-mobile unit which was to be located approximately 15–25 miles behind the front line. We were staffed by 40 nurses, 39 officers, including doctors, and about 200 enlisted men. We did not have enough trucks and other equipment to move ourselves, so trucks were borrowed and loaned as needed. When it came time to move, some equipment would be moved to the new area and the staff would follow.

While in France, we were twice located in buildings, but once we entered southern Germany, we worked entirely in tents. I worked in the operating room having been trained to give anesthesia. The anesthesia consisted mostly of injections of sodium pentothal into a vein or giving drop ether over a mask. When I gave sodium pentothal I would ask the soldier to count backwards from 100 and by the time he reached 90 he had stopped counting. Sodium pentothal works fast.

Surgery was done around the clock. There was a night team and a day team, each consisting of doctors, nurses and enlisted men. We worked 12 hours a day and on Monday we switched from day to night or vice versa. If I had been working days, I worked Monday morning until 1 P.M. and then started the night shift at 7 P.M.

As I recall we had four or five operating tables going at one time. There was also a special room or tent where brain surgery and surgery on mutilated faces was performed. Wounded soldiers were brought into a presurgery area to await surgery. Blood and plasma was given as needed before surgery. Most of the soldiers had bullet or shrapnel wounds or broken bones. Doctors would remove the bullets and shrapnel, clean up the wound area, throw on some sulfa powder, wrap up the area and send the soldier to a tent to recover from the anesthesia. As soon as possible, the soldier was taken by ambulance to a general hospital where doctors would finish the lengthy job of stitching the muscles and skin.

In December of 1944, we were sent to Phalsbourg, France. We were fortunate to be housed in a building that had been a Catholic college. The building had strict blackout conditions and our windows were covered at night, but we had candles available. The surgical unit had electricity powered by our own generators.

All of the nurses wore Army regulation wool shirts and wool trousers, sturdy boots, Army-issue jackets, beanie caps and helmets. We carried a backpack and each of us had our own bedroll. We slept on cots with our bedroll thrown on top of it. Since cots sank in the middle, I would carefully put my extra clothing down the middle of the cot, under the bedroll, thus making the cot firmer in the middle and also keeping my clothing in an almost pressed condition.

We officers had our own mess hall but officers and enlisted personnel ate the same limited food. Breakfast consisted of oatmeal, scrambled powdered eggs, bread, butter and coffee. For lunch we had either canned spam or canned beef. Lunch and dinner were the same. Vegetables and fruit also came from cans, but we had fresh baked bread baked in our own kitchen. Many of us were fortunate enough to receive packages of food from home and these were a real treat.

Showers we did not have. When we were living in tents, we had a stove in the middle of the tent and could heat water for a sponge bath; helmets were used for bathing and hair washing. Our woolen shirts and trousers seldom got washed.

While in our building in Phalsbourg, as the days of December moved along, we began to think Christmas and someone organized a Christmas program. One of the doctors played a musical instruments and a trio of nurses harmonized some current songs including, "I'm Dreaming of a White Christmas," "I'll Walk Alone," and "Deep in the Heart of Texas."

On December 16 the Germans started an offensive that would be dubbed the "Battle of the Bulge" by the American media. Hitler had planned this move as early as September. This was at the center of the American line in the Ardennes Forest. It was a densely wooded plateau, deeply ridged and cut by many streams extending from northern France into Germany. During that December period while we were in Phalsbourg, casualties were very heavy and the surgical teams were operating at full capacity. Suddenly, on the morning of January 4, we nurses were alerted and told to pack for an emergency departure as we were too near the front lines. We collected our personal belongings, threw them into our bedrolls and climbed onto trucks and were driven back to Épinal, where we had first started our overseas service. Our registrar, Lt. Schaefer, had managed by hook or by crook to evacuate all the hospital personnel and approximately 450 patients in about 12 hours. He received a well-deserved promotion to captain.

The Ardennes campaign finally ended in late January of 1945 and our unit returned to northern France and then continued following the battles across southern Germany. By the end of the war we were in Linz, Austria, once again stationed in a building. The large operating rooms were no longer needed and we had few patients. October 24 found me in a staging area named "Camp Philip Morris" at Le Havre, France, waiting to be put on a ship and sent back to the States. My war experience was over.

★ *Biography continued from page 134*

at work. While in Venezuela we adopted three children; the first born in Venezuela and the other two from an orphanage in Germany. We returned to the United States in 1955. In 1964 my husband joined a large construction company with head-quarters in Cambridge, Massachusetts. We settled in Lexington and I enrolled at Tufts University for a master's degree in education. I spent several years as a guidance counselor at a junior high school in Winchester, Massachusetts. My husband and I moved to Brookhaven in 1996.

George W. B. Starkey

Born 1918 · New Britain, Connecticut

Captain George W. B. Starkey, M.D., Autumn, 1944 newly enlisted in the U.S. Army as a battalion surgeon. He served in Europe and was part of the medical team during the Battle of the Bulge. He died in 2000.

George Starkey was born April 3, 1918, in New Britain, Connecticut and graduated from Buckley High School in Hartford. Then came Trinity College on a scholarship. He took two giant steps in the winter of 1944. He joined the Army Medical Corps as a captain having just completed his surgical internship at Children's Hospital in Boston after graduating from Harvard Medical School, and he married Lois MacMurray (Bisi) Starkey in Baltimore on February 5, 1944. She was in her sophomore year at Bryn Mawr College near Philadelphia. They went together to his various posts in the U.S.: first to the Carlyle Barracks in Pennsylvania, then Camp McCoy in Sparta, Wisconsin, and finally to the Army general hospital in Tuscaloosa, Alabama, to join the 76th Infantry Division with whom he went overseas. The couple parted in November 1944: he to go to Europe, she to return to Bryn Mawr from which she graduated in 1946. This was essential as she was going to have to be the breadwinner while he finished the extensive training to be a heart surgeon. After the war he was a surgical resident, 1946–1951, at Roosevelt Hospital in New York City and then received a Harvard Moseley traveling fellowship. He was an assistant resident at Harvard in 1951–1952. Later, he worked at Guy's Hospital in London. A cardiac surgeon, he was on the staff of Children's Hospital, Boston and then on the surgical staff from 1970–2000. At Beth Israel Hospital, Boston, he was Chief of Intensive

★ Biography continued on page 149

Interview

A twelve-year-old grandson, Chris, interviews his grandfather, Dr. George W. B. Starkey, December 1999 about experiences in World War II.

By Dr. George W. B. Starkey (submitted by his wife)

> **"CHRIS**: If our generation was to enter a war, what would be your advice?
>
> **"GEORGE**: Depends what the issues are. World War II had so many angles to it: the fantastic butchery; the uncivilized activities of the Nazis. Are you going to stand by and see innocent people be burned to death with women and children and watch it go on for months and months? I think that's the kind of a war, based on what you think are important principles. I would be less apt to go to war for countries further away. You can't be policeman for everybody."

This was a school assignment to interview a veteran of World War II.

CHRIS: What did you do during the war?

GEORGE: I was a combat battalion surgeon. That means that I was one doctor of 52 in an infantry battalion division of 145,000 soldiers. We were in a combat unit, not in the back of some big building or tent. We were right on the front lines. During the winter of 1944–45 we were in Luxembourg. It's a small place up between France, Belgium and Germany where General George Patton had his headquarters. As the head of the Third Army, he was our chief. We had to cross this river because just on the other side was the German Siegfried Line where a lot of German soldiers were dug

10 to 15 feet below ground. They were able to shoot automatic machine guns and German 88s at us, but they themselves were out of harm's way. They could see us because they used periscopes and we were sitting ducks. Every time we tried to cross the river, we'd put up a Bailey bridge across the river, a metal thing that comes in sections. Then we'd run our wheeled vehicles, jeeps or personal carriers, onto it. Once the front wheel would hit the other side, the German guns would blast our Bailey bridge to pieces and some of my buddies would disappear under the ice along with their vehicles. This happened over and over again. If we finally got to the other side between the river edge and the Siegfried Line, which wasn't too far, the place was mined and caused even more fatalities. We couldn't get anywhere because the Germans would replace the land mines every night.

We lost a lot of boys that I had trained with in Wisconsin and that I had known very well. It was sad to see these young men, 19 to 22, when they stepped on a land mine or got hit by an 88. One of the hard things was how to handle one of these kids, 19 years old, who just had both legs blown off. What can you say to him? It's a nice sunny day? It was different from the safety of the rear corps area.

This was the Bulge along the Siegfried Line. It was so named because it was the last try of Hitler's army to win the war. The Germans were losing, but if they could make a quick move and get through there as they did in World War I, they could beat us. This was in December and January, cold as Willie's ear. We were very depressed, but one day, General George Patton came down in his jeep all by himself with his driver and his silver helmet with five stars on it and his revolvers with pearl handles. I don't know why some German didn't pick him off. He came right down into the foundations of the buildings and gave us big hugs, two, three, four. Our number 2 was a classmate of his at West Point, so Patton was coming down to see what the hell was going on. He jumped in among all the ordinary soldiers, the privates, the corporals and the medics. He slapped us each on the back using a lot of foul language. He said, "We'll get those sons of bitches out of that line!" He was with us for two hours. Pieces of buildings were falling down on him. He was absolutely fearless. He so inspired us that in 2 days we crossed the river, walked through the minefield and into the Siegfried Line. That kind of gives you a view of what we were doing and what a guy like George Patton did. He really renewed our faith in our mission at great risk to himself.

CHRIS: Did you get hurt?

GEORGE: Well, I was right in with the guys. I got banged up a bit falling into ruined foundations, but I never had any serious injury, for which I was very grateful. We doctors couldn't carry arms, but we had helmets with big red crosses on them. We were not supposed to be shot at, so if we got cornered, we had nothing to defend ourselves with. This came from World War I which said medical people are not supposed to be shot at. It worked pretty well. The Germans for the most part respected medical personnel and of course, we did the same for their medics. On occasion, we even worked together on patients: German and American.

CHRIS: What did medics do?

GEORGE: Mike Shallow was one of our bravest medics and he was gay. Anybody who whistled at him or said rude things was usually throttled by his pals, many of whom were big, strong truck drivers. Mike's surgical auxiliary team did an extraordinary amount of work in caring for the American and British wounded. We learned early on that the casualties that we saw were usually in bad shape with their legs or the side of their faces blown off. We saw them before they died. We put tourniquets on them and tried to cheer them up. We would give them a little serrette of morphine to ease their pain. They would usually say, "No, Doc. Got a cigarette?" Of course they were feeling no pain because of all the endorphins that were being released from their spinal cord and the base of their brain. We would light the cigarette and give it to them. Most of them died before they finished it, but the request was always there. We learned from these experiences that a good battalion surgeon should always carry a dry packet of cigarettes in his pocket. We would fuel up our Zippo lighters by dropping the works down on a string into any vehicle's gas tank and then retrieved it. Having removed the flint before doing this, we would then place it back and be ready for combat.

Toward the end of our bit in the war, we ended up in an apple orchard in central Germany, not too far from Dresden. It was there we were supposed to meet the Russians. This German colonel who had been in their army 17 years and had been wounded four times was brought into our medical tent in a big hurry. He was bleeding to death and I immediately got after his problem with my six-stripe sergeant. He almost always in those last days of the war had a little portable radio tuned to BBC. They usually played marvelous classical music. Well, to make a long story short, that radio was going in the background while the sergeant and I were trying to stop the bleeding with sutures and all kinds of things. It looked as though we were winning. Then the program was interrupted and the British announcer said, "Oh, we're terribly sorry to interrupt this Beethoven's Ninth Symphony, but we have very sad news. That is that Franklin Delano Roosevelt has just died in Warm Springs, Georgia." Well, three things happened. One, the colonel that I was operating on sat bolt upright and I had this suture and he was like a big fish on the end of the line. We were working like hell because we didn't have any blood to give him. It was a close thing. The colonel said in poor but understandable English, "Oh, Rosefelt, Rosefelt, great man, great man. Most Germans loved Rosefelt." Then he said "Hoofer" (that's Herbert Hoover) and he gave a little lecture for about five minutes about how Hoofer was hard on the poor and Rosefelt helped them. And then he dropped back and never said another word. My six-stripe sergeant was a very conservative Republican who didn't like the Democrats or Roosevelt. After the colonel spoke, tears rolled down the sergeant's cheeks at the way this German had sat up and said what he thought.

CHRIS: What was Germany like?

GEORGE: At one point, we were camped in Weimar and we opened up the nearby Buchenwald concentration camp. These people we saw were brutalized. The dead were piled up against the fences and the living were walking around bumping into each other. They were just dazed and didn't know what day it was or anything else. I realized this was five miles from Weimar. I went back to this great old city and in my lousy German, I stopped some of the civilians who were pretty well fed, pretty well dressed. I would say to them "Was ist das?" That means what is that over there. And they would say, "Das ist nur ein fabrik," meaning that's just a factory. These people who were living in Weimar had to somehow delude themselves into thinking that was not a concentration camp, but the way they reacted and the fact that most of them gave the same answer suggests that they really didn't know it was a concentration camp. But you'd have to be a real dodo bird not to know what it was. This denial by the Germans was just pathetic and we used to get upset about that.

GEORGE: Also, there were still the SS officers around.

CHRIS: Who were they?

GEORGE: They had a double ZZ on their sleeves like lightning. They were trained to feel that they were superior. They were usually blond, blue-eyed and very, very mean. They often traveled in pairs. Once two came to our medical tent. One of them was wounded. I looked at them closely and saw that one of them didn't look as if he was very wounded. And the other guy I couldn't figure out. So, I asked my sergeants what they thought. They said, "Those bastards probably have hand grenades and loaded revolvers under their coats." I said, "If you really think that, tackle them and nail them to the ground. Open their coats and see if that's true." That's what they did and those SS troopers both had hand grenades in order to blow up our medical unit. This would have been against international law. Then I found that one of them did have a fairly bad wound in his shoulder. As I was looking at his wound, I said in my terrible German that I wanted to see his wounded shoulder whereupon his cleared his throat and spit in my face. They were not nice kids, not to be trusted. So obviously, I didn't do a thing about his wound.

CHRIS: Weren't you relieved when the war was over?

GEORGE: We were fantastically relieved, as our outfit was on its way to Japan, which we hadn't beat yet. We were all on board the *Queen Mary* on the first leg of our trip to Japan when a voice called out from the shore, "The war is over. We dropped the bomb and Japan capitulated!" So many of us rushed to the railing to hear the news that the ship almost capsized. All the decks had been painted with probably hundreds of 3 by 6 foot rectangles. They shifted the sleeping soldiers from the rectangles every eight hours. That ship had about 14,000 men on it. The *Queen Mary* transported 800,000 men back and forth during the war. We were happy to be going home and not to have to go to Japan to fight again. When I came back, your grandmother, Bisi, was in her last year of college. I hadn't seen her for two years. What a joy.

I had been in the combat part of the war, but my last six months of military service, I worked in the plastic surgical center of the Valley Forge General Hospital, outside of Philadelphia. We spent day after day reconstructing the faces and the hands and parts of soldiers who had been burned either jumping out of tanks or parachuting from a plane. These were the kinds of guys I was with back in the war zone. Even with these terrible things that happened to them, they were upbeat and positive. They knew they were lucky to get through. All this gave me another leaf in the book of my war experience.

While I was there, Helen Keller came to entertain the soldiers. She was a famous woman who at the age of 15 months got some infection that made her blind and deaf. She eventually learned how to communicate with people. She traveled hundreds of thousands of miles during the war trying to cheer up these young wounded fellows so they could go back into civilian life, which wasn't easy for them. She was a tiny woman. Now, remember, this lady couldn't hear or see, but she could still talk. She had no idea of the sound of her voice. She would speak in this high voice having no idea how much force she was using. First this voice would disappear and then it would scream at you. When I met her there at the hospital, her assistant would put her hand on my lips and my larynx (my voice box) and by the vibrations, she could understand what was being said. That evening there was a party for her and I asked her to dance. Though she couldn't hear the music, she could feel the vibrations through the floor and she danced surprisingly well.

CHRIS: If our generation was to enter a war, do you have any advice?

GEORGE: Depends what the issues are. World War II had so many angles to it: the fantastic butchery; the uncivilized activities of the Nazis. Are you going to stand by and see innocent people be burned to death with women and children and watch it go on for months and months? I think that's the kind of a war, based on what you think are important principles. I would be less apt to go to war for countries farther away. You can't be policeman for everybody.

CHRIS: How did this affect the rest of your life?

GEORGE: Well, I've never been back to that part of northern France or Germany where we lost so many buddies because of the terrible dreams I had for months after I came back. But, it also had a reverse effect that here I am who came back with two legs and two arms and had made it. We complained very little. We didn't spend any time talking about money or how many Mercedes-Benzes we were going to have. We'd work 24 hours a day, a couple of days in a row, and no complaints. You rolled with the punches. How much more full of beans we were than a lot of our contemporaries who never got into combat. Having gotten through the experience made a tremendous impression on our attitudes. And that continues today.

★ *Biography continued from page 140*

care and a clinical professor at the Harvard Medical School from 1952–2000. He was also chairman of Trustees at Trinity College, Hartford, Connecticut, for twelve years. The George Starkey Award Lectureship is a yearly lecture on teaching given by distinguished doctors from all over the country, established in his honor at Harvard Medical School. He was especially interested in medical ethics and chaired a committee at Harvard Medical School working to crack the glass ceiling for women in medicine. He died February 5, 2000. His wife, Lois MacMurray Starkey, was the daughter of a U.S. diplomat. After finishing Bryn Mawr in 1946, she later was a lecturer at the Metropolitan Museum of Art in New York City, 1948–1952; the Boston Museum of Fine Arts, Boston, Massachusetts, 1970–1990; and the Gardner Museum, Boston, from 1972 to 1990. Bisi's only war work was as a nurse's aide at the Bryn Mawr Hospital and the Children's Hospital in Boston. Her work was ever so tame compared to the bloody battle at the Bulge that her husband was up against. He never mentioned that he was a battalion surgeon on the front lines, so when people asked if she was scared for him, she in her innocence would say, "Oh no, he is a doctor; what luck that he made it through!"

Part Four

★ ★ ★ ★

Women in the Service

ONCE THE UNITED STATES entered World War II, it was time to mobilize. While planners focused on building the armed forces and setting equipment and munitions manufacturing in motion, they also began outlining how women could help the war effort. WAVEs and WACs working in essential jobs freed men for service. These stories about some experiences of women in the service illustrate the contributions of women to the military effort.

Miriam McCue

Born 1917 · Denver, Colorado

Miriam McCue in her Navy uniform ready to ride in the 50th Anniversary of World War II parade in Lexington, Massachusetts, 1994.

I was born in Denver, Colorado, in 1917, the daughter of Miriam Keliher Crowley and Frank J. Crowley. I grew up in Cheyenne, Wyoming, my father's hometown. I graduated from the University of Wyoming in 1939. I studied psychology in graduate school at Fordham University in New York and taught at Rosemont College in Philadelphia, Pennsylvania, while finishing my PhD I joined the Navy in 1944 as a WAVE and was assigned to the Officer Training School at Smith College, Northampton, Massachusetts. I was commissioned an ensign in the Hospital Service and assigned to the Philadelphia Naval Hospital in Philadelphia, Pennsylvania, to work in the psychiatric section. I subsequently was assigned to Hunter College in New York City, Chelsea Naval Hospital, Boston, Massachusetts, and Bethesda Naval Hospital, Bethesda, Maryland. When the war ended, I taught elementary and abnormal psychology at Smith College in Northampton, Massachusetts from 1944 to 1949. There, I met John Joseph "Jerry" McCue and we were married in 1949. We lived in Wellesley, Massachusetts, and I commuted to the VA Outptatient Clinic in Lowell, Massachusetts. When our son was born in 1954, I was happy to switch to my new occupation of "motherhood." After he was in school, I accepted an offer to work part-time at the VA Hospital in Bedford, Massachusetts, eventually working full-time and in charge of a ward.

A Woman's Military Experience, 1944–1948

By Miriam McCue

"Assigned to work in naval hospitals, my orders were the same as those received by men but I was not allowed to attend clinical conferences because I was a woman. Being in the Navy, I could not protest. I did what I was told."

APPARENTLY MY MOTHER did not want me to join the Navy (in 1944), so she delayed our driving from our home in Cheyenne, Wyoming, to Denver, Colorado, a distance of 100 miles, where I could "sign up." I had given up my teaching position at Rosemont College in Pennsylvania, and by October she realized that I was serious about joining the Navy as a WAVE. I had just received my PhD degree in psychology and I knew that psychologists in the Navy worked in the psychiatric section of Navy hospitals. I heard that the enlisted personnel did the "hands-on" work, while the officers "administered," so I tried to join the enlisted ranks. However, I was assigned to the Officer Training School at Smith College, in Northampton, Massachusetts, in October 1944, and after two months became an ensign in the Hospital Service.

Assigned to work in naval hospitals, my orders were the same as those received by men but I was not allowed to attend clinical conferences because I was a woman. Being in the Navy, I could not protest. I did what I was told. My first tour of duty was at the Philadelphia Naval Hospital, where I administered psychological tests to Navy personnel and sat in an office while the men attended classes called "Instruction in Psychiatry," even though my orders read the same as theirs. When the war was over, I left the Navy and accepted a teaching position at Smith College.

Doris Eyges

Born 1921 · Chicago, Illinois

Doris Eyges, taken in 1944 when she was Ensign Doris Kirk, WAVES of the United States Navy, when she was working in communications in Washington, D.C.

I was born Doris Vivian Kirk, in Chicago, Illinois, January 22, 1921. I grew up in Brooklyn, New York, graduating in 1939 from Erasmus Hall High School, an extraordinary public institution that at that time had 8,000 students.

I received a BA in English from the University of Michigan in 1943. I joined the U.S. Navy in 1944 and did my basic training at Smith College, Northampton, Massachusetts. I had further training in communications at Mt. Holyoke College in Massachusetts. I was assigned to Washington, D.C., where I served as a communications officer in the WAVES of the United States Navy. I received an MA from Harvard/Radcliffe in 1947. I married poet/ professor John Holmes who taught at Tufts University, where I also taught part-time. Our son Evan was born in 1950, daughter Margaret in 1954. Widowed in 1962, I moved us to Milton Academy where I taught for eight years. I was remarried in 1970 to Leonard Eyges, a physicist. I taught at Wellesley College from 1948–1950, 1956–1957 and 1968– 1988. Leonard Eyges died in 2006 and I moved to Brookhaven in 2007.

A Voice in the Night

By Doris Eyges

"This brief honoring of Shakespeare's Sonnet No. 29
between two lieutenants junior grade, one male and one
female, across the Pacific, was my favorite experience in
the WAVES of the United States Navy."

WHEN I TELL people that I was in the Navy during World War II, they usually say, "How exciting," or, "You must have some great stories." I've decided to come clean.

I was assigned to communications in Washington, D.C., to use a new system, an electric teletype coding machine. We were first linked to San Francisco, then Guam and eventually Tokyo.

Keep in mind that all of the communications in our office were "Classified." That means RESTRICTED, CONFIDENTIAL, SECRET or TOP SECRET. Most of the content was routine, such as position, course and speed reports. No, it was not exciting, but of life and death importance to the vessels at sea and stations on land.

One night, I was on watch: 11:00 P.M. to 7:00 A.M. Not surprisingly, traffic was lighter than during the day. We had to keep the machines operating at all times. Encoding changes had to be absolutely correct and up to the minute, even if there were no messages. We were to write a few words of anything to use as text if nothing was coming in or out, in order to check the operation. A typical entry might be, "Today is March 12, 1945." But about 3:00 A.M. on this particular "night" I rammed out:

"When in disgrace with fortune and men's eyes

I all along……"

'BING, BING, BING,' ran the signal from Guam that requested a break in the encoded connection.

"Were you English major? I was, and I want to be a teacher. I hope to go to graduate school after the war." He gave his name and rank. We exchanged the information that he had gone to Wisconsin and I had gone to Michigan. It was a short conversation, like those breaks when we discussed some problem in machinery.

This brief honoring of Shakespeare's Sonnet No. 29 between two lieutenants junior grade, one male and one female, across the Pacific, was my favorite experience in the WAVES of the United States Navy.

Joan Keenan

Born 1924 · Danvers, Massachusetts

Rome, 1980. From left, Joan Keenan, Virginia Aldrich and Kathryn McCarthy.

Joan Keenan was born and grew up in Danvers, Massachusetts. Her parents were Arthur Bennett and Audrey Light Keenan. She graduated from Radcliffe College in October 1944 and two days later entered the U.S. Navy as a WAVE. She attended Midshipman's Training School and was assigned to the NSA (National Security Agency) in Washington. She was on active duty for two years and served twenty years as a reservist with the NSA. After the war, She returned to Radcliffe to the Management and Training program, a 10-month program given by the Harvard Business School faculty. She then went to John Hancock Life in Boston where she stayed for 40 happy years. Her responsibilities were largely to develop and administer a personnel program for 1,500 clerical and supervisory employees in over 150 sales offices. She later became responsible for more general administration. She completed a five-year program to get my Chartered Life Underwriter designation, then entered a five-year program at the Cardinal Cushing School of Theology for Laity. She audited theology classes for 20 years with the Jesuits at the Weston School of Theology. She also took a number of Harvard extension courses. Joan was one of five members of a special advisory committee to advise then-Archbishop Law on reorganization of the diocese, and served as chair of an advisory committee for St. John's Seminary studying change for nine inner-city Boston schools. She spent many years as a trustee for Radcliffe College, serving on many committees.

The National Security Agency and Me

By Joan Keenan, Lt. USN

> "My war was not the stuff of which movies were made nor did it demand any great heroism, but I was certainly aware that in a small way, I helped our country when I was needed."

EARLY IN MY senior year at Radcliffe (1944) I became aware that a friend seemed to disappear Tuesday afternoons. She was very evasive when I tried to pin her down as to her whereabouts. Finally, she told me to talk to the placement director, which I did. She asked whether I had ever considered joining the WAVES. Up until then, I do not think I had, but I said I would think about it. I talked with another friend and decided to join.

The placement director told me of a secret course which was given at Radcliffe which would guarantee an assignment at the then Naval Security Station, now the National Security Agency (NSA), in Washington. My friend and I enrolled in the course where we found our missing classmate—and proceeded to apply for the United States Naval Reserve.

All was well until we found that the Harvard Corporation, which awarded Radcliffe degrees, was not scheduled to meet until two days after we were to report to Midshipman's School. We could not go there without a college degree, so the Harvard Corporation met three days earlier than planned and we received our degrees in the nick of time.

Because we were on an accelerated schedule, we graduated in October 1944 and were in the last midshipman's class during wartime. After two months, we were bright young ensigns and reported for duty at the NSA.

Joan Keenan, December 1944,
Northhampton, Massachusetts.
Newly commissioned as ensign in the
U.S. Navy.

At that time, we were not allowed to say where we worked and were forbidden to discuss our work. We had to sign statements to that effect. Actually, as the years went by, I was grateful for that discipline and I learned not to talk shop. Often, I wished others in civilian life had taken the same oath!

Then, as now, the NSA did important and highly secret work. All intelligence work is top secret and we were Top Secret Ultra. Some of the people at the NSA—not me—did work that was vital to our ultimate victory. For their work, we were awarded the Presidential Unit Citation. The people I worked with were quite wonderful and I made good friends with whom I am still in touch.

I liked the Navy and particularly the NSA. After the war, I joined the Naval Reserve and for 20 more years I took correspondence courses continuously, went one night a week to Reserve meetings and two weeks a year to the NSA in Washington. As a result, I am now a Former Naval Person. Some joined the Navy to see the world; I apparently joined so I could buy my cat food at the Hanscom Air Base Commissary at 20 percent off! I enjoyed my NSA Reserve time and helped to set up two new units where I typically was the personnel or training officer.

When, as new young ensigns, we used to go through the gate at the NSA, the cute Marine guards would often greet us with "Good morning, Admiral." Years later, I got on the elevator at the John Hancock building and the operator said, "Good morning, Admiral." Instinctively, I said, "Good morning." Then a bass voice behind me said the same thing and I turned around to see Admiral McCrea, the commandant of the First Naval District and a member of the Hancock board. Weakly, I tried to explain but the admiral was not amused. The ride to the 20th floor had never seemed so long!

My war was not the stuff of which movies were made nor did it demand any great heroism, but I was certainly aware that in a small way, I helped our country when I was needed.

Florence Trefethen

Born 1921 · Philadelphia, Pennsylvania

Florence N. Trefethen, taken at Brookhaven, Lexington, Massachusetts.

Florence N. Trefethen was born in Philadelphia on September 18, 1921, the daughter of Emma and Otto Newman. She graduated from Philadelphia High School for Girls and Bryn Mawr College. During World War II, she and her husband, Lloyd MacGregor Trefethen, served as U. S. naval officers. When the war ended they both attended Cambridge University for advanced degrees. Mrs. Trefethen lived in Lexington, Massachusetts, for 57 years. During that time, she taught English at Tufts University, the Northeastern University Graduate School and the Radcliffe Seminars. She spent 18 years at Harvard University as executive editor for the Council of East Asian Studies. Her column "The Poets' Workshop" was a bimonthly feature in *The Writer*, when that magazine was published in Boston. In retirement, Mrs. Trefethen served as a volunteer docent at the Harvard University art museums and as manuscript editor of the *Radcliffe Culinary Times*.

The Secret of All Secrets

By Florence Trefethen

> "The prize example of intense security was the presidential citation that our entire organization received…we never knew (not to this day) why we were being decorated. Whatever we'd done was so secret that we couldn't learn which of our activities was deemed meritorious, even at our own presidential citation! That's real security!"

WHEN I THINK BACK to the war years, I think first of SECURITY. Security seemed to dominate my life. I knew I had been recruited as a senior at Bryn Mawr for a hush-hush job, but the intensity of our security program became oppressive. My Navy classification was TOP SECRET ULTRA, and ultra it was. Like others in our establishment, I wore two badges, kept under my clothing on the way to work, then pulled out to show to two rows of Marine guards (resting up from Guadalcanal) who encircled our building. When a document entered our office space, it was immediately stamped RESTRICTED, CONFIDENTIAL, SECRET or ULTRA. Our offices had no wastepaper baskets; everything that had to be discarded was put into a burn bag, to be collected at the end of each watch and, presumably, burned. The corridors were decorated with posters that warned "Loose Lips Sink Ships" and similar admonitions against revealing Navy secrets.

My apartment mate, a close friend, who worked in the same building but in a different office, never knew what I actually did; I was similarly in the dark about her activities. When I got married, my husband never knew what I was up to for eight hours each day. Here's what I really did. At first, I was a watch officer, who sat at an entry desk presumably to guard the premises, actually to log in visitors and documents. As such it was deemed necessary for me

Florence N. Trefethen and Lloyd M. Trefethen, at their
wedding in Philadelphia, Pennsylvania, May 17, 1933.

to learn how to use a gun. So, for several weeks, I went from the
office three afternoons a week to target practice until I "checked
out" on three guns. (I think they were called a 22, a 34, and a 45.)
There was a .45 in a holster in the watch officer's desk and I was
obliged, if on duty during a blackout, to wear the gun. It's fortunate that I never needed to use it, since I had proved a mediocre
shot at target practice. Through all the war, I never heard a shot
fired in anger.

When I graduated from being a watch officer, I became the
editor of a semi-weekly report. (It seems that in my life, whatever
job I take I end up being an editor!) Naturally, the report, reproduced on a copy machine, was TOP SECRET ULTRA and confined
to seven copies. Three were distributed within the building. The
other four I delivered by reserved car elsewhere. One of the else-
wheres was the White House. I was driven up to a door which
opened, and I handed in my document to an unknown person,
then was driven on to the next recipient.

Life under security had some lighter moments. Our main office
wall held a photograph of the chief of Naval Operations, our "boss"
many steps up the line. He was in uniform and had a purposeful,
somewhat grim expression on his face. His image failed to enchant

a few of the enlisted WAVES in the office. They turned the picture face to the wall and on the back taped a colored photograph of Lord Louis Mountbatten, a spectacularly handsome British naval officer. "He's our ally" was their excuse for the alteration, which remained until V-J Day, except for captain's inspections, when Admiral King was temporarily restored to visibility. One time, a WAVE officer on midwatch, midnight till 8 A.M., lowered a slice of layer cake out her window to a Marine guard below. This was deemed unseemly if not a breach of security, and she was obliged to apologize to the entire Marine battalion. Fortunately, she was a fun-loving southern belle who regarded it all as a great joke. Nothing happened to the Marine who ate the cake.

The prize example of intense security was the presidential citation that our entire organization received. We were all lined up in the garden of the building (which had earlier been a school), and someone from the White House came and pinned a green ribbon on each person's lapel. (To save materials, no medals were issued, but the ribbons could be exchanged for medals "after the war.") The maddening part of the whole exercise was that we never knew (not to this day) why we were being decorated. Whatever we'd done was so secret that we couldn't learn which of our activities was deemed meritorious, even at our own presidential citation! That's real security!

Part Five
★ ★ ★ ★ ★

Winning the War at Home

THE UNITED STATES was not prepared for warfare. Preparations began immediately after war was declared: young men were drafted; factories were converted to build ships, planes, weapons; and the home front was organized, including organizing women to help with military duties at home. All this took time but when the wheels began to roll, the war effort was a massive and eventually powerful force. Everyone pitched in: men, women and children. Looking back, the dedication and cooperation of American citizens was a heroic effort. Their common goal united Americans in teamwork and effort unmatched since that time. World War II created an America that had become a force to be reckoned with worldwide. These next stories are a reminder of how citizens helped the war effort in so many different ways.

Frederick L. Hafer

Born 1925 · Reading, Pennsylvania

Fred Hafer. Graduation picture, U.S. Military Academy, 1946.

I was born in Reading, Pennsylvania, to LeRoy I. Hafer and Esther Wertz Hafer on July 21, 1925. I grew up in Pottsville, Pennsylvania, and graduated from Pottsville High School in 1942. I attended three semesters of the Pottsville branch of Penn State University before entering the United States Military Academy at West Point in 1943. I graduated from West Point, June 4, 1946, with a commission in the United States Army Air Corps, silver pilot's wings and gold second lieutenant's bars. On June 8, I married Mary Stewart in Newburgh, New York. I had met her the previous year on my 20th birthday. I flew B-29s at McDill AFB Tampa, Florida, and was sent to MIT for a MSEE in electrical engineering. I worked on engineering matters connected to atomic testing at Johns Hopkins Applied Physics Lab, Silver Springs, Maryland; Sandia Base, Albuquerque, New Mexico; and Washington, D.C. In 1957 I was sent to Cape Canaveral, Florida, where I was in charge of developing telemetry and tracking that was magnitudes better that what we had. I then was sent to the University of Chicago Business School for an MBA. After another stint in Washington, I was sent to the Air War College in Montgomery, Alabama. There was a shortage of pilots in Vietnam then, and older, grounded pilots were sent back to flying school and to Vietnam as much-needed replacements. I received the Distinguished Flying Cross for a pair of dangerous missions. I retired from the Air Force as a lieutenant colonel after 24 years of service. I then worked as an engineer in a variety of civilian jobs in train transit and air traffic control. I also did volunteer work and served on town commissions in Bedford, Massachusetts, where I retired.

A Flat Tire on the Way to West Point

By Frederick L. Hafer

"Finally, 1942—(after a slow start)—the United States was changing to an active wartime status....almost everything was rationed: leather, gasoline, rubber, foods. And I entered West Point."

I HAD ALWAYS wanted to fly. I built "flying models" out of bamboo and rice paper, and powered them by a twisted rubber band that turned the propeller. They never flew very far, but they did produce some spectacular crashes. I also built "solid models" out of balsa wood. We neighborhood boys would engage in spectacular dogfights in our Spads and Fokkers, and later on in Spitfires and Messerschmidts.

September 1939: Nazi Germany invaded Poland. World War II had begun. I was a 14-year-old sophomore in Pottsville (Pennsylvania) High School. Except for a funny Walt Disney cartoon called "In Der Führer's Face," this situation meant little or nothing to me.

The Selective Service System was drafting young men for Army service. Several friends of my family were called up for the specified one year of service. Sadly, the training was half-hearted and equipment and supplies were scarce. I remember a photograph of a mortar team practicing with a baseball bat because no actual mortar equipment was available. Morale was low—what are we training for? That stupid war will never reach us—there is the whole Atlantic Ocean between us and Germany. OHIO began to appear painted on building walls in the training camps. OHIO meant Over the Hill (desert) In October, but more and more of my older friends were being called to active duty.

9 April 1940: Germany attacks Denmark and Norway.

10 May 1940: Germany attacks Holland and Belgium.

22 June 1940: Germany and France sign an armistice. I am still a sophomore at Pottsville High. More and more friends are being drafted. Suddenly the war seems closer to everyone.

22 June 1941: Germany attacks Russia. The war is now much, much closer.

7 December 1941: Japan attacks the United States (Pearl Harbor Day). In the next several days Japan attacks the Philippines, Malaya and other military targets throughout Southeast Asia. I am now a 16-year-old senior at Pottsville High.

The United States finally started changing to an active wartime footing. Rationing was instituted by use of ration coupons, books and tokens. Leather shoes were limited to two pair per year. Regulation W limited women's skirts to being short and tight to conserve fabric. Gasoline was rationed because military vehicles had first priority for the reduced fuel supply. I very quickly learned to walk at a dog-trot to get anywhere. The nearest movie was four miles from home, and I could make that distance in well under one hour. Rubber was extremely scarce, as the Japanese had captured the rubber plantations of Malaya, which were the primary source of raw rubber. New tires were available only to top-priority emergency personnel such as doctors. Others had to make do with shoddy, unreliable recaps. And this situation led to one of the most significant events of my life. Food was also rationed, most especially sugar and meat. Extra sugar could usually be obtained for the home canning of food, so that imposed little hardship. Everyone had some sort of Victory Garden, so raw food was usually available on a seasonal basis.

Early June 1942: I graduated from Pottsville High School; turned 17 six weeks later. I immediately entered the local branch of Pennsylvania State University in an engineering curriculum. I applied for both Army and Navy pilot training programs but was told I was too young and did not have two years of college education. They recommended that I stay in Penn State as long as possible. I also started actively seeking an appointment to the US

Military Academy at West Point. There was a lot of talk that the war would last ten years before the United States finally won.

7 August 1942: U.S. forces land on Guadalcanal. I have been out of high school all of two months and have celebrated my 17th birthday. There is no chance of getting into a regular pilot training program at this time. Colleges are operating on a three semester per year schedule, so the pace is pretty demanding. I make the first significant contacts for a West Point appointment.

2 March 1943: The Battle of the Bismark Sea begins. This battle was a major disaster for the Japanese; their losses were so great that they could no longer adequately reinforce and resupply their garrisons in that area. In early March, I took the entrance exams for West Point in New York City. Wartime conditions had finally arrived; the lenses on all the traffic lights were painted black (except for a small strip in the center) to create blackout visual conditions. This was done to help protect the ships at sea from being seen by attacking submarines.

1 July 1943: I entered West Point on a three-year program. At that time, there was active combat in the South Pacific, in Southeast Asia and in Russia, but western Europe was relatively quiet, except for training and resistance operations.

Our training program was a very compressed and demanding mixture of academic and military work. We had three days off over Christmas but were in the classroom on New Year's Day. On New Year's Eve the warden at nearby Sing Sing prison announced over the PA system that the inmates at West Point would NOT be allowed to rattle their "cell" doors at midnight.

The traditional Army-Navy football game had been moved from Baltimore to West Point for obvious reasons. In the spirit of friendly rivalry, it was decided that, since the midshipmen could not attend the game, the cadets would take their place. So half the cadets (the First Regiment) sat on the north side of Michie Stadium, yelled Navy cheers and sang Navy songs. Half the band played Navy music. The other half of the cadets (the Second Regiment) sat on the south side of the stadium and yelled and sang the usual

Frederick Hafer at the United States Military Academy, 1946.

Army football encouragement. Unfortunately, Navy won, 13–7.

6 June 1944: D-Day. The Allied invasion of Europe had begun. It was also graduation day for the West Point class of 1944. I became a third classman (Yearling) and got two weeks of leave before reporting back to the academy. As we left the academy we were each issued a packet of food ration coupons to provide our families with food to compensate for all the home cooking we would eat. Leave was rather dull, as all my buddies were now in the Army and the girls were in college. We also got more time off (with ration coupons) at Christmas. Otherwise, our lives were little changed.

15 April 1945: I departed West Point for pilot training in Florida. In the very early hours of 15 April, over 350 of us formed ranks in the barracks area and marched to the railroad station to travel to four different pilot primary flight training schools. We each wore a tan summer uniform with brown shoes and carried a large duffel bag containing all our belongings. Yes, it was cold! The rest of the cadets formed ranks immediately after we left and marched to a fleet of buses to go to New York City to march in President Roosevelt's funeral parade. My train to Florida stopped in Washington for a crew change, and we were given about two hours to stretch our legs. Washington was totally closed. Nothing was open: we could not even get a cup of coffee. Then back to the train and on to Lakeland, Florida, and to primary flight training. Since the war was almost over, there was no need for additional pilots and the washout rate was horrendous. Fortunately, I made the cut and continued my training to become a pilot.

7 May 1945: Germany surrenders.

8 May 1945: Formal declaration of V-E Day. The war in Europe ends.

15 June 1945: Primary flight training completed. We are released on leave, to report to Stewart AAF (West Point) NLT 5:00 P.M. on 1 July.

Now back to the unreliable recapped tire. My father had arranged a car ride from Pottsville to New York for me. I would then take a train and a bus to Stewart AAF. Somewhere in New Jersey a tire failed, and we lost more than two hours repairing the failed tire. As a result, I missed my connections and was late reporting in. My punishment was to "walk the area" (walk back and forth across the barracks courtyard) for a specified number of hours. On Saturday night, after walking for several hours, I went to the Saturday night dance. It was my 20th birthday. The cadet hostess kindly telephoned a young lady in nearby Newburgh and asked if she would go to the dance and celebrate my birthday with me. Yes! A short time later a very lovely young lady arrived and we went dancing. A year later this lovely lady became my bride. Talk about a delightful chain of events, all of which could be traced back to a rotten tire.

George Hanford

Born 1920 · Cambridge, Massachusetts

Naval officer George Hanford before departure for the Battle of the Great Salt Lake.

I was born in Cambridge, Massachusetts, in 1920, the son of Alfred Chester Hanford and Ruth Hyde Hanford. I grew up in Cambridge and graduated from Exeter Academy in 1937. At Harvard University I studied mathematics, graduating in 1941. I graduated from the Harvard Business School in 1943. As a lieutenant, senior grade in the U.S. Naval Reserve, I was sent to Salt Lake City, Utah, where it seemed as though the Navy had forgotten me. I married Elaine Halstead and we had two daughters. After the war, I served for 2 years as an assistant dean at Harvard Business School; then 7 years as business manager and teacher at the North Shore County Day School in Winnetka, Illinois; and finally 32 years in a variety of positions at the College Board (the SAT, Advanced Placement, etc.), the last 7 as president. Then I wrote a book, *Life with the SAT*. Earlier, on sabbatical in 1973–74, I authored a lengthy report on a study I had done on the sorry state of big-time intercollegiate sports.

The Battle of the Great Salt Lake

"What We Don't Know Can't Hurt Us"

By George Hanford

> "I got as far as San Francisco when the Marine officer in charge of the base-to-be made it clear that he wasn't going to have HIS base defended by some 60-day amateur....After the war, I found out that I was kept there that long as part of a ploy by the Bureau of Ordnance to have replacements ready to take over for the expected heavy casualties in the invasion of Japan."

THIS TALE BEGINS on December 5, 1941. I was a student at the Harvard Business School and some Navy recruiters showed up to sell the idea of service in the Reserve. The next week a bunch of us signed up. For reasons which escape me, the Navy left us—on inactive duty and at our own expense—to finish our degrees some 15 months later in the spring of 1943 when I went on active duty.

By the fall I had been transformed by a series of crash courses from a budding businessman into an antiaircraft artillery naval officer destined to be assigned to an advanced base on a Pacific island where I would repair the guns on PT boats and, incidentally, protect the base from Japanese bombs.

I got as far as San Francisco when the Marine officer in charge of the base-to-be made it clear that he wasn't going to have HIS base defended by some 60-day amateur. So I was shipped back to Utah on what was called "90-days temporary additional duty." I arrived in Salt Lake City on November 30, 1943, and departed same on November 30, 1945—on the same train—the Exposition Flyer headed east. Thus it is that my "Battle of the Great Salt Lake" lasted exactly two years.

The battleground was the Clearfield Naval Supply Depot on the Bamburger Railroad in some of the best farmland in the state of Utah—halfway between Salt Lake City and Ogden. Then the largest such facility in the world, it was located there—inland to avoid possible bombing by the Japanese and equidistant from Pacific port facilities near Los Angeles and San Francisco, California, and Seattle, Washington.

After the war, I found out that I was kept there that long as part of a ploy by the Bureau of Ordnance to have replacements ready to take over for the expected heavy casualties in the invasion of Japan. (Parenthetically, that's given me a somewhat different view of the use of the atomic bomb than that of a lot of people. It meant I didn't have to invade Japan.)

In any event, Clearfield had an oversupply of ordnance officers. As line officers, as differentiated from supply officers, we pulled a lot of shore patrol duty, mainly bringing back hungover sailors from the Salt Lake City and Ogden jails and escorting Italian prisoner-of-war work details from their camp in Ogden. We also ended up with some nonordnance assignments in addition to our regular duties of overseeing ordnance shipments. I had four of these assignments.

On one nonordnance assignment, I ended up as officer in charge of the Navy's photographic equipment being sent to the Pacific. That was easy. I had a couple of photographer's mates who knew what they were doing.

A second nonordnance assignment was the same but for aerological (the Navy's term for meteorological) equipment, except that in this instance my one aerographer's mate got what he called "ulsters" and had to be sent to the naval hospital in San Francisco. For a while, the Pacific fleet was lucky to have any weather.

For my third assignment we were to ship equipment to Admiral Nimitz's print shop on Guam and needed somebody to assemble the equipment. The Navy doesn't have printer's mates, so we had to scour the base to find men who had some print shop experience. The volume of print output from Guam was testimony to our success.

My fourth assignment came when the officer in charge of the Advanced Base Section called me in and asked me, "Hanford, isn't your father dean of Harvard College?" When I allowed as how he was, my superior officer said, "You're in charge of the Advanced Base newsletter." So much for sequitur.

Not an exciting battle perhaps, but one that in microcosm demonstrated not only how we outmanned the enemy but also how we used our ingenuity in using that manpower.

Robert Preyer

Born 1922 · Greensboro, North Carolina

Robert Preyer after returning from flight in the open cockpit of a Stinson trainer, Glenview Naval Training Base, 1943. He is wearing equipment from an earlier decade and recovered from storage, issued to flyers in training in 1943.

Robert Preyer was born in Greensboro, North Carolina in 1922, the son of William Yost and Mary Norris Watson Richardson Preyer. He graduated from Choate Preparatory School in 1940 and began his studies at Princeton. He spent 1943–1946 in the USNR, then returned to complete a Princeton BA and Columbia MA (1948) before marriage and the birth of his first child. Two more daughters were born while he taught English at Smith and Amherst colleges. A PhD from Columbia in 1954 led to a long career at Brandeis University where he was some-time chair of the Faculty Senate and the Department of English and American Literature. He retired in 1987 as full professor. He is the author of numerous scholarly publications. His other interests include minority education; politics; theatre; opera; poetry; baroque music; symphony; foreign travel; swimming and climbing the Adirondacks; and Perry, Maine. He is or has served on the boards of the Posse Foundation, ACLUM, NAACP/Legal Defense Fund, Museum of Afro-American History, and Backsides, Inc. He also served with the advisory presidential boards at Brandeis and Princeton. Summers spent with a growing number of great-grandchildren and their predecessors keep things lively indeed!

A Nagging World War II Memory

By Robert O. Preyer

"And I now honor an unknown number of gallant pilots and feel great sorrow for those heroic pilots from many nations who had the bad luck to be a few months ahead of my cadre in naval aviation, struggling with inferior equipment in the terrible months of our entry into World War II."

EARLY SPRING, 1943. After months of ground training at RPI (Troy, NY) and UNC (Chapel Hill) orders came to proceed to Lenoir-Rhyne, N.C., an obscure regional college town deep in the Blue Ridge Mountains. It was at such rudimentary bases that naval cadets had their first experience of flight training. Instruction was handled by civilian pilots—among them leather-faced crop dusters and barnstormers with many a yarn to enthrall their 20-year-old flight students, mostly college students in V-5 programs. Our "flight base" was located at a bulldozed wooded hilltop surrounded by taller mountains; it consisted of a hanger and a flight shack, and a wind sock near the single bumpy airstrip which had been carved to resemble the dimensions of a carrier deck. Student pilots had to make a full throttle sharp right turn as soon as they were airborne to avoid a mountain, as to suggest the way pilots took off from ships at sea.

A "skipper" and "exec" of this improvised civilian flying school were the only ones there in regular Navy uniforms—and they had at their disposal a large fighting plane which none of us had glimpsed in hours of Airplane Recognition study. We stared at it with wonder, speculated on how or why it was present at our rinky-dink base. Word got around that it was too hot to use on carriers; someone had heard that hundreds of this discarded design were shipped abroad to help hard-pressed British and Dutch allies struggling in Burma and other Asian areas under invasion by Japanese forces. There seemed to be confirmation that this reject, equipped with pontoons or snow skis, was performing miracles as the gallant Finnish pilots wreaked havoc on the invading Russians. Frigid weather conditions were just right for its nine-cylinder power plant. A third set of rumors came from Marine pilots in our tropical outposts in the Pacific—they called it a "flying coffin." This was all idle "scuttlebutt"—and we soon turned our attention to a final test of flying skill which must be passed before authorization to proceed to the next stage of training. A second landing strip had been prepared, shorter and narrower than the accustomed one, and surrounded on all sides by an endless expanse of pine trees. Our final exercise consisted of timing our altitude and speed precisely and then crossing the controls as we reached the beginning of the strip, a maneuver which stopped forward motion and led to a precipitous flat stall as near as possible to where the short runway commenced. Hitting the ground with a stunning jolt or bounce, it was imperative to instantly apply full throttle in hopes of clearing the fully grown trees looming up at the not very distant end of this uneven incision in the dense forest. Precision flying or else—it fully absorbed our attention. Those who managed this feat were given orders to entrain for Glenview Air Station.

And then it happened. On a quiet southern afternoon loungers on the tarmac watched with interest as the exec and the skipper made their way to the hangar, rolled out their special machine and blasted off the runway with a tremendous roar, rapidly disappearing from sight. They did not return.

In the early twilight, word got out that something terrible must have happened—strange new officers appeared; we were told that the skipper and executive officer had apparently landed their mystery craft in a farmer's field for reasons unknown—taking off they were unable to clear the surrounding pine forest—the two bodies had been extracted from the shattered hull squashed into splintered trees above and spread about in the forest floor below. I was driven in a jeep to the crash scene to make sure that

night prowlers, human or animal, would not disturb the site before investigative officials arrived next morning. It was a lonely
and strange duty—filled with the snuffling sounds of nearby bears
and other nocturnal creatures, the soft patter of tiny feet, howls
of distant dogs, hooting of owls—and it brought memories of Boy
Scout overnight wilderness fears of a twelve-year-old on his first
pup tent experience in woods not far away in this same forest.

And then we were gone, in transit to a huge naval air station with instructors who had seen combat in the Pacific, flying
each day new and sturdy Stinson open cockpit trainers, whose
wide margin of safety was fiendishly reduced by "spoilers" on
leading edges of wings so that slight errors led to tailspins and
stalls in midair. This was a new kind of experience, more serious,
more thrilling and far more dangerous, since we were not inside
a closed cockpit. Weekend leaves in wartime Chicago, USO invitations to local Polish weddings, exciting girls, jazz nightclubs,
bars and dances were now available. At Lenoir-Rhyne the initial
wonder came from hovering over rooftops and forests, master-
ing a three-dimensional world through the windows of a slow-
moving Taylor Cub. Instead of a flight office shack and a hangar
with six homely Taylor Cubs surrounded by blue mountains and
lonely villages, we cadets, now in our hundreds, savored the wonders available in wartime where civilians honored our distinctive
green uniforms with every form of hospitality. USO invitations
to join in celebrations of Polish marriages were a delight; exciting girls showed us where to find the best jazz, bars, nightclubs
and dance bands. Then back to work: entire squadrons broke the
morning quiet with the barking sounds of engines warming up,
testing controls, then rolling into takeoff positions and blasting
off with a roar. Planes were in the air constantly, night and day.
Solo flying and acrobatic maneuvers with unrestricted visibility
offered new wonders—the horizon tilted alarmingly as we rolled,
dove and went into spins. At one moment the earth was above
us and the sky below; at the next we were hanging upside down,
restrained only by a safety belt and close enough to smell the

freshly ploughed soil a few hundred feet below our open cockpit, almost regretting that we were losing altitude and must act immediately to alter our situation. And so the events and feelings associated with the mystery plane and the unexpected death of its two occupants were no longer in the forefront of consciousness.

The passage of time—decades—tend to haze over one's recollections; books remind us, documentary films show us what it "looked like," but a rich, full recovery of a moment in our past usually requires some trigger in the present that makes it happen. My "shock of recognition" came on January 2, 2012, when the *New York Times* provided a remarkably full account of the discovery of the engine and propeller of a Brewster Buffalo that had crash-landed just short of the runway in the lagoon of Midway Atoll in June 1942—shortly before the commencement of the epic battle of Midway. The writer, Eric Eckholm, was given a two-page spread, illustrated with two pictures, one of which showed the fighter/bomber in question, the other a touching snapshot of four Marine pilots on Midway. One of them was the pilot of the submerged wreck only recently located. (He had the good luck to be transferred from Midway shortly before the Zeros and bombers appeared.) What I saw in that photograph was one of the several versions of the plaything the bored commanding officers had managed to bring to our lonely flight school—and in which they died.

Eckholm began to unravel the mystery of what he called a "famous flying Dud found 10 feet deep below the waters off Midway Atoll...the plane had its day of ignominy in the epic battle of Midway in June 1942 when 19 Marine pilots valiantly engaged Japanese Zeroes in dogfights above Midway Atoll, a strategic speck some 1,300 miles northwest of Honolulu. Only five of the pilots and planes returned." He quoted from an action report by a surviving Marine pilot: "the Japanese Zero fighter can run circles around the F2A-3" (the designation for a fighter plane version of the Brewster Buffalo that had been handed over to land-based Marines as unsuitable for carrier landings). Navy pilots noted that its wheel struts broke during the hard landings on carriers—it was nicknamed "the flying coffin" and was rapidly replaced by much more reliable crafts. Eckholm quotes a furious Captain P. R.White of the Marines who were stuck with the Buffalo: "It is my belief that any Commander that orders pilots out for combat in a F2A-3 should consider the pilot as lost before leaving the ground." Replacement Marine pilots, equipped with aircraft that could equal and/or surpass the Zero, were spared this ordeal. But already several hundred Brewster Buffaloes had been sent out to the Navy from a former car factory in Queens, New York. Knowledge of their whereabouts was restricted information in war conditions and of little concern to the general public in subsequent years. Eckholm: "Of the hundreds of Brewster Buffaloes produced at a former car factory in Queens, only one largely intact plane survives, a modified model...sold to the Finns. That craft was fished out of a Russian lake in 1998."

I saw years ago (1944?) a confidential Navy film of mock combat between a (captured) Zero and a variety of U.S. fighters, with commentary. The Buffalo was not mentioned. I also recall newsreel images of Finnish Buffaloes with pontoons or skis—a version that destroyed hundreds of Soviet aircraft with minimum losses. Apparently squadrons of Buffaloes were also provided to the Dutch, British and Commonwealth pilots locked in mortal combat with superior Japanese aircraft. Eckholm has now cleared up the mystery of why these lend-lease Buffaloes were brilliant performers in icy Finland but had a rotten record in warmer climes. To quote Eckholm again: "The story is told of a New Zealand Buffalo pilot, based in Burma, whose vision was obscured in the heat of battle by oil squirting onto the windshield. He removed his shoe, and took a sock, slid back the canopy and reached around to wipe the window clean." The fate of the Buffaloes sent to the aid of Finland was completely different—refitted with skis and pontoons it became a superior fighting machine. It is no wonder then that the single surviving Buffalo is on loan to Finland. A final word from the *New York Times*: "Only one largely intact plane survives, a modified model that was sold to the Finns…That craft was fished out of a Russian lake in 1998." The loan is from the National Naval Aviation Museum in Pensacola, Florida. So ends my tale.

Called by various names, this discard from the Navy had a checkered career indeed. I now believe that it was the plaything that caused the death of a commanding officer and his second-in-command at a lonely civilian base where naval cadets learned the rudiments of life off the ground. And I now honor an unknown number of gallant pilots and feel great sorrow for those heroic pilots from many nations who had the bad luck to be a few months ahead of my cadre in naval aviation, struggling with inferior equipment in the terrible months of our entry into World War II.

Mary T. Simonds

Born 1917 · Auburn, Maine

Mary Trafton Simonds, 1917–2012.

Mary Trafton Simonds was born August 23, 1917, to Willis Allen Trafton and Frances Dain Trafton of Auburn, Maine. She attended Abbot Academy (now part of Phillips Academy), Andover, Massachusetts; Colby Junior College (now Colby-Sawyer College) in New London, New Hampshire, class of 1938; and Mount Holyoke College, class of 1940 with a major in economics. She then worked at the Babson Institute, Wellesley, Massachusetts, and the Liberty Mutual Life Insurance Company, Boston, Massachusetts, as a financial analyst.

She married John Langdon Simonds of Boston and North Andover, Massachusetts, the day of the Cocoanut Grove fire, November 27, 1942. They were married 57 years and lived in Cambridge and Belmont. They had three children, a daughter Virginia and sons Robert T. and William T. Her husband, an attorney, died in 1999. Mary was very active as a volunteer for Mount Auburn Hospital in Cambridge. She was president of the Ladies Auxiliary and head of the Thursday Morning Talks Committee for three years. She was a hospital incorporator and overseer for many years and served on the hospital's development committee. She also served on the Board of Trustees of Colby-Sawyer College, serving as secretary of the board from 1953 to 1973. She was named a Life Trustee Emerita of the college. She was also a member of the National Society of the Colonial Dames in the Commonwealth of Massachusetts.

You've Got to Stop It!

By Mary T. Simonds

> "'You've got to stop it! You've got to stop it!' They were
> loading bombs on one vessel and detonators on another,
> making the bombs useless if the detonator vessel was
> sunk or the ships became separated."

JOHN L. SIMONDS had one year at Harvard Law School when he entered the U.S. Navy. He trained at Dartmouth College and in Washington. D.C. We had planned a Maine wedding for November after he was commissioned with two weeks' time to his new assignment—not in the same city! The captain said, "Go, collect your orders on Monday." So. Along with the wedding guests, John arrived Saturday, we were married and then driven to Boston after the wedding by an officer from Ft. Devens who had gas for his vehicle. We found the city of Boston a mass of smoke and flames and sirens, too. It was the night of the Cocoanut Grove fire!

Early Monday morning John checked in for his new job...solving naval problems primarily in the United States, often concerning ammunition. He found the work interesting and it kept him busy and happy. Then after eight months he was told to go to Pontiac, Michigan, where he would work with H. Klingler, producing bombs. (There was no room in Pontiac for a new bride, but I went along anyway.) The United States had only two working bombs in 1942 and badly needed more. The operation was successful. We then spent a few weeks at the Great Lakes Naval Base, until John was recalled to Washington.

The next assignment was in the port director's office in New York City. John boarded foreign vessels, planned inspections and checked security. We lived in a New York hotel, and then on Long

Island. There were more problems in New Jersey, so we quickly moved to an area inside Sandy Hook, where a two-mile pier had been constructed. Trains from the Midwest brought ammunition which had to be loaded on ships bound for the Pacific. Timing and scheduling was not easy. I remember a frantic call to the captain in Washington, "You've got to stop it! You've got to stop it!" They were loading bombs on one vessel and detonators on another, making the bombs useless if the detonator vessel was sunk or the ships became separated. Our next move was to Newark and so it went.

When the war was over, John, now a full lieutenant, returned to Maine to collect me and our two babies. He completed his education at Harvard Law School.

Mary's story

APARTMENTS IN WASHINGTON, D.C., were impossible to find. We moved in with another naval officer and his wife. They were Mormon. We alternated weeks cooking. She sang in the Tabernacle Choir and I took a Red Cross nurse's aide course. Once trained I volunteered at George Washington University Hospital, caring for patients and working in the nursery. They were so short-handed that the hospital trained three of us to work in the delivery room. I sat with patients, cleaned and autoclaved instruments and was on call for whenever extra help was needed.

In Pontiac I again volunteered and the Red Cross even helped by recommending an apartment! On Long Island, because I was pregnant, the Red Cross preferred that I help home patients rather than continue working in the hospital. This early training developed my interest in hospital care, making it a lifetime interest.

Harry Baldwin

Born 1918 · Waltham, Massachusetts

May 1943. Harry Baldwin on furlough from Scott Field, Illinois. Picture taken at his home in Belmont, Massachusetts.

Harry Heath Baldwin was born January 2, 1918, in Waltham, Massachusetts. He was a beloved only child and named for his father and grandfather. He grew up in Arlington, Massachusetts, and attended schools there until 1934 when his family moved to Belmont. Harry went to Bowdoin College in Brunswick, Maine, graduating in 1940. He was hired (by the father of a classmate) as an outside messenger at the Merchants National Bank in Boston. Drafted in 1942, he became a radio instructor at Scott Field in Belleville, Illinois, and later studied ground control approach at Columbia, South Carolina. He became a corporal. Harry married Eleanor Wright in 1943, and after the war they lived in Arlington with their four children. He returned to his former job at the Merchants National Bank, by then the Bank of New England, and remained there 42 years, retiring as a vice president. As a trustee of Symmes Hospital in Arlington, he was interested in the building of Brookhaven. In 2004 he and Eleanor happily moved there. In spite of excellent health care, he died in January 2005 of heart failure.

From the Journal of Harry Baldwin, Belmont, Massachusetts

By Harry Baldwin

Excerpts selected by Eleanor Baldwin

"I received a disappointment, having passed written examinations and board interviews for Communication Cadets, I was rejected on account of my eyes."

SEPTEMBER 1942—"After taking a two-week furlough following induction, I found myself an acting corporal taking the Belmont delegation to Camp Devens, Massachusetts. In spite of the fact it was September, it was very hot. After a couple of days taking physical and mental tests, getting uniforms and the dreaded shots, we found ourselves entrained for Atlantic City, New Jersey. Arriving that first night in a blacked-out city was very weird. We were marched to the Hotel Claridge where we bunked with nothing but beds—no blankets at all. The following day found us marching down the famed boardwalk to our quarters (for the next few weeks) at the Ritz Carlton and the 923rd T.S.S.AAFTCC."

October 1942—"Looking back now at Scott Field, Illinois, I think of the amount of work—in our basic training—drill, drill from 7:00 A.M. to 5:00 P.M.—what a memory. Corporal R., Sgt. C. and a few others are unforgettable as typical tough basic training non-coms. Fortunately, I finished basic training and spent the after basic training period dodging KP and as much work as possible wondering where I would ship. October 30 found me at Scott Field drenched to the skin and dead tired from a 43-hour G.I. troop ride. My Scott career has been very hectic however and overloaded with disappointments—the biggest—was my rejection for O.C.S. after board interviews—I'll try again."

Harry Baldwin on furlough from Scott Field, Illinois, with his fiancée Eleanor Wright of Dedham, Massachusetts. Picture taken May 1943 at Harry's home in Belmont, Massachusetts.

April 1943—"I graduated with class 28 from Scott Field as radio operator and mechanic. Were it not for my eyes, I might be headed for gunnery school and then combat as a radio man and gunner—then I discovered that I was to become an instructor whether I wanted to or not....We all attended ITD or Instructors Training Division for two weeks. Following graduation we eagerly awaited for furloughs but due to payroll formations, we had a short period of observation at school."

May 1943—"On furlough in May, Eleanor and I became engaged—and then in June, as I was to teach in the Receiver Phase, I was assigned to the 20th Academic Squadron—a pleasant change. Oh yes, June also brought another stripe and I am now a corporal."

January 1944—"I received a disappointment, having passed written examinations and board interviews for Communication Cadets, I was rejected on account of my eyes. By the way, ratings have long been frozen and a corporal I remain. On December 4, I married Eleanor in Cambridge and then returned to Belleville, Illinois."

March 1945—"The news came—we are to leave—goodbyes are said to our friends and 35 of us (unfortunately under me) head for our new base, Fort Dix, New Jersey, and a fate unknown. Almost sure we will soon be overseas.—We were shipped to Columbia, South Carolina, winding up in the School Squadron and went through Pre-control and Ground Control Approach finishing Sept.

30th. Since completing school, war is over and due to my points "48" I have been deleted from a team."

December 1945—"Tomorrow I leave for Westover Field, Massachusetts—and should be out of the army by end of the week."

Eleanor Baldwin

Born 1920 · Boston, Massachusetts

2010 photo of Eleanor Baldwin as she recalls the uncertain but happy years of being a serviceman's wife.

In 1920, I was born Eleanor Wright in Faulkner Hospital in Boston. Sadly, my mother died two years later, and my sister and I were brought up by housekeepers. Fortunately, we lived next door in Dedham to my mother's parents. After graduating from high school, I attended the Sacker School of Decorating in Boston. There I received a lifelong appreciation of antiques, decorating and historic preservation. In 1943 I married Harry Baldwin from Belmont, Massachusetts. We settled in Arlington where we brought up our four children. When the youngest was in college we moved to a small saltbox in Winchester, more manageable than our Victorian house in Arlington. In 2004 we settled comfortably at Brookhaven, coincidentally "up the street" from Chapel Hill school where Harry lived in the early thirties! In spite of excellent care, Harry died six months later from heart failure.

My Essential War Work

By Eleanor Baldwin

> "My conscience (would 'guilt' be a better word?) for leaving
> my 'essential war work' was eased a bit by working at
> the local USO. I was urged to stay in the kitchen making
> pancakes, etc., as the single girls preferred waiting on the
> soldiers."

IN JANUARY 1943, I heard that Bendix Aviation Corp. in Norwood, Massachusetts, was hiring women for assembling fire control panels for fighter planes.

As I was living with my sister and grandmother in Dedham, the next town, I applied for a position. I wish I could say it was patriotism that motivated me, but I think it was the $35 a week salary, more than I had ever earned.

A friend offered to drive me with others to the plant for the 7:00 A.M.–3:00 P.M. shift. In our blue coveralls, we checked in. Some of the women I knew from Dedham but most were from other towns. Young or older, it was a congenial work force.

Our job consisted of lacing with stout cord heavy wires set on boards in a nailed pattern so that the ends of the wires could be connected to panels in the planes. The work was hard on the hands but ours soon toughened up. With no electrical engineering knowledge, this is a very hazy recollection of how we connected the wires, which were then lifted off the board, inspected and sent to plane factories.

After a few months I was transferred to the drafting department which raised my salary to $45 a week. In May, I became engaged to Harry Baldwin from Belmont, Massachusetts, and a small wedding was planned during Harry's next furlough, which came suddenly on December 1. We were married on December 4 and went together to Scott Field in Belleville, Illinois, where Harry was teaching radio.

My conscience (would "guilt" be a better word?) in leaving my 'essential war work' was eased a bit by working at the local USO. I was urged to stay in the kitchen making pancakes, etc., as the single girls preferred waiting on the soldiers. Eventually I got a job at Scott Field correcting code tests. This job continued until January 1945 when Harry was sent to Columbia, South Carolina, for radar school. I went home to Dedham.

Mary Stewart Hafer

Born 1924 · Newburgh, New York

In the winter of 1945–46 Mary Stewart and U.S.M.A. cadet Frederick L. Hafer were beginning to think seriously about marriage. Note saddle shoes and bobby socks. Silk or nylon stockings were not available.

Mary Sterwart Hafer was born September 7, 1924, the daughter of Thomas Archibald Stewart and Mary L. Warden Stewart. She graduated as valedictorian from Newburgh Free Academy in June 1941. She received a BA in chemistry from Swarthmore College in 1945 and a BS in library science from Simmons College in 1968. She married Lt. Frederick L. Hafer on June 8, 1946. Living in Bedford, Massachusetts, she became a member of the Bedford Friends of the Library and organized a library volunteer program in 1971. The program is still active. As a member of the Bedford Historical Society she curated the society's collection and then curated the Job Lane Historical House in Bedford. She was named Bedford's Citizen of the Year in 1988.

Defense Plant Work: A Wartime Education

By Mary Stewart Hafer

"The WWII generation matured really fast. After Pearl Harbor, every able-bodied male either volunteered for service or was drafted. Many of them had life or death responsibilities and they knew it. The lives of women and children also changed.... [Our] testing jobs were routine and boring.... I quickly realized the benefit of a higher education.... factory work educated me in ways that I probably would never have learned otherwise."

THE WWII GENERATION matured really fast. After Pearl Harbor, every able-bodied young male either volunteered for service or was drafted. Many of them had life or death responsibilities and they knew it. The lives of women and children also changed. Women were encouraged to work and many new kinds of work became available to them. Homemakers had to cope with shortages, rationing and a black market. Many kids helped with Victory Gardens, collecting metal and other useful tasks.

I was 17, a freshman, majoring in chemistry at Swarthmore, a Quaker college near Philadelphia, when the bombing of Pearl Harbor electrified our country. In spite of its Quaker roots, the college accepted a Navy V-12 unit and went on a three-semester-a-year schedule in order to graduate students sooner. Out of about 250 freshmen in my class, I was among the 17 who actually graduated in June of 1945, our original graduation date. I was among the younger members of my class and disliked the idea of spending hot, humid summers there.

The summer of '42, I was still 17 and fell under the child labor laws forbidding me to do factory work. I could probably have gotten a variance but didn't try. I taught riding at a girl's camp instead.

The next summer, I worked at the DuPont Fabrikoid plant in my hometown of Newburgh, New York. They took on a couple of college students for the summer for the minimum wage of 50 cents an hour. The other girl was from my high school class and was a chemistry student at Russell Sage, the female affiliate of Rensselaer Polytechnic Institute. They also hired as a permanent employee a girl who had been valedictorian of my high school two years ahead of me. The other summer employee and I worked in the testing lab. This was in an all-metal building which was incredibly hot under the summer sun. The factory made plastic-coated fabrics and was now engaged in making tarpaulins for the military. Some of their products used highly explosive nitrocellulose. They kept miles of antique nitrocellulose movie film in barrels under an artificial pond and handled it with extreme care. I believe smoking was cause for instant dismissal.

Our testing jobs were routine and boring. The head of the lab was a woman with a doctorate, but none of the workers had a college degree. The boring work was okay for a summer—but for a lifetime? I quickly realized the benefit of higher education. Occasionally, one of the engineers would have a bit of spare time and take the two summer employees and the new graduate on a tour of the factory and explain the processes to us. One time, it involved quite a lot of calculus. I had struggled with calculus under Arnold Dresden, a world-class mathematician, but I understood what the engineer was explaining. The new graduate, who had distinguished herself at a much easier college, hadn't a clue.

The other lesson I learned was about money. At the end of my employment, I made out a long shopping list for clothes and headed for New York City by myself. Previously, my mother had always paid for my clothes. When I looked at price tags, I suddenly realized that this dress would cost two weeks labor, or that suit, four weeks. My list immediately dropped by about 90 percent.

The summer of '44 was spent in Dearborn, Michigan. My father, who had been too young for World War I, volunteered for service in World War II. He wound up as Army Air Corps resident representative at the Ford Motor Company's River Rouge plant where they were manufacturing Pratt & Whitney R-2800 aircraft engines. Mother and my younger sister joined him. I now joined the small group of students and one young professor who traveled to Detroit for Christmas for end of term. We took the "Red Arrow," a night sleeper from Philadelphia. Railroads had been pushed to their limits by wartime needs. All old rolling stock had been pulled out of storage. Parts and skilled labor were in short supply. Breakdowns were common. I always took an upper berth because it was cheaper. This had other advantages. I once slept through an altercation a couple of berths away when a drunken sailor climbed into some woman's lower berth and had to be hauled out by other passengers. I don't think the "Red Arrow" ever arrived on time. Sometimes we were many hours late. At least once, we ran out of both food and water and arrived hungry and dirty. Fortunately, the young professor took care of our required excuses for returning late to school.

When I walked into the Consolidated Vultee Stinson aircraft factory in nearby Wayne, Michigan, I was hired on the spot as an assistant materials & process engineer at the amazingly high wage of $1.05 per hour plus time-and-a-half for Saturdays on a six-day week.

This was much more interesting work. They made small L-4 observation planes for the Air Corps at the rate of one a day. They made a somewhat larger seaplane for the British Navy for submarine patrol in the Caribbean at the rate of one per week. These planes were held together with rivets that suffered from galvanic corrosion. I tested various waterproof coatings for protection from salt water and wrote company specifications, which I signed with my initial rather than Mary. Engineering was still a man's world. I also helped work on the preparation of aluminum sheet for welding, which was then a new and tricky process.

Getting to and from work was another part of my education. The plant had an office devoted to setting up carpools and paid rides. I lived about twelve miles from the factory and didn't have a car. They arranged that I would be a paid rider in a pool. I was expected to be standing at the edge of the road at a certain time each morning. I rode in a car with people the likes of whom I had never before encountered. Their conversation was gross. They seemed to be friends and worked a second shift at another factory somewhere. I wondered how they found time to eat or sleep. On the way home they stopped at a bar and invited me to join them. I didn't drink and simply waited in the car. No doubt they thought I was snooty. On about the third day, I was a few paces from the roadside. They rolled on past. I hastily borrowed my mother's car, got to work and went back to the carpool office. This time, I was the only rider with a fine young man who was a hunchback. He was delighted to have paid skilled work, to own a car and to no longer be dependent on his parents for support. His body odor (never mentioned) was explained by telling me about how difficult it was for hunchbacks to bathe. At this point, we were winning the war and he was worrying about taking an office job at less pay, in order to be employed when the veterans came home. Our factory was filled with women and handicapped workers who were probably all in the same boat.

In September 1945, shortly after the end of the war, I went back to say "hello" to all my old friends and found the factory closed except for the engineering department. Again, I was hired on the spot to do paperwork for a 56-hour week with double pay for the additional overtime, while the engineers were frantically trying to figure out what consumer products they could now manufacture. I worked for a couple of weeks, went on my merry way to other things and never went back or found out about the products. I realized that factory work had educated me in ways that I probably would never have learned otherwise

Lucien Theriault

Born 1914 · Salem, Massachusetts

Lou Theriault, taken in 2002 at Brookhaven..

I was born in Salem, Massachusetts, and graduated from Salem High School. I then attended radio school and passed my exams, but could not find work. I went to work for Raytheon as a machine operator and repairman in 1933. Early in 1941 I was promoted to foreman and subsequently department head. I continued to work for Raytheon throughout my career, in receiving tubes and microwave power tubes for the duration. I retired from Raytheon after 46 years. I was married in 1940 and we had one son.

Seven Deferments

By Lucien Theriault

> "During the war I supervised 300–400 workers; about 80 percent were women."

I STARTED WORKING at Raytheon, Radio Receiver Tube Division in 1933. During World War II, Raytheon was providing radio receiver tubes to the armed forces for their communications equipment. The four departments that I supervised were responsible for providing all parts and other materials to the assembly and finishing lines.

Many of the parts were very small, wire the size of a human hair or less. Many parts had a tolerance of less than +/− .0002 of an inch. The need for preciseness meant we needed operators with good eyesight and nimble fingers. After the tubes were completed, they were tested to specifications. All good tubes were shipped to a military supply depot. During the war I supervised 300–400 workers; about 80 percent were women. Many of our employees were bused to our plant from the inner city. We worked three shifts per day, six days a week. After the war, we reduced our shifts from three to one, working five days a week.

I was given seven deferments between July 1941 and October 1945. These deferments were because my work at Raytheon was considered essential for the war effort. They were issued by the War Board usually every three to four months. My last deferment was issued August 1945. It expired in October 1945.

Rosemary Fitzgerald

Born 1917 · Center, Colorado

Rosemary Fitzgerald, retirement at Brookhaven.

Rosemary Fitzgerald was the daughter of Frank and Mildred Hudson. She was born near Center, Colorado, in 1917 then moved to Tuttle, Oklahoma, where she and her two brothers grew up. As a child she rode to a one-room school in a horse and buggy. After graduation from Oklahoma University in 1936, she took a train east to do graduate work in physics at Wellesley College, specializing in optics. During World War II she worked in research and development on flight simulation for the Navy. In 1941 she married Arthur Eugene Fitzgerald (Gene), an electrical engineering professor, consultant and author. They had three children. The family moved from Cambridge to Lexington, Massachusetts, in 1949. There she served in the Lexington Town Meeting and the Capital Expenditures Committee. She was active for decades in the Lexington League of Women Voters and sometimes represented the League in testimony on taxation issues at the Massachusetts state house. Rosemary served for many years as a docent at the Boston Museum of Science and was a teacher at the Harvard Institute for Learning in Retirement. She also participated in archeological digs with Earthwatch.

I Did the Math, the Shopping and the Machining

By Rosemary Fitzgerald

"I took time off just once from my R and D job for an MIT wives luncheon. Mrs. Compton spoke and said that we shouldn't be there; we should have defense jobs....My job was with the Howe Laboratory of Ophthalmology....Our major job was to make a trainer that would work like the Mark 4 range finder for oncoming airplanes."

I SPENT THE WAR YEARS in Cambridge, Massachusetts. We were married in September just before Pearl Harbor. My husband taught engineering courses at MIT that the Army wanted lots of soldiers to take. We lived in Shaler Lane, which was Harvard housing but available at the time to some MIT people. We could both take the T to work and were allowed very little gas; after about a year our car was disabled and we couldn't get another one until years after the war.

I took time off just once from my R and D job for an MIT wives luncheon. Mrs. Compton spoke and said that we shouldn't be there; we should have defense jobs. My job was with the Howe Laboratory of Ophthalmology, which was part of Harvard; we were housed in the old Eye and Ear infirmary and were working on contract for the Navy. Our leader was a delightful eccentric Viennese Harvard professor. He was a devotee of prizefighting and made great friends with a young semipro heavyweight. He said the fighter had a very high IQ so he sent him to Wentworth to learn machinery and set him up in a little shop in the basement, where we could all go down and use the lathe. Others in the little group were a practicing ophthalmologist from Belmont who was also a lieutenant commander in the Naval Reserve, a young man who had been teaching math in a prep school and another girl with a math major and typing skills.

Our major job was to make a trainer that would work like the Mark 4 range finder for oncoming airplanes. My part was to build a machine that would damp the movements of the controls so they would feel like the real ones. It was fun, since I did the math, the shopping and some of the machining and waived my patent rights. When our trainer was done and tested we all went to Chicago to demonstrate it to a firm that had been making hair dryers.

Meanwhile my brother was over in the radiation lab working on the radar that made the Mark 4 obsolete. My other brother was drafted but never got overseas. Shortly, before the war's end I quit work and became a stay-at-home mother.

Barbara Kirchheimer

Born 1919 · Chicago, Illinois

Barbara Kirchheimer at Brookhaven.

It is hard to summarize an account of 94 years in a few words, but I'll try! I was born in Chicago in 1919 and lived there until I went to college. I graduated from Swarthmore College in 1940 and received an MA from American University in 1990. Returning to school was a fun time with all those much younger classmates. I married Joe Kirchheimer in 1940. I've lived in Marmaroneck, New York; New York City, New York; Palm Springs, California; Washington, D.C.; Cambridge, Massachusetts; and finally Brookhaven. My husband died in Washington, D.C., in 1989. My "career" has been entirely volunteer work , a variety of projects with the elderly in the Bronx, then the same for the New York Housing Authority, and past years in the environs of Boston. Now I suppose I have to say that I am completely retired and my work is to keep on going!

Serving at Home and Abroad

By Joseph and Barbara Kirchheimer

> "I remember both happy and sad times.... Now, after more than six decades, I have so many memories of those years that they are like stars in a dark sky. Some are bright and others dim as the years go by."

I MUST GO back to the summer of 1940, almost a year and a half before Pearl Harbor, to write about my husband's and my experience of World War II. That year Joe volunteered for active duty in the United States Cavalry. He had been in ROTC (Reserve Officer Training Corps) at the University of Arizona. Germany's invasion of France and the Netherlands in 1940 motivated him to volunteer. We were married in the autumn of 1940 and I accompanied him to Ft. Riley, Kansas, where he joined the Second Cavalry Division. The horses were soon replaced by jeeps, and early in 1941 he was off to the 4th Armored Division—tanks and jeeps—and after that to the 8th Armored Division. On October 8, 1944, he went to Europe with that unit; he was the G-2 (intelligence officer) of the division. He left for England and then to Europe in October 1944.

During those four years, from 1940 to 1944, I went with him from post to post: Ft. Riley, Kansas; Pine Camp, New York; Ft. Knox, Kentucky; and Camp Polk, Louisiana. Wherever we went I volunteered with the Red Cross Home Service, which connected families at home to their soldiers, through Red Cross field directors who were with the troops. I could never have done the things I did in a city Red Cross office, but in the small towns where we lived—Watertown, New York; Elizabethtown, Kentucky; and Leesville, Louisiana—my help was welcome and essential.

On the way to Louisiana, 1943; from left, Ed Binkert and
Joseph and Barbara Kirchheimer.

I remember both happy and sad times. The saddest was the
result of a phone call from Ft. Lewis, Washington, where a soldier
requested a loan and leave to visit his sick brother in the back country of Kentucky. I made my long way over the dirt roads and found
a small run-down shack. The odor was terrible. A pale youngster
lay on a bed, looking almost comatose. I asked if a doctor had
seen him to verify his illness. I was given the name of a doctor in
Elizabethtown, but when I called him he said, if the boy "ain't dead
yet he ain't gonna die." He refused permission for a leave for the
soldier. At Christmastime I saw a notice in the local paper that the
soldier had committed suicide at home. I'll never know whether
he couldn't bear to live away from his home or whether it was because his brother had died.

In Leesville I had to stop volunteering for the Red Cross and
switched to Travelers Aid in the USO. I find it hard to believe now,
but the fact was that the families I usually saw were too illiterate to
fill out Red Cross forms. They couldn't understand my accent, nor
could I understand theirs, so I was unable to fill in the paperwork.

That life ended when Joe went overseas with the 8th Armored Division in October 1944. The division landed in England, where they stayed until they went to France the first week of January 1945, and then to Holland and Germany. They crossed the Rhine in the north on March 26 and did some fierce fighting in the Ruhr and the Harz Mountains. One day I received an elegant, silk-lined box with a medal in it. I had no idea what the medal meant, but at least I saw that it was not a Purple Heart. It was a Bronze Star that Joe was awarded, I think, for apprehending spies. (He passed it off as a "buddy badge" but I was impressed.) Following V-E day (May 1945) the 8th Armored was ordered to Czechoslovakia to process prisoners of war and guard a munitions plant. They returned stateside after V-J Day (August 1945) and were deactivated in November 1945.

And where was I in 1944: I was living near family in a Chicago suburb, with baby Anne, who was born on January 3, 1945. I had no idea where Joe was on that day and he told me later it took three weeks for him to learn about the baby's birth, and then it was another three weeks until I heard from him. Six dreadful weeks in all.

The Bronze Star Medal is the fourth-highest Individual military award and the ninth-highest by order of precedence in the U.S. military. It may be awarded for acts of heroism, acts of merit or meritorious service in a combat zone. (*Wikipedia*)

Thanksgiving Day, 1943. From left. Jonathan Strong, Ann Strong, Joe Kirchhheimer, Susie Robbins, John Corrigan, Barbara Kirchheimer, Monty Robbins.

Now, after more than six decades, I have so many memories of those years that they are like stars in a dark sky. Some are bright and others dim as the years go by.

Mary Lou Touart

Born 1923 · Utica, New York

Mary Lou Touart, photo taken in 1980s in Lexington, Massachusetts.

Born in Utica, New York, Mary Lou Touart was the daughter of Louisa May Stephenson and John William Charley. Her father was the vice principal of Middletown High School where Mary Lou graduated. She then attended Hood College in Frederick, Maryland. After graduation she was given a scholarship (she was one of two women in the United States to receive this scholarship) to the Tobé-Coburn School for Fashion Careers where she studied for one year. She then worked for Simplicity Pattern Company, editing a teen fashion magazine; then with an ad agency with Anne Klein as a client. She was a fashion editor at *Woman's Day* in 1948 when she met Chankey Touart, who was doing graduate work at New York University.

College Years in World War II

By Mary Lou Touart

"That memorable night of delirious joy in New York City
in Times Square when World War II ended is a night I will
never forget."

AS I LOOK back on the four years I spent in a sedate women's
college, those years were dominated by a war in which the whole
world seemed to be involved. When I started college in the fall of
1940, the rumblings were loud and clear as Poland's serene farm-
lands were being engulfed by Nazi tanks and the initial chords of
Beethoven's Fifth Symphony were repeated over and over on Poland's radio, until the music was suddenly silenced by Nazi guns.

My roommate and I took our news seriously. She subscribed
to the *New York Times* each Sunday and I read the *New York Herald
Tribune,* so we read both political sides of the war, sides the newspapers usually agreed upon. We knew that some of the boys with
whom we'd graduated from high school had already enlisted and
those in college had joined ROTC or equivalent Navy programs,
postponing temporarily the inevitable call-up to service. That
first year seemed relatively normal. I attended a weekend college
Christmas house party and invited a beau from another university
to our spring prom. There were still dates and a smattering of normalcy that first year. But we knew things would change.

At the start of sophomore year, many of our classmates didn't
return. They'd left to be married to their men who were off to war.
These newly-marrieds were deemed unsuitable to return to school.
God forbid they should tell us what went on in the marital bed! In
early December, our college choir, of which I was a member, sang
on a trip to York, Pennsylvania. As we boarded the bus to go back

to school, we learned that the Japanese had bombed Pearl Harbor. We all were very silent on the bus back to college that night, thinking our own thoughts about what lay ahead for us. The next day, our dining room was hushed at lunch as we listened to President Roosevelt announcing the bombing of Pearl Harbor and the U.S. declaration of war against Japan. The room remained silent as a prayer was offered and we all filed silently out of the room.

The college determined that it was time for us to mobilize along with the rest of the country. We were assigned work in the college laundry. Rationing began. Meat and sugar rationing changed the menu in the dining room. We took home ration cards so our mothers could buy a festive roast while we were home, or bake a cake and cookies with our sugar coupons. Much later, we rolled bandages and the talented among us knit caps for servicemen in cold climates. We rode the train home from Baltimore to New York, sitting on upended suitcases surrounded by sailors from the nearby Maryland Naval Station. The men were eager to talk, flirt and carry on with us. Rarely did we get a seat on that train!

We began to wear the insignia of Army, Navy, Air Corps and Marine unit pins on our clothes. One classmate wore several on her pajamas to signify her devotion to her many beaux. Only occasionally did we have dances with servicemen from nearby colleges and other units on limited assignment nearby. We wrote to servicemen endlessly. V-Mails to men we knew, and those who needed to hear from stateside friends, both old and new. The news of friends and "boyfriends" killed and wounded started to come in. There was the Marine officer, a VMI graduate, killed the third day on Iwo Jima. He had lived up the street from me and used to walk his Irish setter past our house every day. A skinny uncool high school classmate was killed early in a friendly fire accident. The handsome football player who did not survive the Battle of the Bulge was another. My roommate's beau, a flyer shot down over the Ploesti oil fields, survived three years in a Nazi prison camp. News kept overwhelming us. We could do nothing but write notes of sympathy and cry into our pillows at night.

And we studied and worked jobs in the summertime, sometimes jobs that had been held by men. I was lucky and was hired back by my local newspaper after my high-school stint with it. I took the place of a reporter going to war. It was lonely and sad those summers, only soothed by family and high-school girl friends. The Christmas of my senior year, a friend from home gave a New Year's Eve hen party for all her single and married friends. There must have been 15 or so of us. We shared news of all the servicemen we knew and their whereabouts. What else was there to do?

So, finally, finally, I graduated from college and headed to New York City, as I'd been awarded a fellowship to a fashion school there. It had been my ambition and my dream. There opened up a whole new world of excitement, study, and yes, culture. I made new friends, gulped down city sights and waited for the war to end.

It finally became reality but not before that last piece of devastating news. A former beau, a navy pilot, was shot down over the Pacific that summer of 1945 just before the Japanese surrendered. I know I cried and cried and thought about the aborted promise of this bright and charming man. It was the tragic cap to my war experience.

Of course, Japan finally did surrender but only after our ugly Hiroshima bombing. A friend from Minnesota and I were having dinner with two sailor friends of hers, just off the carrier *Enterprise*. We could scarcely eat our dinner that night at the Jumble Shop in the Village, for we knew rumors were flying about a surrender. We headed for Times Square in a frenzy of anticipation. And there it was! JAPAN SURRENDERS! THE WAR IS OVER! And on and on the news went, around and around, on the lighted billboard that circled the top floor of the *New York Times* Building. There was a roaring delight as New Yorkers came running into the square, crowding tightly together and not caring a bit. The scene has been captured for all time in the photo of a sailor bending a nurse backwards over his arms in a long victory kiss.

There were hugs, kisses, screams, shouts, tears and crazy hilarity among perfect strangers. This was helped along by a drunken ecstasy and the generous sharing of whatever alcohol any person had brought along.

That memorable night of delirious joy in New York City in Times Square when World War II ended is a night I will never forget.

Part Six

★ ★ ★
★ ★ ★

The Children's War

MOST CHILDREN IN the United States were not exposed to the fear and dislocation so many European children suffered. But World War II was real for any child old enough to sense the anxiety and worry of their elders. Children wanted to help and found many ways to do so. Early in the war, the Germans were a real threat and officials and citizens worried about invasion. Japanese-Americans on the West Coast were interned. War—and the need to help in whatever way anyone could—was the prevailing attitude.

The following stories describe just a few of the ways children found to help—there were many others. They certainly convey the sense of the concerns and cooperaton of children.

Mary L. Bundy

Born 1925 · Boston, Massachusetts

Summer 1942. Mary Lothrop (Bundy) feeds the chickens next to her grandmother's Victory Garden. The chicken coop hides the view of their beautiful pig with long auburn eyelashes named Rita in honor of the gorgeous actress Rita Hayworth.

I was born in 1925, Mary Lothrop, and raised in Boston, Massachusetts. When the war began in Europe, I was a sophomore in high school, and when it ended, I was a junior at Radcliffe. After college, I worked as a teacher, a college admissions officer and a faculty wife when my husband taught at Harvard. I was a full-time mother of four boys and later a clinical social worker. Like many professors in Cambridge and their families, we moved to Washington, D.C., in 1961, where we spent five intense years of government service. After Washington, we moved to New York, where my husband was with the Ford Foundation; then we moved to Brookhaven.

A Teenager Follows the War from the Home Front

By Mary L. Bundy

> "President Roosevelt's speeches to the American people made a powerful impression of determination, fortitude and wisdom on this teenager. Listening to his broadcasts after the fall of France and following Pearl Harbor gave a sense of confidence and hope in adverse circumstances. The president was definitely a source of information and inspiration for the American public."

PREPARATIONS FOR WAR were evident in the summer of 1939 when my family visited relatives in France, England and Scotland. Bomb shelters were being dug in Paris. Blackout rehearsals in Oxford were accompanied by the songs of drunken undergraduates joyriding in the dark. In Scotland, our cousins advised us that return reservations for early September should be changed to a mid-August date. We were happy to reach home and to have avoided a voyage threatened by German U-boats.

Keeping track of wartime news was a problem at boarding school. Radios were forbidden to students. Few 14-year-olds read a daily paper at that time—at least, not this one. But periodically throughout the year, Helen Hill Miller, an American who served as the Washington columnist for *The Economist*, would come to a school assembly to report on heroic efforts by British aviators, matched by the courage of English civilians learning how to survive German bombing. The success of the German invasions and the submission of Europe was depressing news. By mid-June our handsome French cousin Xavier—the aviator who gave his American cousins the most wonderful chocolates—had been shot down

Americans were strongly urged to plant "Victory Gardens." The government wanted people adequately fed and to grow their own food as much as possible. (*U.S. Government Printing Office*)

and killed in the defense of France. The Scottish cousins were in the army, or deeply engaged as civilian leaders.

President Roosevelt's speeches to the American people made a powerful impression of determination, fortitude and wisdom on this teenager. Listening to his broadcasts after the fall of France and following Pearl Harbor gave a sense of confidence and hope in adverse circumstances. The President was definitely a source of information and inspiration for the American public. Paul Fussell's book *Wartime: Understanding and Behavior in the Second World War* raises interesting questions as to how much information was actually released to the American public, and whether the media focused too much on journalism through rose-colored glasses, failing to give an accurate account of the vicissitudes of war.

By the end of December 1941 my father was gone, without the opportunity to say goodbye to his children away at school. He enlisted—at the age of 43 he was still subject to the draft—and spent the war in North Africa and in Foggia, Italy. He served as the intelligence officer with a squadron of young fighter pilots who defended the huge planes that bombed the oil fields of Ploesti. It was his sad duty to gather up the belongings of the young men who were shot down and to write letters of condolence to their parents and wives. We did not see him again until May of 1945.

Shortly after Pearl Harbor, a strict rationing system began. Shoes, meat, butter, sugar, certain canned goods and, above all, gasoline could only be purchased with points from a ration card. Everyone saved gas points for special occasions and traveled by Boston's fine system of public transportation. My least favorite task was mashing a huge five-pound piece of white and oleaginous margarine with an envelope of orange, Tang-like powder to produce a truly revolting spread. Cans of Spam, requiring points, were everywhere. Most brands of cigarettes were reserved for the armed forces, and civilians formed lines to purchase the unpopular brands that were left.

News of casualties became more common as the war continued. Close friends of my parents lost an only son at sea, and a Radcliffe classmate mourned the death of her youngest uncle, who used to take her dancing. Because my contemporaries were only 16 or 17 when the war began, many were in training in the early years. Only later did I have the personal losses of two dear friends, one shot down over the Pacific and the other obliterated by a Japanese shell that sank his destroyer. It came as a terrible shock to know that I would never see them again.

Letters meant so much during the war. From overseas, they generally arrived by V-Mail, which was a piece of airmail paper that could be written on and then folded to form an envelope. Sometimes these letters were reproduced in an early form of mimeograph, or were censored, with whole sentences blocked. All envelopes were marked with the rank and name of the sender, his or her unit and an APO (Army Post Office) number.

My contemporaries' letters contained many accounts that couldn't be descriptive because of the hazardous conditions the writer was experiencing, like the Battle of the Bulge or the huge naval battles in the Pacific. Sometimes the writer was in training for, or worse, permanently assigned to routine tasks in some deserted corner of the United States. Most letters spoke of how much fun the last leave had been and when the next break might be expected. At the end of the war in Europe, one letter described the thrill of being welcomed with blossoming cherry branches, hugs and kisses by residents of a village in northern Italy.

On the home front, there were plenty of volunteer jobs. My grandmother sponsored a Victory Garden, over half an acre of every sort of vegetable and berry, with volunteers supervised by a retired professional gardener, who was also responsible for a flock of chickens, a few ducks and a resplendent pig, named Rita Hayworth for her luxurious auburn eyelashes. Any former Victory gardener can recall the satisfaction of a job well done. One memorable day, my sister Jane and I pulled, washed, cooked, peeled and canned 40 quarts of beets on a coal stove. We were purple to the shoulders, but triumphant.

Attending college and volunteering at the Massachusetts General Hospital did not get in the way of other lighthearted duties like being a hostess at the USO or the officers' club. There were plenty of parties where we danced to the sentimental strains of "I Don't Want to Set the World on Fire" or the more upbeat tones of "Boogie Woogie Bugle Boy."

The most heartwarming of duties was to join Red Cross volunteers in welcoming the troops back from Europe to the port of Boston. The troopship came in slowly, canted toward the dock with a boatload of solders lining the port side, all cheering, shouting and roaring their joy at being home. As each soldier made his way to the waiting train, the volunteers would hand him a carton of milk (unobtainable in wartime Europe) and two doughnuts. They were a motley crew in incomplete, disheveled uniforms, some weighed down with an exotic wartime souvenir like a German helmet or antique sword, or even a stray puppy on a rope leash.

It was a thrill to be part of that homecoming.

Phyllis Hinsey

Born 1934 · Caldwell, New Jersey

Phyllis Hinsey, fall 2013, taken at her home.

Phyllis LaRue Hinsey was born in 1934 in Caldwell, New Jersey. She graduated from the College of Industrial and Labor Relations, Cornell University, and worked for Realty Hotels, Inc., New York, New York. She was then a stay-at-home mom in Scarsdale, New York, caring for three daughters. Active in the community, she served six years on the Board of Education (Edgemont) including a term as president, and also served as vice president of Scarsdale/Edgemont United Way. She spent six years as a docent at the Neuberger Museum on the campus of SUNY Purchase, New York, and twenty-four years as a gallery instructor at the Boston Museum of Fine Arts. She is also active in the P.E.O., a national philanthropic and educational organization.

We Were All in This Together

By Phyllis Hinsey

"I… well remember December 7, 1941 [when the Japanese bombed Pearl Harbor]. I was called in from playing, and we all gathered around the radio. No one spoke—you could have heard a pin drop. I had no idea what a war would mean for our family, or for our country, but it soon became very clear to me that we were all 'to do our part.'"

I WAS IN elementary school when the Japanese bombed Pearl Harbor and well remember December 7, 1941. I was called in from playing, and we all gathered around the radio. No one spoke—you could have heard a pin drop. I had no idea what a war would mean for our family, or for our country, but it soon became very clear to me that we were all "to do our part."

My mother took a course in first aid "to be prepared." She also became a "plane spotter." When there was an air raid, she would put on a one-piece jumpsuit, go to a nearby hilltop and look for planes. I have no idea what she was supposed to do if she spotted one! She also planted a Victory Garden, and we all had tasks related to its success.

My father had a travel agency, but there would be no travel now. He was able to get a job in the personnel department of a munitions plant.

I had many responsibilities. I was in charge of stacking and saving newspapers. I would take them to my Girl Scout meetings, where we made thousands of disposal bags to be used by our veterans (I was told). I can still make a bag from a piece of paper in a matter of seconds! Our scout troop also knitted squares, later to be made into afghans for our servicemen. I remember we were to put 30 stitches onto a large needle, and the squares were to be 6 inches square. I felt good each time I completed one.

At home, I was also in charge of flattening our tin cans, after removing the tops and bottoms (needless to say, there were no electric can openers). It was also expected that I would save what I could from my small allowance and, at lunchtime at school on Wednesdays, purchase 10-cent stamps. These would then be pasted in a book, and when I reached $18.75 (I have no idea where the extra nickel came from), I could purchase a war bond. This would support the war effort, and ten years later would be worth $25.00!

In music class at school, we learned and sang every verse to every anthem from the various military forces. My favorite line was singing, "Yea, nothing will stop the Army Air Corps!"

I would also grocery shop nearby with ration book in hand. One time we saved up our meat coupons for my father's birthday celebration. However, all I remember from that festive occasion was walking into the dining room and seeing the cat on the table licking the steak! Fortunately, I have no recollection as to what ensued following this infraction by our beloved pet.

My sister Claire, who was ten years older, had a boyfriend in the Navy. Gordon would send me postcards from his ship in the Pacific and I would take them to school for "show and tell." While showing a picture of his ship and reading the message, I felt

FOOD IS A WEAPON

DON'T WASTE IT !
BUY WISELY - COOK CAREFULLY - EAT IT ALL

FOLLOW THE NATIONAL WARTIME NUTRITION PROGRAM

Part of America's war effort was being sure enough food was available and that it was being used wisely. (*U.S. Government Printing Office*)

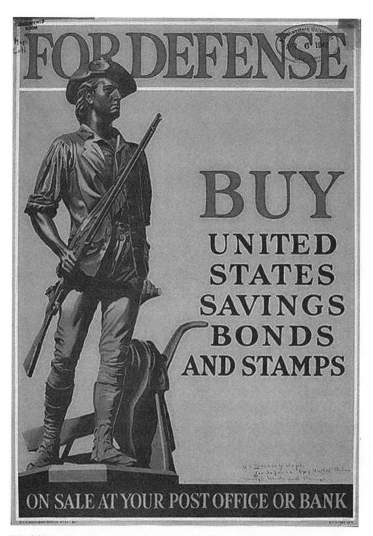

World War II poster urging Americans to buy savings bonds. (*U.S. Government Printing Office*)

very important! Gordon was a good artist and was the cartoonist for his ship's newspaper. He would send us these cartoons—he found humor in some amazing situations. Claire and Gordon were married for 65 years.

My strongest memory is that we were all in this together. We were one with each other, and one with our community, and we lived for the day when there would be NO more war.

Jean Hall

Born 1927 · Somerville, New Jersey

Jean Hall, September 2012, Cote d'Azur, France taken during a tour of Southern France

Jean Hall grew up and went to school in Somerville, New Jersey. After college and a year of teaching in Scotch Plains, New Jersey, she moved on to graduate school at the University of Pennsylvania in Philadelphia, where she received her MA. She was awarded a scholarship and fellowship at the University of Minnesota, where she majored in political science and government and also taught an undergraduate course. She then moved to Washington, D.C., where she worked for nine years at a job with the federal government and where she met her husband. She and her husband Henry moved to Belmont, Massachusetts, where they raised two sons. Active in local affairs, Jean was also a substitute teacher and then worked with special needs pupils in the middle school reading and math programs. After retiring she volunteered at the Boston Museum of Science.

Never Buy Rationed Goods Without Ration Stamps

By Jean Hall

"Cooperate with your local Salvage Committee."

I GREW UP in Somerville, New Jersey, and attended the Somerville public schools through high school. During World War II, in 1943, families were issued a book of coupons to be used to purchase meat, butter and sugar. Gasoline coupons were also issued. These were especially important for people who needed their automobiles for transportation to and from work. My father was an engineer with a defense-related industry that required him to have transportation.

This poster illustrates government efforts to prevent black market participation. (*U.S. Government Printing Office*)

Our book of coupons included a warning:

"NEVER BUY RATIONED GOODS
WITHOUT RATION STAMPS"

and

"NEVER PAY MORE THAN THE LEGAL PRICE."

The book also had a statement:

"IMPORTANT: When you have used your ration, salvage
the TIN CANS and WASTE FATS. They are needed to make
munitions for our fighting men. Cooperate with your local
Salvage Committee."

(See illustration on facing page.)

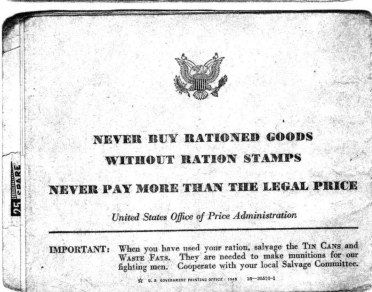

World War II ration book. During the war—on the home front—a number of items were rationed, including meat, butter and sugar and also gasoline, tires and fuel oil. Coupons were issued to civilians to limit the amounts of rationed items they could purchase.

Henry Hall

Born 1931 · Sandwich, Massachusetts

Henry Hall, September 2012, Cote d'Azur, France, from a tour of southern France.

Henry Hall grew up on Cape Cod, Massachusetts, where he graduated from high school in 1949. He was the son of Henry and Edith Hall. He graduated from the University of Massachusetts, Amherst and went into the Army. He spent three years in the Army, studying Russian for a year at the U.S. Army Language School in Monterey. California. After he was discharged from the Army he graduated from the George Washington University School of Law, Washington, D.C., where he met his wife Jean. They then moved to Belmont, Massachusetts, when he joined a major Boston law firm, Ropes & Gray. He and Jean raised two sons. Henry was active in Belmont town politics for many years both as a Belmont town member and serving as town moderator for 17 years. He also spent 12 years as the Belmont representative on the School Committee of the Minuteman Regional Vocational Technical School District.

Air Raid Warden and Plane Spotter

By Henry Hall

> "My wartime contributions…spot unlawful lights and …keep watch for suspicious airplanes."

DURING WORLD WAR II, I lived in East Sandwich on Cape Cod, Massachusetts, a short distance from Cape Cod Bay. My father was an air raid warden. One of his tasks was to drive around the neighborhood, on call, making sure that no lights were visible through any window. From time to time, when my father was called out, I accompanied him as a spotter of unlawful lights.

Another of my wartime jobs was to assist my mother as an aircraft spotter when I wasn't in school. She and I were required to take a course conducted by the military personnel stationed at nearby Camp Edwards or at the East Sandwich Coast Artillery base. We learned how to recognize German aircraft. After we passed a test, my mother was assigned from time to time to a high spot overlooking the bay, with a small shack and a telephone. The spotters were to report any suspicious aircraft or any planes they did not recognize.

My wartime contributions were helping my father spot unlawful lights and helping my mother to keep watch for suspicious planes.

World War II civilian defense poster.
(*U.S. Government Printing Office*)

Nancy Hubert

Born 1935 · Syracuse, Kansas

Nancy Lansdon Hubert, 1944, during World War II, age 9.

Nancy Hubert was born in western Kansas, Syracuse, in 1935. She was a Dust Bowl baby. She lived in various places during World War II while her father was in the Marine Corps. She graduated from Garden City, Kansas, high school in 1953. She and her husband were high-school sweethearts. They married while he was still in college, and they lived in Lawrence, Kansas, where they attended the University of Kansas. With a new job for her husband in Massachusetts, they moved to Winchester in that state in 1961 with their four children; a fifth child was born in Massachusetts. After a year in Massachusetts, they moved to Kwajalein in the South Pacific, where they would live for two years (her huband worked for MIT Lincoln Laboratory). They returned to Lexington, Massachusetts where their children attended the Lexington schools. Nancy had not finished college earlier, so when the children were in school she returned to school, receiving a BS from Simmons College, Boston. After graduation she then worked in the publishing field for 20 years.

Preparing for War in Kansas

By Nancy Hubert

"We learned to identify airplanes with cards printed with silhouettes of enemy planes, and I did wonder how an enemy plane would make it to Kansas. I had scary nightmares about the Germans invading our community and home (I planned to hide in the barn)."

MY FIRST MEMORY of the threat of Hitler and Germany was when Hitler invaded Poland. It was September 1, which was my fourth birthday. What I remember is the solemnity of my parents and grandparents as they discussed what had happened. I certainly didn't understand why it was important, but it was clearly momentous to them.

My next memory is the Sunday Pearl Harbor was bombed. I was in the first grade. My father went out to his car to listen on the car radio. There were three little children and a new baby in the house and we did not understand "quiet." We had no changes in our daily life immediately after Pearl Harbor, but I was aware my father wanted to volunteer. With four children it was not likely he would be drafted, but he was eager to serve.

My father finally got my mother to agree he should enlist and my mother moved us to Arkansas, where my grandparents had retired not long before. I was very fond of my grandparents and the move was welcome to me. My father joined the Navy and we happily waved goodbye when he left for basic training. We lived on a farm and did not have a telephone. When my father called us, a local restaurant would send a messenger to our house to tell us my father planned to call at a certain time. Since it was usually around mealtime, I liked his calls because we also got to eat in a restaurant. On his way to training camp, two Marines came onto the bus and announced they needed two Marines; they "volunteered" my father and one other. My father loved the Marines. Having grown up in Oklahoma and owning a rifle since he was seven, he was an excellent marksman. He sailed right through basic training and then was sent to Camp Pendleton in California for additional training and where he became the champion marksman of the base. It was an easy accomplishment for a man who had been shooting squirrels, rabbits and birds since he was seven or eight.

As a result of his marksmanship my dad became an MP (military policeman) and was sent to Honolulu. There he worked with the shore patrol and as a bodyguard to a Marine Officer. Their mission was to fly or go by boat onto islands in the Pacific where they either buried or dug up packages presumably for the armed forces. My father never knew what was in them.

As a child, the war for me was just a part of growing up. I was impressionable and since I was very young when the war started, I took it for granted this was just a normal part of life. My family often told me there was another kind of life, no gasoline or tire rationing, no ration cards—no Gold Star mothers. No shortages of the many things we took for granted. One lasting memory is of listening to the evening news. Every evening when Edward R. Murrow broadcast we had to be totally quiet—we were sent from the room if we spoke. After the news, my family would talk about the war and how it was going.

In school we talked about what we could do to help the war effort. We bought savings stamps every week and when you filled a book with stamps, you received a war bond. My husband learned to knit during the war, making knitted squares which were joined to make blankets. We also had scrap metal drives and were encouraged to bring any scrap metals we could find. Again, in my husband's school, there was a prize for the student bringing in the most scrap metal—50 years later he was still irritated that one boy's father donated an old car, winning the prize for his son. We saved foil, even peeling the foil from the wrappers on chewing gum.

We learned to identify airplanes with cards printed with silhouettes of enemy planes, and I did wonder how an enemy plane would make it to Kansas. I had scary nightmares about the Germans invading our community and home (I planned to hide in the barn). My grandfather would comfort me, pointing out we would have plenty of warning, and time to escape, if the Germans got as far as Arkansas.

V-E day came in May 1945, less than a month after the death of Franklin D. Roosevelt. There was still the war with Japan. I remember V-J day more clearly. We were in the car in town when all the church bells began ringing and sirens sounding. I was confused and my grandfather told me it could only mean the war was over. My father returned home in the fall. I was in the fifth grade. What I remember best about my father's homecoming was a huge Halloween party he, my mother and my grandparents organized. Each of us got to invite all the guests we wanted to. It was the first and best Halloween party I ever attended. The weather was fair and we were outside. We wore costumes, bobbed for apples and played all kinds of games. After Christmas we moved back to Kansas. Putting our lives back together and adjusting to peace was probably a lot more difficult for my parents than I realized, and it was strange to have my father home permanently. But my sister, brother and I were young and I'm sure we adjusted more quickly than they did.

Barbara Rediker

Born 1938 · New York City, New York

Barbara Zenn, in her Sunday best, in front of her home, Woodmere, Long Island, New York, 1944.

Barbara Zenn Rediker worked as a social worker and a grassroots volunteer in community organizations, continuing a family legacy of volunteering that began with her great-grandfather, who enlisted as a captain in the New York State Guard during the Civil War. She was born in New York City, June 26, 1938, to Max and Ethel Bauman Zenn. She and her family moved to Cedarhurst, New York, where she graduated from Public Elementary School No. 5 and Lawrence High School. She received an AB from Smith College and an MSW from the School of Social Work, Boston University. She also attended the Harvard Extension School/ Harvard School of Public Health for a certificate in public health. Her three, very satisfying, careers in social work included pediatrics and a four-year faculty appointment to Simmons College School of Social Work, for a student unit; geriatrics; and housing. She married Robert H. Rediker in 1980 and they have two sons, four granddaughters, one grandson, one great-granddaughter and two great-grandsons.

A Little Girl Gives Away Her Toy Teapot

By Barbara Rediker

"'We are collecting tin pots and pans to make into ammunition for the war.' ...I went to get my tin doll dishes, including the teapot, to give away. Later...we saw the pile of metal things that had been collected....(I)t was up to my waist at the edges, much higher in the middle. I couldn't see my teapot."

I MUST HAVE been between three and seven years old. I lived in a house on Long Island, New York, with my mother, father, grandmother and ill grandfather, who had big blue eyes and a German accent. My father loved the corn we grew in our Victory Garden, and my mother canned the delicious tomatoes we grew for the winter. I helped plant seeds and watered with my watering can. My grandmother was a good cook. Sometimes she had to put yellow coloring in the margarine because we didn't have real butter. No one really liked it, but it was better than white butter. My mother made chocolate pudding and we all liked that. My parents rode bicycles because we had to save gas for the soldiers. I sat in my father's front wicker basket.

Sometimes at night sirens rang for an air raid and we all had to go to the cellar with our flashlights until we heard the all clear. We had cans of food and dried food and some old chairs and a table there in case we got stuck in the cellar.

My father volunteered to work on Sunday nights to receive wounded soldiers at Mitchell Air Force Base, New York. He worked all night and went Monday morning, without sleep, to work in New York City. He went every Monday night in his uniform with friends to practice being a soldier for the New York State Guard just in

Barbara Rediker: My father, Max Zenn, in his New York State Guard uniform. Between 1942 and 1944.

case we had a war here. In the summertime my father had to go to camp for military training in the woods and fields. He crawled through poison ivy and got a terrible case of it. He was sent home with a fever and fainted in the bathroom. On his legs and arms were the largest blisters I ever saw. I wasn't allowed to visit him in his room, but could stand at the doorway for a short time. I brought him red and yellow zinnias in the teapot that belonged to my tin tea set.

My mother volunteered at the Hebrew Immigrant Aid Society to help Jewish people who had escaped from Hitler come to this country. She also volunteered for the Red Cross and the USO. She gave cookies and cake to wounded soldiers who came back from the war and danced with them. My mother loved to dance.

My father's grammar school friend, "Uncle Irwin," was on an island, New Guinea, in the South Pacific. He sent us a coconut at holiday time and sometimes postcards, which made my father very happy. My father wrote letters to him whenever he had the time. New Guinea was very far away on our map of the world. We invited "Aunt Jeannie," Uncle Irwin's wife, to come visit us on lots of Sundays. She took the train from New York City and brought me the best things—candy, books and toys, and a playsuit like my mother's.

One day, Mr. B., with a German accent, came to our front door. He said, "We are collecting tin pots and pans to make into ammunition for the war." While my father was talking to him, I went to get my tin doll dishes, including the teapot, to give away. Later, at the Cedarhurst, Long Island, railroad stations, we saw the pile of metal things that had been collected. It was surrounded by a very high chicken-wire fence, and it was up to my waist at the edges, much higher in the middle. I couldn't see my teapot.

Our neighbors, who had a television set, came to tell us the war was over. All the neighbors were laughing and crying and yelling. We piled into the car and went to town. It was like a circus parade. Cars were going up and down the main street honking and dragging tin cans on ropes. People, on the streets and from their windows, were throwing paper streamers and confetti. Then we went to have our favorite food, ice cream.

That fall my parents bought a television set and I became a big sister!

Janice Rittenburg Rossbach

Born 1929 · Boston, Massachusetts

High school graduation of Janice Rittenburg (Rossbach) taken spring 1946 at Jeremiah E. Burke High School for Girls in Roxbury, Boston, Massachusetts.

Janice Rittenburg was born May 29, 1929, in Boston and grew up in the Roxbury and Mattapan sections of Boston. She graduated from the Jeremiah E. Burke High School for Girls in 1946 and the University of Massachusetts, Amherst, in 1949 with a BS in mathematics, summa cum laude; and an SM in mathematics from Massachusetts Institute of Technology in 1951. She attended Brown University Graduate Division of Applied Mathematics 1954–1957. She married Leopold Jerome Rossbach in 1951. Janice worked as a mathematician and military systems engineer at Arthur D. Little, Melpar and GTE. She and her husband lived in Westwood and Weston, Massachusetts. She moved to Brookhaven in 2003 after her husband's death.

Jewish in America and Locating Survivors

By Janice Rittenburg Rossbach

"Germany surrendered. After that there was a very sad time for my family. My mother and my Rittenburg grandma left early every morning for the crowded office of HIAS, the Hebrew Immigrant Aid Society, to look in their lists for any survivors of my grandma's family. Then a bittersweet day: my grandma found a nephew and a young grandniece who had survived in the woods of Lithuania....The rest were presumed dead, except we heard that the girl's mother was killed by a German soldier when she resisted his advances. Probably true."

FOR ME THE WAR started in 1933 right after the Reichstag burned down on February 27, 1933, while Hitler was in power. My mother was crying and I asked my father why. He explained the situation, how Hitler had been elected but now had taken over as a dictator and how serious that was for Jews in Europe because he was so anti-Semitic. So that was why my mother was crying. My father said it might get better but he couldn't tell me who could stop them with Hitler in charge as a dictator. So I decided it could only get worse but said nothing, not wanting to upset everybody more. I turned four in May.

Friday nights we went to the movies and always saw Pathé News. I remember the Anschluss early in 1938, when Hitler annexed Austria, and Kristallnacht in November of 1938. It was getting worse and I was very worried. I also have memories of newsreels of the massive rallies with Hitler Youth in their uniforms, so enraptured and fanatic, giving the Seig Heil salute; and hearing "Deutschland Uber Alles" which I understood because it's the same in Yiddish. I realized I was seeing mass craziness and saw what propaganda could do. I decided that Hitler would be glad to come to America or send someone to kill me, but I said nothing. I thought he had to be beaten. At some point my father was invited to join the German American Bund, the American Nazis, because of our German name. My father said he thought they might kill him if he showed up, which he didn't plan to do. I wasn't happy to know we had Nazis here. The boys who came every now and again from South Boston to break neighborhood shop windows were bad enough.

My father got a job testing aircraft superchargers at GE in Lynn but then got a job at Polaroid more suited to his mechanical engineering degree, where he worked until the war ended. I was very interested in and proud of the work he did in developing plastic lenses and in 3-D photos that had to be viewed with Polaroid glasses. I visited their building in Cambridge and then on Route 128. Very exciting for a kid who wanted to be an engineer. We went to the annual skating party at the Boston Skating Club and I met Edwin Land. Happy memories!

In the meantime when my father and I visited my Rittenburg grandparents every Sunday morning, my grandma would sometimes be crying and they would be talking to each other in a language I did not understand. But my father told me my grandma was crying (out of character for her) because she couldn't convince her three brothers and a sister in Lithuania to come to America as she and her other two sisters had done. Each one in Lithuania had a reason: business, sick in-laws, etc. I just remember being worried about all those relatives "over there," far away. I remember that we listened to Hitler's speeches on the radio. His ranting gave me chills. I was particularly upset on Yom Kippur in 1938, I think, when my grandparents were listening to his speech. We never could listen to the radio on Saturday or the high holidays so I didn't like that they were listening to Hitler, of all people. I was so shocked, I told my mother.

During those years, we talked a lot about the isolationists, primarily in the Midwest, and how we didn't think we could avoid getting more involved because Hitler had a world plan. President Roosevelt, we knew, supported the Allies and we supported him. It had been a thrill when they took us out of my grade school, the William Lloyd Garrison School in Roxbury, in the fall of 1936 to see President Roosevelt drive down Seaver Street in an open car on his way to a rally in, as I remember, Mattapan Square.

Then in 1941, Germany invaded Russia. For me, it was a positive development because I didn't like the dictator, Stalin. My grandpa Bloom was delighted, even gleeful in a somewhat dia-bolical way. He told me about Napoleon in Russia and that the Germans had forgotten how the Russians handled that (scorched earth). So we followed that battle as my grandpa came frequent-ly after having a schnapps at the synagogue, telling me how it was going to get cold in Russia soon. "Now it's really cold; the Germans think they are winning but their supply lines are only getting longer....The Russians will give up territory and people because they have lots more, etc....Germany is experiencing what Napoleon experienced." He used to rub his hands together and dance up and down; so little and old and cute. We had our own news analyst/expert. He had deserted from the czar's army in the Caucasus Mountains and walked home to Odessa, so he took a very personal interest in Hitler's Russian campaign and didn't like either side. I never considered Russia an ally either. I used to fan-tasize that Hitler would beat Stalin but would be so weakened in the process that the Allies would defeat him more easily and the world would be rid of both of them.

Then Pearl Harbor and we were in the war, not just support-ing England and the other Allies with Lend-Lease, etc. My cous-in Sumner joined the Seabees; neighborhood boys enlisted and relatives of relatives showed up in uniforms. A few never came back; I remember one in particular. My mother and I went to my cousin's high school graduation as moral support for my aunt and his younger brother, as Sumner was in the service somewhere. My uncle, Captain Isadore Edward Rittenburg, was in the Coast and Geodetic Service stationed in Washington. For the duration of the war, military convoys very often rumbled down Blue Hill Avenue in Mattapan (Boston) where we lived. Trucks and jeeps full of young soldiers were going from Camp Edwards on Cape Cod to Boston and then overseas. I always waved to them; my mother initially objected to this until I reminded her that some of them would not be coming back. Such a waste, I thought. My aunts and I knitted sweaters and socks for the troops through the Red Cross. I was the go-between because I was in that neighborhood every week when my mother and I went for our allergy shots.

Even before Pearl Harbor we dealt with rationing. After school my classmates and I could be found with family ration books in the neighborhood market to buy butter and other rationed items or walking along the avenue to see if any fruit market had bananas. My grandpa Rittenburg drove around a lot for his business, limited by gas rationing, and whenever he saw a line outside of a market he would park and stand in line for whatever he could buy for his family. He had one of his brothers and five (out of eight) children and their families living in Boston so there was always some place to drop off whatever he got. My great-uncle used to load up his car with my aunts and me and take us to the kosher slaughter house to buy chickens for Friday night and the rest of the week. My mother couldn't take it. I didn't mind but I was glad she could clean them, as I couldn't do that.

A younger girl appeared at my high school, the Jeremiah E. Burke High School for Girls in Roxbury (Boston), in 1945, a refugee from Finland, which had been invaded by Russia in 1939. I thought she looked so typically Finnish, so blond and blue-eyed. I didn't know her well, as she was very quiet and didn't speak English very well yet. Many years later we were both MIT alums; at a meeting, we caught up with each other and I found out she was Jewish too. Don't jump to conclusions!

We had a big school assembly a month before my 16th birthday in 1945 to tell us that President Roosevelt had died. Many tears; he was the only president we knew. Then four days before my 16th birthday, Germany surrendered. After that there was a very sad time for my family. My mother and my Rittenburg grandma left early every morning for the crowded office of HIAS, the Hebrew Immigrant Aid Society, to look in their lists for any survivors of my grandma's family. So many days my mother came home so discouraged and exhausted with no results. Then a bittersweet day: my grandma found a nephew and a young grandniece who had survived in the woods of Lithuania and gotten themselves smuggled into Berlin (the girl is still there). After contacting him through HIAS, my grandma found that there was another nephew and his new wife in Berlin with him. The rest were presumed dead, except we heard that the girl's mother was killed by a German soldier when she resisted his advances. Probably true. My grandpa started the process to bring here the couple who wanted to come to the United States and they did. The other nephew corresponded with my grandpa, sending him money and deceiving the censors until he had enough for my grandpa to send it to a New York rabbi who sent Jewish religious items—bibles, tallesim, etc.—to him in Berlin, as they understandably had very few there. This went on until he was arrested in Berlin for being a black marketer. I was sorry he got caught. That was how new family branches in Germany, Israel and the United States began.

The next year just before my senior year in high school, the United States dropped the atomic bombs; V-J day came and the war was over. I couldn't come to grips with the killing of civilians then and even before with the bombing of Germany by the Allies, but I felt that the whole world situation was crazy and in some way beyond right and wrong. But off we went to Boston's Chinatown to celebrate with thousands of others the relief of the end of a nightmare. The dragon was snaking its way all along the streets—no cars; the restaurants and clubs sent musicians to play atop the cars in their parking lots. Very soon my father lost his job because the war was over, and I was seriously worried about how I was going to go to college to study mathematics and be able to take care of myself. My cousin came back from the Seabees but wasn't quite right. Decades later I found out that my uncle, stationed in Washington, had gone on "business trips" that really were to the South Pacific to plan where our forces should land to take over the islands held by the Japanese. His son only found out when Navy and Marine representatives came to his funeral in Arlington Memorial Cemetery.

Janet Linn

Born 1930 · Bellefonte, Pennsylvania

Janet Linn in her Girl Scout uniform, February 1943, State College, Pennsylvania.

Janet Denithorne Linn was born in Bellefonte, Pennsylvania, to George and Janet Scott Denithorne and grew up in central Pennsylvania. She graduated from Oldfields School near Baltimore, Maryland, and from Smith College in 1952 with a degree in art history. She worked at the Dayton, Ohio, Art Institute and then married Andrew Linn in 1954. They have three children. Over the years they lived in New Haven and Middlefield, Connecticut, then Wilmington, Delaware, and back to Farmington, Connecticut, where she worked as a library assistant at the school where her husband was teaching. She and her husband retired first to Peterborough, New Hampshire, and then to Brookhaven. Over the years she participated as a volunteer in civil rights, nuclear freeze and antiwar movements.

A Girl's War

By Janet Linn

"My 'war effort' was with the Girl Scouts. Our troop plunged wholeheartedly into any chance to show our patriotism. We marched in parades and wore our uniforms to church and on all public occasions. We worked for badges in Morse code, first aid and home nursing as well as the usual cooking, sewing and baby care."

I WAS ELEVEN when Pearl Harbor was attacked. We were living in the small town of State College, Pennsylvania, where Penn State, then a small college, is located. My father, a veteran of the First World War, volunteered again and was gone from home by the next April.

There was a great deal of hysteria in the first months of the war. There were some German nationals on the faculty and staff of Penn State, some of whom had lived in this country for a long time, and the FBI came around asking questions of their neighbors and townspeople. Throughout the war, the possibility of sabotage and spying hung over research projects at the college, and we children were sure that Mr. Miller, the recluse across the street who never let us come onto his lawn to retrieve lost balls, was a spy (Miller = Mueller?). Because our valley was not too far from the Pennsylvania Railroad line from New York to Chicago—the main transportation artery from the Midwest to the East Coast— State College quickly developed an air-raid warning system under the aegis of the National Guard. It was thought likely that the Germans would bomb the railroad's Horseshoe Curve near Altoona and disable the entire war effort. My uncle became an air raid warden and plane spotter, and we had blackout curtains throughout the house.

My "war effort" was with the Girl Scouts. Our troop plunged wholeheartedly into any chance to show our patriotism. We marched in parades and wore our uniforms to church and on all public occasions. We worked for badges in Morse code, first aid and home nursing as well as the usual cooking, sewing and baby care. I learned about hospital corners for sheets, how to apply tourniquets and splints, and spotting planes. When we went to camp, we learned "survivor" skills. We participated in community drives, bundling newspapers and collecting "tin" cans which had to be stomped on to flatten. Households were encouraged to pour used cooking grease into cans (whatever for?), which we went from house to house to collect. I remember using my red wagon for transport.

Rationing was a big part of our lives. Food ration books of stamps were carefully guarded. Each member of the family had a ration book, and it required careful planning and shopping on my mother's part to provide a balanced diet. She invented a wonderful dish using lamb neckbones, which I have never been able to replicate. Meat and sugar were in short supply, and I learned to drink my coffee black because my mother treasured her sugar allotment. We learned about spaghetti with sauce and other meatless dishes. One of my jobs was to mix the yellow food coloring into the lard-like substance called "oleomargarine." It was always streaky and unappetizing. Fortunately, we lived in a farming area and there was plenty of produce, if you had enough gas to drive out into the countryside. Canning and preserving went on all summer, as long as we had sufficient sugar.

Gas rationing certainly impacted our lives. State College was a small enough town that children could walk, roller-skate or ride bikes wherever we needed to go. Mother took driving lessons at age 48 and ran into the back of the garage coming back from getting her license. She drove to the train station to meet my father after the war and never got behind the wheel again, but that's another story. Cars were given stickers to indicate priority at the pump. My uncle had an "A" sticker because he drove to work, but our old Ford had a lowly "B" or "C."

Like most of my classmates, I wore braces during the war years. The closest orthodontist was 40 miles away in the mining town of Osceola Mills. State College mothers organized carpools which drove us once a month for the 15-minute ordeal of wire tightening. We had time then while waiting for the others to explore the empty streets of Osceola Mills and sense the impact of a closed mine and a male population away at war. We knew rural poverty from the farms around State College and the scrub pine area known as "The Barrens," but this was my first experience of abandoned buildings and a whole community devoid of hope.

Movies were a big part of my life in the war years. The Saturday matinees cost a nickel, and I spent a lot of time with Jane Withers and Tom Mix, seeing wicked Nazis and dastardly Japanese fighting our soldiers, of whom every unit had at least one black, one Italian, one "Brooklynite" (Jewish, but never identified as such) and one blond WASP. Mrs. Miniver and the Brits were noble, as were all Russians.

Penn State participated in the Navy V-12 officer training program and the Army Specialized Training Programs, so our streets were filled with uniformed young men marching to and from classes, chanting the cadence as they went. I can still hear "SOUND off—HUP-two-three-four." We were deemed too young to fraternize with the military, which of course made them all the more appealing. There was a "Church-Door Canteen" which served as a supervised mixer for the older girls.

My father, in the Corps of Engineers, was first assigned to Milwaukee to convert a candy factory into a small-arms manufactory. After a tour in Brazil building an air base, he was sent back to Milwaukee to retrofit the bullet-making process back to confectionary. We went to live with him on this second assignment, and I got familiar with a different part of the country. Going back and forth to visit family provided me with an opportunity to "train-watch" the steady stream of freight trains, more than a hundred cars long, passing through Altoona, and a sense of the great war effort and patriotism of the American people.

All in all, I had a "good war." I learned a lot of valuable life skills, had my horizons broadened considerably and, most important—I met my husband, the handsomest Marine in the V-12 program!

Part Seven

Fighting in the Pacific

UNTIL THE BOMBING of Pearl Harbor on December 7, 1941, America stayed out of the war in Europe. After Pearl Harbor, the U.S. Congress declared war on Japan on December 8, and three days later, December 11, Congress declared war against Germany, Italy and the other Axis countries.

The bombing of Pearl Harbor destroyed much of the American fleet, and the American forces had serious losses in the war in the Pacific, but the Battle of Midway, June 4–6, 1942, turned the tables. With a decisive win over the Japanese navy, the Americans proceeded to cross the Pacific, island by island. The strategy was to acquire landing strips for the B-29 Superfortress within flight range of Japan. The B-29 Superfortress airplanes bombed targets in Japan and flew over the Himalayas (the Hump) to bomb Japanese bases in China. Once the atom bomb was dropped, Japan surrendered and an invasion of Japan was not needed.

The stories in this section—sea battles, the air war and intensive action on each island—are the story of the war effort in the Pacific.

Opposite: Internment notification for Japanese Americans posted shortly after Pearl Harbor. (*Courtesy Elizabeth Toupin*)

In 1942, shortly after the attack on Pearl Harbor, President Roosevelt issued this Executive Order ordering
the internment of all people of Japanese American
descent, including those who were U.S. citizens. More
than 127,000 people were interned in camps scattered across the United States. This is a copy of the
order which was posted in California.

NOTICE

Headquarters
Western Defense Command
and Fourth Army

Presidio of San Francisco, California
April 30, 1942

Civilian Exclusion Order No. 29

1. Pursuant to the provisions of Public Proclamations Nos. 1 and 2, this Headquarters, dated March 2, 1942, and March 16, 1942, respectively, it is hereby ordered that from and after 12 o'clock noon, P. W. T., of Thursday, May 7, 1942, all persons of Japanese ancestry, both alien and non-alien, be excluded from that portion of Military Area No. 1 described as follows:

> All that portion of the County of Los Angeles, State of California, within the boundary beginning at the intersection of Western Avenue and Redondo Beach Boulevard, northwest of Gardena; thence easterly on Redondo Beach Boulevard and Compton Boulevard to Atlantic Boulevard; thence northerly on Atlantic Boulevard to Artesia Street; thence westerly on Artesia Street to Alameda Street; thence southerly on Alameda to Carson Street; thence westerly on Carson Street to a point at which a north-south line established by Western Avenue intersects Carson Street; thence northerly on said line and Western Avenue to the point of beginning.

2. A responsible member of each family, and each individual living alone, in the above described area will report between the hours of 8:00 A. M. and 5:00 P. M., Friday, May 1, 1942, or during the same hours on Saturday, May 2, 1942, to the Civil Control Station located at:

> 16622 South Western Avenue,
> Torrance, California.

3. Any person subject to this order who fails to comply with any of its provisions or with the provisions of published instructions pertaining hereto or who is found in the above area after 12 o'clock noon, P. W. T., of Thursday, May 7, 1942, will be liable to the criminal penalties provided by Public Law No. 503, 77th Congress, approved March 21, 1942, entitled "An Act to Provide a Penalty for Violation of Restrictions or Orders with Respect to Persons Entering, Remaining in, Leaving, or Committing Any Act in Military Areas or Zones," and alien Japanese will be subject to immediate apprehension and internment.

4. All persons within the bounds of an established Assembly Center pursuant to instructions from this Headquarters are excepted from the provisions of this order while those persons are in such Assembly Center.

> J. L. DeWITT
> Lieutenant General, U. S. Army
> Commanding

Liz Toupin

Born 1925 · Honolulu, Hawaii

Elizabeth Ann Toupin, at home in traditional Korean dress with ancient Korean calligraphy screen. A reminder that Korea, too, was a victim of Japanese aggression. Her parents, W. K. and C. S. Ahn were leaders of the Korean Independence Movement in the United States.

Liz Toupin was born in Hawaii, the youngest of five children born to Won Kiu Ahn and Chung Song Ahn. Her parents were active in the Korean Independence movement and were buried with honors in the Korean National Cemetery, 1998. As a young woman, she often participated in Korean dance programs. She is a graduate of Bennington College in Vermont (BA) and the University of Hawaii (MA industrial relations). She is a dean emeritus of Tufts University, where she was from 1969 through 1992. She has three children, Christine, Cecile Lee and John P. A. She is the author of articles in the *Journal of Cross-Cultural Psychology*, *American Journal of Orthopsychiatry* and the *Journal of College Student Personnel*. She is also the author of *The Hawaii Cookbook*, 1967, and *The Entertaining Wife (The Hostess Cookbook)*, 1958, 1963 and 1971.

Young, Korean and Pearl Harbor

War Changes the Social and Economic Face of Hawaii

By Liz Toupin

"As calls poured into the radio stations, one exasperated announcer shouted, 'This is not a maneuver. This is the real McCoy!'...As Hawaii became the major staging area for the military in the war in the Pacific against Japan, every branch of the military was increased. With another 220,000 defense workers—increasing the civilian population by a third—the whole socioeconomic fabric of the islands changed."

ON DECEMBER 7, 1941, 350 Japanese planes attacked Pearl Harbor and adjoining airfields, killing about 2,400 people and wounding about 1,200. I was 16 years old, a naive adolescent who was to learn that the ensuing war would test the melting pot myth that held the Hawaiian interracial society together, and eventually destroy the myth of Aryan superiority that held Hitler's Germany together.

The racial makeup is critical in understanding Hawaii: 42% percent of the islanders were of Japanese ancestry, 10% were Chinese, 7% Koreans, 10% Caucasians, almost 20% Hapas—those of mixed ancestry; the rest were Filipinos, Portuguese, Samoans and others. Over half of the population were Asians whose homelands were now enemies. Many of these people had been brought to work the sugar and pineapple fields, the key industries in Hawaii. And to accommodate each ethnic group, each was encouraged to have their own churches, language schools and business groups. So there were Congregational, Presbyterian, Methodist churches for whites, and separate but smaller churches of the same denominations for the Chinese, Japanese and Koreans where the sermons were presented in their native language. In addition, there were Buddhist temple; a Korean Christian Church; Japanese, Chinese, Korean language schools; even Chambers of Commerce for each group. The YWCA, open to all groups, was arranged by race. Each group shared and perpetuated their culture through cooking, dance and folk tales. As national organizations like the Red Cross grew, they followed these cultural patterns; there were Japanese, Korean, Chinese Red Cross groups that met separately to wrap bandages, prepare packages for servicemen and knit wool socks for them.

On December 7, 1941, my brother had turned on the radio to listen to the early morning concert. It was abruptly interrupted with a call that all military personnel—Army, Navy and Marine Corps—were to report to duty at once. The appeal was repeated at 15-minute intervals, and then all police and firemen were asked to go to their stations. The announcements seemed unreal, a bad joke like the "Attack from Mars" radio show in 1939 by Orson Wells. Then at 8:40 A.M. the announcement was made that "a sporadic air attack has been made on Oahu…enemy planes have been shot down…the rising sun has been sighted on the wingtips!" We were stunned. We sat around, waiting for the radio to speak to us again but heard mostly static. As calls poured into the radio stations, one exasperated announcer shouted, "This is not a maneuver. This is the real McCoy!"

The sounds of planes and distant explosions were not unusual, as the Army and Navy often had their war games. On December 7, announcements calling servicemen back to their posts were followed by grim calls by name for doctors and nurses, then civilian workers of the Army and Navy. As almost every non-Japanese doctor was called, my mother commented that the attack must have been serious. We were told to stay off the streets, not to use the telephones and to leave the radio on. There were ominous silences, static; then further instructions on filling tubs and buckets with water and getting cars off the street. Just before noon, we were told to leave our radios on. The commercial stations would be going off the air so that they could not serve as "beams" to guide enemy planes.

We lived on the edge of the Punchbowl, a crater overlooking Honolulu, where antiaircraft had been placed. We ran out to see the "war." We saw one war plane with a bright orange circle—the rising sun—painted on its wings and smoke puffs in the clear blue sky from the antiaircraft that missed it. The plane just flew away. The antiaircraft fire continued. The shells fell close by, setting fires that eventually left 31 families homeless, mostly alien Japanese.

At 4:25 P.M. martial law was declared. The announcement was repeated twice in English and once in Japanese for the first-generation population. Thereafter our only contact with the world outside our front door was with the two radio stations and they were "on" only nine times on December 7. Before sundown, blackouts of all buildings and homes were ordered. The static of the radio was the official sound and only sound we all heard. In a strange way it was comforting; it was our only contact with everything that was happening outside our front door, in Honolulu, in the islands, in this war, in this world. Without news and music, we lowered our voices, whispering as if the Japanese could hear us. The general quiet was eerie and ominous. The neighbor's dog barking took on a different meaning—intruders, enemies, fifth column?

We slept dressed, ready to leave on a moment's notice. We whispered and imagined all kinds of scenarios: "Were the Japanese landing on some of the beaches? Where?" There weren't enough people living on the other side of the islands to provide any kind of resistance. "How far do you think they got?" A few nights later, in the blackout, I overheard my parents whispering in Korean about "moving the girls" (there were three of us living at home; the fourth was studying at Julliard in New York City). They talked about "what if...the Japanese returned and landed" and "their savage behavior toward Korean women." My parents were political leaders among the Koreans in the United States, and were in continuous contact with the Korean independence movement in

Liz Toupin in her senior prom dress, 1943, Hawaii.

China, sending money and supplies; they must have known about the "Comfort Women." My two older sisters traveled to the mainland to join the eldest in early 1943.

As on the West Coast, there were no acts of espionage. After Pearl Harbor, a small group composed of the Japanese Consulate staff, Shinto priests, Japanese language-school teachers, an active labor leader and their families were sent to the internment camps on the mainland. The only person convicted of espionage was a German resident. Members of the Hawaii's second-generation Japanese petitioned the military governor to serve in "whatever you may see fit to use us." Most were University of Hawaii students. They worked as a labor battalion clearing land and stringing barbed wire. Eventually they were accepted to service in the Army and became members of the famed 100 and 442 combat teams who won the most medals in World War II.

All the public schools were closed for two months, since they were being used as evacuation centers, then as centers where identification cards were issued. The entire population was inoculated against smallpox, informed of dengue and malaria fevers and had the option for tetanus shots against shrapnel wounds. Gas masks were issued and we dutifully carried them everywhere.

When the schools opened in February, the Army and Navy "brats" were gone, along with other *haoles* (whites) who were evacuated out of the war zone. A quarter of the faculty left their jobs, some for higher-paying jobs with the military, others to return home to the mainland. Some of our classmates left for higher-paying jobs with the military; others held jobs that deferred them from the draft.

One day all the girls in my high school were called to an assembly. We chatted nervously, wondering why we were asked to attend and not the boys. We were addressed by a Navy intelligence officer who stressed that there were 287 single men to every single girl in the islands—the number was so overwhelming that we let out a spontaneous whoop—the officer soberly continued—it was important when we dated servicemen, that we not pass on information such as times when they were leaving the island or the unit or ship to which they belonged. A lot of us giggled because the idea of dating servicemen seemed so crazy and absurd. Had he not heard of the famous Massie murder case in 1931 where the wife of a naval officer accused five local youths of rape? They were acquitted by the local jury. Mrs. Massie's husband, mother and two sailors then took the law into their own hands, kidnapped and murdered one of the accused youths. They were convicted of murder. The sentence brought the wrath of officials and complaints from Washington. A private investigator hired by the governor supported the jury. The governor was ordered to commute their sentences to a day. Thereafter, the Massie case became part of the legends of Hawaii encompassing the ongoing issue of military versus civilian population, federal power versus local rule and blatant racial prejudice. For middle-class nonwhite islanders, it was set in stone; the military was strictly off limits.

As Hawaii became the major staging area for the military in the war in the Pacific against Japan, every branch of the military was increased. With another 220,000 defense workers—increasing the civilian population by a third—the whole socioeconomic fabric of the islands changed. Some of the newcomers were eager to live the "melting pot" idea; others brought their racial prejudices with them, but racial slurs were not common. White-collar and managerial jobs in the defense sector became available to local residents, a new experience for second-generation Asian Americans. With full employment and money pouring into the economy, plantation workers left the fields in droves for higher-paying jobs. Using a banking system common among peasants in their homelands, the Hui (Chinese), Tanomoshi (Japanese), Kay (Korean) and other Asian immigrants were able to purchase real estate, small businesses, banks and even an airline, by pooling their resources.

As a teenager, a whole new world of opportunity opened up for me, opportunities that had not been available to my older siblings. My first job was in the cashier's office at the Hawaiian Pineapple Company, a job previously held by the children of white managers. Cannery employees were not known by their name but by a number, a demeaning relic from the earliest days of contract labor as field hands.

From a coworker, Barbara Silverman, whose parents were faculty members at Punahou School, I learned about slights to Jews among the white islanders, enough so that she was concerned about the reception she might receive in a college on the West Coast.

"I'm a Jew. Can't you tell?" My response was "No, what's that?" She went on; I should know she was Jewish by her name. To me she was another "haole." She was surprised that Asians didn't differentiate among the "haoles."

In the fall of 1943, I entered the University of Hawaii as an engineering student. I did not do well and decided to take some time off. My drafting professor suggested that I look into a job he just posted for an engineer in Quartermasters. He thought I could do the job. If the colonel was shocked at the appearance of a young girl with one year of college drafting for the job in combat loading, he did not blink. I worked for three months on the Saipan invasion, fascinated by the intricacies and the details required in planning. It was not only the booms and hatches

Photo for application to Bennington College, New Hampshire. Departure for the mainland, fall 1944.

and position of ships; it also required teaching the troops to survive, swim, recognize poisonous vegetation, etc.

That winter I was offered a job teaching math in an inner-city school. The salary was appealing. I had applied to colleges in the United States against my parents' wishes and needed money to pay for my first year, confident they would not let me starve after a year. I taught three sections of algebra and three sections of high-school math. I felt great on learning that my algebra students received the highest grades at the year-end test.

I returned to Quartermasters for a final seven weeks of drafting in the summer of '45. We were drawing up ships that were still in the European theater where the war had ended, but that would be needed on the invasion of Japan. There was a restless feeling and dread, as we knew from the island-to-island combat in the Pacific how furiously and fanatically the Japanese fought. Protecting their homeland would have been the Battle of All Battles.

I left Hawaii in late July and caught a troopship to San Francisco on my way to Bennington College. The atom bombs were dropped. The war ended while I was on a train en route to college.

Leonard Rothman

Born 1925 · New York City, New York

January 1946. T/5 Leonard J. Rothman aboard the SS *Stanley Matthews* between Okinawa and Yokohama, Japan. The war had ended 3 to 4 months before, so transport ships were busy returning troops to the states. "Our small remaining company had to go to Japan, so we were placed on a merchant marine cargo ship. The food was good and I had a private cabin: couldn't complain."

Len Rothman enlisted in the Navy in 1943 after graduation from DeWitt Clinton High School in New York City. He was born in 1925 to Jack and Nettie Rothman and grew up in New York City. After his enlistment he was sent to Fort Benning, Georgia, for infantry training. At Fort Benning he was selected to train as an engineer at the Army Specialist Training Program known as ASTP. He was sent to Rose Polytechnic Institute in Terre Haute, Indiana, to begin his studies. The ASTP program was disbanded a short time later and he was transferred to Camp Crowder, Missouri, where he was assigned to the 4025th Signal Corps Group. When he finished this training, he was sent to the Pacific. He was discharged in 1946 and returned to school at George Washington University, Washington, D.C. After his marriage to Elaine Kravitz in 1951, they raised two sons in New Jersey. He was employed as an international examiner for the IRS and was eventually transferred to Connecticut to follow the international corporations. After retirement, they built a house in Litchfield, Connecticut. After many years in Connecticut, they moved to Brookhaven, Lexington, Massachusetts, to be closer to family.

Army Life at the Age of Eighteen

By Leonard Rothman

> "One day I read on the bulletin board that a bomb equivalent to 'x' number of tons of TNT had just been dropped on Hiroshima. I had no idea that this was the beginning of the end."

SHORTLY AFTER MY 18th birthday in 1943, with one year at City College in New York under my belt, I joined the Army. My basic training was at Fort Benning, Georgia, after which I was selected to be trained as an engineer under the Army Specialized Training Program, known as the ASTP. After my three-month infantry basic training I was sent to Rose Polytechnic Institute in Terre Haute, Indiana, to get an engineering degree.

That was not to be. After one glorious semester, living in Hotel Deming, the Army disbanded all ASTP programs. From there I was assigned to the 4025th Signal Corps Group at Camp Crowder, Missouri. Having purposely failed a Morse code test (I couldn't see myself listening to dots and dashes all day), I was trained as a teletype operator. From there my company was sent to the Pacific theater.

After 57 days aboard the USS *Sea Corporal*, zigzagging across the Pacific (we were not in a protected convoy), we stopped in Hollandia, New Guinea, to pick up more men and supplies, and eventually went ashore in Manila. It was on this segment of my voyage that I learned a lesson. Being a nonsmoker, I had voluntarily given up my cigarette rations. While our ship was waiting in Leyte Gulf, natives in outrigger canoes came out to the ship to trade handicrafts for cigarettes. Watching my buddies trading, I kicked myself and said, "Stupid! Where are your cigarettes?"

August 1944, Camp Crowder, Missouri. Len Rothman is third from left. The men are learning how to advance into "enemy" terrain and set up communications lines.

To keep us busy in Manila, we assembled radio transmission towers that were to be raised on golf courses. Eventually, we flew to the northern part of Okinawa to serve as a radio transmission relay station in the event that the expected surrender negotiations could not reach from Tokyo to Manila and back. This waiting was a time of leisure where I could wade out into the very clear blue ocean teeming with colorful tropical fish, and also take refuge in the native cave-like burial tombs during typhoons. One day I read on the bulletin board that a bomb equivalent to "x" number of tons of TNT had just been dropped on Hiroshima. I had no idea that this was the beginning of the end.

After the Japanese surrendered, my remaining company had to wait for a ship to take us to Tokyo, where our new captain eagerly awaited us. His jaw dropped several inches when we explained that we were all eligible to go home and wanted to do so. After we turned down his offer of an immediate promotion, he sent us to Atsugi, Japan, to await a ship for the trip home. After my discharge in Fort Dix, New Jersey, I promptly took advantage of the G.I. Bill to complete my college education at George Washington University in Washington, D.C.

Harry Foden

Born 1924 · Boston, Massachusetts

Last visit home before leaving for the Pacific, Roslindale, Massachusetts.

I was born in Boston, Massachusetts, in 1924. On October 30, 1942, I enlisted in the Signal Corps, with an assignment to begin my training on January 1, 1943, at Boston Teachers College. I reported to Fort Devens, Massachusetts, for active duty September 20, 1943. I was finally assigned to Tarawa in the Pacific. Following discharge from the service in 1946, I enrolled at MIT and (with the help of the G.I. Bill) graduated in 1950 with a BS in chemical engineering practice. Following 4½ years with DuPont, I joined Arthur D. Little, Inc., as a process engineer. As a result of an assignment in 1955 and 1956 in Iraq to develop an industrial development plan for that country, I joined an economic development section of the company. This led over the course of my career to a variety of assignments in 25 countries and 48 states working for local, state and federal governments, nonprofits and educational and health organizations whose operations affected economic development. I retired from Arthur D. Little in 1993 as vice president of institutional development. I have been married to my wife, Fran, for 61 years. I am the proud father of one daughter, Lynn.

My World War II Memoir

By Harry Foden

"I never saw combat. I had become accustomed to picking up and moving at short notice, as part of a group or as an individual. I had learned to adapt to conditions on a small island in the Pacific, where I stayed for 11 months after moving 13 times in 11 months in the States prior to leaving for overseas…. The radio teletype equipment that I learned how to maintain and operate served a very useful purpose in providing vital information that contributed to the need to move aircraft and personnel all over the Pacific area."

The War Begins

THE DECEMBER 7, 1941, attack on Pearl Harbor by the Japanese not only changed the future of the United States and the world, but it also significantly changed the direction of my personal life.

At 17 years of age and a recent high-school graduate, I was not eligible for the draft at the time of the Pearl Harbor attack. When I turned 18 on January 12, 1942, I was classified as 1-A, that is, eligible to be drafted. Because the Navy, Marines and Coast Guard depended on volunteers rather than draftees, those who were drafted had no choice but the Army and no control over what part of the Army they were assigned to, with the infantry the most likely place they would be assigned. I recognized that if I were drafted, I would most likely face a real possibility of assignment to an Army ground-fighting group. I was delighted, therefore, to come across an opportunity to enlist with the Signal Corps attached to the Air Corps and to attend a six-month radio training course as a reservist before going on active duty prior to being sent to Officer Training School and commissioned as a second lieutenant. On October 30, 1942, I enlisted in the Signal Corps, with an assignment to begin my training on January 1, 1943, at Boston Teachers College.

Training for My Role in the War

I knew nothing about the repair of radios of any kind but was eager to learn. The six-month course taught the theory and repair of basic radios. At the end of the six months, the Signal Corps, in what proved to be the unreliability of Army promises, said they had enough officers, and I was sent to Philadelphia to a ten-week course operated by the Philco radio corporation. Here I learned about the operation and repair of specific types of radios used in Army Air Corps aircraft. Upon completion of the Philco course, I reported to Fort Devens, Massachusetts, for active duty on September 20, 1943.

After four days, I was sent to Columbia Air Base in Columbia, South Carolina, to begin my basic training. There I had another physical and received some more shots. The physical exam became a part of every transfer. I could never figure out why the Army gave us a physical every time we moved. Was it because the doctors at each base didn't trust the doctors at other bases? Was it because the paperwork never caught up with me as I moved 11 times in the 11 months I was on duty in the States? Or was it just to keep us busy while they got around to deciding what they wanted us to do next? At any rate, as I recall, once I was overseas, I did not receive any more physicals until I was discharged.

For reasons we never learned, after only two weeks in Columbia, we were sent by truck convoy 75 miles to Daniel Air Base in Augusta, Georgia, for the rest of our basic training. At the conclusion of our basic training, we were sent back to Columbia Air Base for post-basic training—and another physical exam. In the next few weeks at Columbia, we never had a chance to get near a radio or an aircraft. I was beginning to be frustrated about the changes of direction and the inactivity toward getting me into a situation where I could begin to contribute to the war effort.

To add to the frustration, after only a few weeks at Columbia, I was part of a shipment of 90 men to Godman Field, which is located within Fort Knox, Kentucky. When we arrived at Godman Field, we learned that our destination was apparently a mistake. We arrived early in the morning as the troops there were just getting up. Many of them wanted to know our Military Occupational Specialty (MOS). When we told them it was 547, for the maintenance of aircraft radios, they said they had never heard of it at their base. After discussions among the officers at Godman Field, the decision was made to keep us in the Air Corps and take advantage of the technical training we had already received from the Signal Corps. We sat around for several days not knowing what was going to happen. A cigar-smoking sergeant assured us we would be reassigned. We weren't convinced he knew what he was talking about, but he was right. Consequently, the 90 of us were divided among six groups of 15 each and sent to different installations. I was sent to Chanute Field, Illinois, for training in the maintenance of radio range, a device to provide direction to aircraft planning to land at certain fields. At this point I began to wonder whether the Germans and Japanese could be any less efficient than the U.S. Army.

Just as we completed our training on the radio range equipment at Chanute Field and then at Selfridge Field in Mt. Clemens, Michigan, our small group was surprised to learn that we were changing directions once again. We were sent to Philadelphia to attend a school operated by American Telephone and Telegraph Company to train personnel in the maintenance of a new type of equipment—radio teletype. This equipment combined the teletype machine, used to send telegrams and telexes, and radio signals to replace the usual telephone lines. This would make it possible for ground stations, for example, Hickam Field headquarters in Hawaii, to send messages quickly to other stations located on various islands in the Pacific, more efficiently than the older method of messages sent by Morse code.

At the completion of our training in Philadelphia, we were given a ten-day leave, and then sent to Smyrna Airfield just outside of Nashville, Tennessee. One of the other men sent with me to Smyrna was a good buddy, with whom I have maintained communication to this day, by the name of Jack Hopkins. In late August, after six weeks at Smyrna, we were sent to Fort Lewis, just outside Seattle, Washington, to await shipment overseas.

Achieving My Role in the War Effort

After a short stay at Fort Lewis, our group was trucked to the Port of Seattle for an unknown destination. We were surprised to see crowds at shipside, with bands playing Hawaiian tunes. We thought that in wartime, there would be more secrecy. We seemed to be the only ones that didn't know where we were going.

Aboard ship, our sleeping quarters were in the hold of the ship, one of the Liberty ships produced in great numbers by the Kaiser Corporation. The bunks were five deep, from the bottom of the hold to the ceiling. If I turned over in the bunk, my knees would bump the fellow above me. Once we had been at sea for a couple of days, many of us chose to sleep on the outside deck, although in the morning it felt as though someone had been kicking me in the back because the deck was so hard. After nine days, we arrived—surprise, surprise—in Honolulu and were sent to Hickam Field, the site of some of the heaviest attacks by the Japanese. There were still signs of the attacks on many of the buildings at the Field.

After a few days at Hickam Field, our group was finally to get the opportunity to do what we had been trained to do. We were sent about 30 miles outside Honolulu to an installation at Kipapa Gulch, in the middle of a pineapple field. Here, the government had built two underground tunnels after the Japanese attack, to contain all of its transmitting and receiving equipment. Each tunnel was air-conditioned, with special locks to isolate areas in the event of a chemical attack. The new radio teletype equipment was to be set up in one of the tunnels.

The staff lived above ground in small cabins, each housing six men. I lived in a cabin where one of the occupants was a regular Army master sergeant, who had been in Hawaii for many years. The master sergeant relied on a radio station for his wake-up call every morning. In those days, the radio station went off the air at night and came on the air at 5 A.M. Each day as the station came on the air, it usually announced, "There will (or will not) be work in the pineapple fields today." This was the way the company that produced the pineapples informed its workers whether they were needed that day. The first few times I was awakened by this announcement, I could not figure out where I was, but I soon became used to it.

Hawaii proved to be a delightful place to be assigned. I was able, for example, to visit Waikiki Beach on days off from duty. The Royal Hawaiian Hotel, the most luxurious hotel in Hawaii at the time, had been taken over by the government as housing for Navy personnel. All service personnel were able to use the hotel's beach, so it was a favorite place to spend a day. Little did I realize at that time that, after the war, I would stay several times at this hotel, which was completely refurbished after the government returned it to the owners. Nor did I realize, or even imagine, that I would return to Hawaii more than 30 times in later years. In fact, at one point in the late 1980s, I had a project that took me to Hawaii 20 times in an 18-month period.

By late December, our group had installed, tested and achieved operational status for the radio teletype equipment. On Christmas Day, just after the noon dinner, I was notified that I was to report at the Hickam Field flight line at 6 P.M. for a trip to Kwajalein Island in the Marshall Islands. Before leaving for Hickam, I had to give away many of the Christmas gifts and goodies to my cabin mates since I didn't have room to carry them. When I arrived at Hickam, I learned that because of the heavy rains, the flight would be delayed. The plane finally left at midnight. What a way to spend Christmas Day!

My Longest Stay in One Area

My stay at Kwajalein was short, for within two days I was airborne for Tarawa Atoll in the Gilbert Islands, the site of one of the bloodiest battles of the Pacific war. The facilities at Tarawa were located on Betio Island where the battle actually took place. The island was two miles long and one-half mile wide, very white because it consisted of coral. One part of the small island had been left as it had been at the end of the battle, with stubs of palm trees and wreckage of equipment, as a constant reminder of the battle that had taken place there.

I was part of a small group charged with the responsibility of getting the radio teletype equipment in operation there on Tarawa. In the early days, there were many difficulties due to static caused by atmospheric conditions, which resulted in garbled messages and necessitated the return to Morse code until the static could be cleared. Of course the men who were handling messages from point to point by Morse code took great delight in poo-pooing this new radio teletype method of communication. However, we were able to achieve reliable operations, thus making it possible for much more effective communications concerning aircraft moving from one island to another in the vast Pacific Ocean.

During the weeks we were trying to achieve reliable operations, we would communicate with the maintenance personnel on the other islands. By FAA regulations, we were not allowed to communicate personal information, but we always knew who was on the other end of the teletype, particularly if it were Jack Hopkins on Majuro Island or Garland Gentry, another buddy, on Johnston Atoll.

Life on Tarawa took on sameness as day to day there was little change in routine or in the weather, other than changes in the shifts we were assigned to for our work. The island was small; there were no places for recreation other than swimming and outdoor movies every night, rain or shine. However, it was satisfying to realize that, after all the various types of training and moving around, sometimes without apparent reason, I was able to do something that helped the war effort. Tarawa served as an intermediate stop for small aircraft going to and from islands closer to the ongoing war effort as the battles took place closer to Japan. It also served as a stopover for larger aircraft that were returning from the forward areas with the wounded being airlifted to Hawaii and the mainland.

On August 15, 1945, the Japanese surrendered after the United States had dropped two atomic bombs, one on Hiroshima, the second on Nagaski. On September 2, 1945, Japan's surrender was formalized with the signing of documents aboard the battleship USS *Missouri*. I remained on Tarawa until November, when I was sent back to Kwajalein Island for a brief stay before returning to Hawaii and the station at Kipapa Gulch. Once the war had ended, discharges of the troops proceeded on a point system, one that awarded points for the number of months in the armed forces, the number of months overseas and any special awards and medals that a serviceman had received. Since I did not have enough points to merit discharge, I was to continue to remain in Hawaii. While we still worked at Kipapa Gulch, we now had our quarters at Schofield Barracks, another major recipient of the Japanese attack.

Finally, in February 1946, I had enough points for discharge. I sailed from Hawaii on a faster ship to San Francisco, one with better accommodations than on our trip to Hawaii and requiring only five days for the crossing. The Air Corps refused to give us any winter clothes, saying we would get them in San Francisco. Of course only two days out of Hawaii, the weather turned really cold and our summer chinos and thin flight jackets were not much protection on deck. As a result, we spent most of our time inside. When we finally arrived at Fort Stockton, just outside San Diego, the first stop for all of us was to get an overcoat.

After only two days at Fort Stockton, where we received our winter uniforms, had time to have all the necessary patches sewn on for the units we were in and for the stripes of rank, mine being a sergeant by this time, I was on a train for a five-day trip to Fort Devens, where I was discharged from the service.

Return to Civilian Life

It was great to return home after so long away. Except for two ten-day leaves, I had been away for two and one-half years, not as long as some service men and women, but long enough to be delighted to get back home. I had been very fortunate. I never saw combat. I had become accustomed to picking up and moving at short notice, as part of a group or as an individual. I had learned to adapt to conditions on a small island in the Pacific, where I stayed for 11 months after moving 11 times in 11 months in the States prior to leaving for overseas. I had met a number of servicemen who became very good friends. I had lived with and traveled with a wide variety of men from all backgrounds and from all parts of the country. I had learned some new skills that enabled me to play a useful, if not combat-involved, role. The radio teletype equipment that I learned how to maintain and operate served a very useful purpose in providing vital information that contributed to the need to move aircraft and personnel all over the Pacific area.

After a week at home, I returned to my prewar job at Dewey and Almy Chemical Company and began to review my high-school work prior to taking exams in June for entry to MIT, for it had been five years since I had left Boston Latin School. The studying paid off, for I learned shortly after the exams that I had been accepted at MIT, but, because of the size of the class that was expected, I would not start until February 1947, then go all summer to catch up with those who started in September 1946.

Thanks to the G.I. Bill that had been enacted, a large portion of my tuition at MIT was paid for by the government, and there was a weekly payment to help defray living expenses. I provided much of the rest by working in the dining halls 20 hours per week.

I was attending the university that I had always wanted to attend and was on my way to the career I was hoping for.

Florence Wallach Freed

Born 1933 · Riverdale, New York

This photograph of Florence Wallach Freed was taken in their Lincoln, Massachusetts, home sometime in the 1990s when she was in her 60s. They had two granddaughters, Sara and Rachel, born in 1995 and 1999. Florence and Charles happily babysat for them for many years while their daughter Lisa and her husband Ted were working.

I was born May 31, 1933, and grew up in Riverdale, the Bronx, and New York City, New York. I graduated from PS81, the Barnard Preparatory School, Barnard College and Harvard Graduate School. I worked as a school and clinical psychologist and professor of psychology, Middlesex College in Bedford, Massachusetts. While teaching, I also had research articles published in psychology journals. In 1956 I married Charles Freed, a Holocaust survivor who became a senior scientist at the Massachusetts Institute of Technology's Lincoln Laboratory. He received awards for his pioneering research on lasers. We had two daughters, Lisa and Josie, and lived in Lincoln, Massachusetts. Later we had two granddaughters, Sara and Rachel; they live in Lexington, Massachusetts. Charles died at Brookhaven in 2010. After retiring I had stories, memoirs, and poetry published in literary journals. I am an amateur pianist, playing mostly classical composers. Also, during World War II, my uncle Captain Bernard Wallach was a medical doctor caring for the wounded in the Pacific. I strongly believe that war is NOT INEVITABLE and that someday there will be Peace on Earth.

My Cousin Jackie

By Florence Wallach Freed

Part I is written in stream-of-consciousness style to vividly project the child's point of view. Part II is written in straight essay style—from the adult point of view—50 years later.

Part I, 1945

THE FIRST LETTER said you were missing in action, the second said you were dead, the third finally arrived in April 1945, describing how it had happened, so my Uncle Julius, your father, slips the letter into his pocket, takes the subway from 86th Street uptown to 242nd Street, the Bronx, he's jostled by indifferent crowds, they don't realize he's a Gold Star father, we huddle around the dining-room table, Mom serves tea with poppy-seed pastries, I gaze intently at my teabag bobbing up and down in the boiling water, first it stays up for quite a while, then it gets soaked through, gets heavier, sinks to the bottom, never to surface again…

The letter, written by a commanding officer of the United States Navy, explains that your plane encountered violent winds, ran out of fuel, landed in the Pacific, you clung to a life raft with a few other sailors, but extremely rough seas capsized the raft, all climbed back onto the raft, but "your son, Jack, noting that some of the provisions and gear were floating about, re-entered the water of his own volition to retrieve them," they threw you a life jacket, you managed to get it on, they paddled furiously to reach you, but the heavy seas…

I remember that winter day when you were fourteen and I was eight, you came to visit, we take my Flexible Flyer sled with the American Eagle painted on, hurry out to the snowy hills of Van Cortlandt Park, this is my Cousin Jackie, I boast to all my friends, I'm so proud to be with you, tall, strong, with thick shining black hair, piercing blue eyes, you're only my cousin, but I pretend you're my big brother, we take turns, belly-whopping down the steepest hill, around that curve, past the oak tree, over those bumps, and later, mittens caked with ice, we ride down together, sitting up, I in front, you behind, your sturdy legs wrapped around me, your big boots firmly on the steering bar, your arms hugging me tight, we whiz safely over the last bumps, shrieking, laughing, we roll off into the snow, and afterwards, tired out, we have hot cocoa with floating marshmallows, and play checkers, you always let me have the reds, but you don't let me win, King me, I cry, and you King me, my King...

A few years later, only 17, you lie about your age, tell them you're 18, and enlist in the Navy, they don't look carefully at the date on your birth certificate, the Navy needs many tender young boys, next thing I know, a package comes in the mail, it's a beautiful deep blue satin apron, with a gorgeous golden anchor embroidered on, and the words, all in capitals, UNITED STATES NAVY, I wear it for good, when I help my mother serve the company, I'm very careful, never spill a spot of pot roast gravy on it, I still have that deep blue apron...

You request to be assigned to the Atlantic Fleet to help fight Hitler, you've got personal reasons as well as patriotic ones, the Nazis are killing off all our relatives in the Warsaw Ghetto, but in that senseless shuffle of the careless cards of life, you get sent to the Pacific instead, after that we get a few flowery postcards from San Francisco, and an enlarged photograph, of you in your Navy uniform, with those smart white stripes on the collar, your tie perfectly knotted, your bars showing your rank, Aviation Radioman, Third Class, your shiny silver eagle, your straight smile...

A few days after the letter, we go downtown to visit Uncle Julius, he lives alone in a small apartment, a pharmacist doesn't make much money unless he owns his own store, but Uncle Julius knows what's good, he's got shelves filled with art books, Rembrandt, Vermeer, Chagall, biographies of the great artists and composers, Renoir, Mozart, Brahms and, best of all, almost a hundred classical records, Beethoven, Schubert, Chopin, right now he's listening to the *Pastorale* Symphony, trying to drown out his grief, this was Jackie's favorite, he says, I could turn on any one of these records and he knew what it was, the composer, the piece, even which movement, Uncle Julius cries, a grown man crying, Julius we say gently, Julius, you've got to eat something, we drag him out to Slatkin's Deli, he takes a few bites of his hot pastrami sandwich, he continues, Jackie could have become a great music critic, he could write, he had a perfect ear, he could hum any melody, even complicated ones like Debussy's *La Mer*, The Sea, oh, the sea...

The following summer, at Camp Wahanda, Winsted, Connecticut, I'm twelve years old, I keep pretending I'm drowning, I climb up on the raft, do a running dive off the bouncy board into Laurel Lake, and stay underwater as long as I can, I force myself to stay down until my lungs are bursting, and then I come flailing up at the last second, thinking, so this is what it's like to drown, this is almost what it's like, I keep doing this until one day Millie, the head counselor, grabs hold of me and yells, what are you DOING? Are you crazy, Florrie? for God's sake, we thought you were never coming up, Debbie Vogel dove in to save you already, now cut that out or I'm going to have to dock you for a week, I come shivering to my senses, pull on my terrycloth robe, sit on the sand and dry off, I never do that again, I realize, way deep down, I can't get back to you, Jackie, my handsome Cousin Jackie...

Part II, 1995

FIFTY YEARS LATER, my husband Charles and I fly to Honolulu on the island of Oahu. We settle into a little Hawaiian hotel and take our first swim in the mighty Pacific Ocean at Waikiki Beach. The golden sun is beginning to set; waves pound the shore. Early next morning, we drive out to Pearl Harbor where it all began. In the midst of shimmering beauty, where ancient Polynesians gathered pearls from oysters, the bombs exploded. We walk silently through the USS Arizona Memorial built over the sunken ship in

This is a picture of my cousin, Jack Wallach, taken soon after Pearl Harbor. Jackie immediately enlisted in the U.S. Navy. He sent copies to all his family members before he was sent to the Pacific. He was killed just before the war ended in 1945. I think he was only 22 when he died.

which over one thousand sailors are forever entombed. Oil still bubbles up from the mangled vessel to the surface of the ocean.

Next we drive about ten miles to the Punchbowl, the National Memorial Cemetery of the Pacific. We drive uphill, almost six hundred feet above sea level, and find ourselves in the midst of an enormous volcanic crater, shaped like a punchbowl. Before the arrival of the missionaries, this place was known as "The Hill of Sacrifice," as it was the setting for human sacrifices of people who had violated the kapus, or taboos, of ancient Hawaii. We park the car and enter a small building where a kindly woman looks up my Cousin Jackie in a huge book containing the names of all the service men and women who are either buried here or remembered here. She quickly finds his name and information, in alphabetical order, and turns the book around so we can see it clearly. She also gives us a map and explains that we can find Jackie's name on panel number two, in the Court of the Missing.

We walk straight down a long, wide path toward the Court of the Missing. Along the way, on either side of us and stretching up the grassy slopes, are the graves of over 37,000 service men and women who were recovered from the Pacific battles and buried here. We arrive at the Court of the Missing, which consists of a wide staircase flanked with ten huge white marble columns. Each column is twelve feet high and all the ten columns contain the names of over 28,000 missing service people whose bodies were never recovered. They are mainly from World War II, but there are also names from the Korean and Vietnam wars.

We locate panel number two and his name jumps out at us. "JACK WALLACH, RADIOMAN THIRD CLASS, US NAVY, NEW YORK." My heart beats faster. I want to touch his name, to glide my hands over it, but it is too high up and I cannot reach it. We lay an armful of deep, blood-red, Hawaiian ginger flowers under Jackie's name. At this moment, through the silent air, I seem to hear a chorus of all the voices of all our long-gone family saying, "It's a good thing you came here, Florence, to this very place, to honor Jackie's memory." For one magical, transcendent moment, we are all here—grandparents, parents, uncles, aunts, brothers, sisters, cousins—together again, alive and happy. The vision passes and I look back up at his name and see that there are other Wallachs listed before and after him. The flowers are for them too, I think— for everyone on this panel, on all the white marble panels, in all the deep, dark graves.

Eventually, we continue up the stairway to the white marble statue of a woman called "Columbia," symbolizing all the American mothers who lost their sons or daughters. Then we enter a chapel where we sit quietly for a while. The chapel includes a Jewish Star of David, a Christian cross, and a Buddhist wheel. Next we go out to study an extensive gallery of friezes of maps depicting in colorful crushed glass all the major battles of the Pacific where so many suffered and died for us. I realize that I have no idea which battle Jackie was in when he drowned.

As we descend the marble stairs, I see images of my Cousin Jackie before me—his bright blue eyes and shining black hair, his sturdy body, going sleigh riding, playing checkers, listening to Beethoven's *Pastorale*, wearing his Navy uniform, out on the raft in the Pacific, trying to rescue the provisions, being overwhelmed by the terrible sea, and finally—drowning. My Cousin Jackie—another human sacrifice in the endless chain of human horrors. But, in a strange way, after 50 years, I feel I got back to him—at least a little bit. Yes, I got back to you, Jackie. My handsome Cousin Jackie…

Will Cochran

Born 1923 · St. Paul, Minnesota

Wildcat F4F like the one in which Will Cochran used to train.

Born in St. Paul, Minnesota in 1923, Will Cochran and his parents Moncrief and Margaret moved to Massachusetts when he was 14. He went to Belmont Hill School, Belmont, Massachusetts, then graduated from Andover School in Massachusetts. He attended Harvard as an undergraduate and Harvard Medical School. He went into the Navy in 1942 and spent four years training to be a pilot and then a night fighter pilot at various bases across the United States. He was based on the USS *Saratoga*, where a focused kamikaze attack off Iwo Jima tried to sink the ship. The *Saratoga* sustained five suicide plane hits as well as aerial bombings, damaged but surviving. As a result of the damage, Cochran's front-line career was extremely short—three missions—since the *Saratoga* was sent back to the naval repair yard in Bremerton, Washington for repairs. He met his wife Mary Rolls at a Radcliffe "Jolly-Up" and they married in 1946. After medical school Will Cochran specialized in pediatrics, practicing in New London, Connecticut. Gradually, he became more and more focused on the care of newborns (now known as neonatology), and he returned to Boston in 1960 where he practiced at Boston Lying-In Hospital, Children's Hospital and finally at Beth Israel Hospital. He and Mary raised five children.

Chewing Gum

By Will Cochran

> "To this day I praise the human brain which can compute
> so many facts so fast—give each one a relative weight—
> that variable not easily available to a computer—and then
> include fear in the equation."

IT WAS 1 O'CLOCK in the morning, obviously dark and now, mixed with rain, snowing lightly. I sat apprehensively in my Hellcat, chewing gum, when a fist banged on the wing telling me to open up my cockpit hood. My pulse quickened as I cranked the hood open. The launch crewman told me to start my engine and turn on the radio because "they've got something on the radar!" Sitting in my F-6-F-5N night fighter already positioned on the catapult, engine now started, I heard over my radio the voice of the carrier's C-I-C (combat information center) this curt message, "Launch immediately and report in at 'Angels 20' [20,000 ft.]." Chewing gum with renewed enthusiasm—but now with lessened saliva—I rewarmed my engine once again to operating temperature, all within one minute, went through the check-off list for a catapult takeoff, then blinked my running lights as a signal I was ready and all seemed OK. The routine for such a night launch was that I run up the warmed engine to full ear-splitting power, check the instruments (glowing red on the panel lights) for normalcy, set the trim tabs for a slight climb, put down full flaps, tighten the throttle quadrant knob lightly so the throttle would stay on full against the huge G force of the catapult's kick, then, with the cockpit hood briefly cranked open, "so you can jump clear of the plane should you land in the water," I put my head back against the headrest to keep it from being snapped back by the thrust of the catapult. By that huge jolting force I was quickly catapulted—0 knots to 90—into the black and snow. My launch was timed by the catapult officer as a wave lifted the bow of the carrier just above the horizontal. The hood now cranked shut, but the engine roaring at full power drowning out all else, my wheels tucked in, I climbed on instruments, breaking out of the clouds into a moonlit sky at about 15,000 feet.

The date was February 18, 1945, and now, for the first time in World War II, a huge U.S. naval armada of carriers, cruisers and destroyers, coming north from our rendezvous, the tropical island of Ulithi, was some 150 miles off the southwest coast of Japan for planned air strikes on the Japanese, mainly the Tokyo area. We were the first planes to carry out such a low-level bombing since 1942 when Jimmy Doolittle's B-25s had made their daring raid, flying off the deck of the carrier *Hornet*. Now the war was obviously going our way, but still appeared to have a long way to go. Our air group, based on the USS *Saratoga*, represented one of just two night air groups now readily available, the second on the USS *Enterprise*.

Air strikes on Japan had been carried out earlier that day in waves, starting just after dawn with most of the two night fighter and torpedo bomber groups going in as the last wave of the day. Hence, these two night air groups had been expected to find their way back in darkness, flying at sea level to avoid radar detection. Earlier, Stew Doty, one of our more senior pilots, on his way back had taken it upon himself when well out to sea to climb to 12,000 feet, enabling him to see, on the small radar each of us carried in our plane, the whereabouts of our task force, somewhere ahead. But by so doing he had had to burn an excessive amount of fuel in his climb, though from this higher altitude he had seen the task force some 50–60 miles ahead—and not quite in the direction his returning group flying below him was headed. He radioed down the correct heading. Unfortunately, now arriving over the carrier a little ahead of his group because he had picked up extra speed as he partially glided back down to sea level, he requested immediate permission to land having little or no gas left. But it turned out the *Saratoga's* captain had refused to turn the carrier prematurely into the wind just for him alone to land, as such a move might eventually put the carrier even farther out of her central position in the task force than she soon would be likely to need as she spent time retrieving the main body of her planes. Hence Doty had been told if he didn't have enough gas to remain aloft he would either have to parachute near a destroyer or try to land in the water near one and hope to be rescued. What kind of options were those? Since it was night and rather stormy we never knew which he attempted!! He was never heard from again. Such a decision by the captain (maybe coming down the chain of command from some admiral) made the untested young ensign pilots like me feel, needless to say, suddenly more vulnerable. Never before had we encountered such "crisis management." Previously the ambience among us pilots (obviously spoiled) had built to the point it seemed the Navy felt we were irreplaceable, everyone there to support us, to make every effort to get us back alive. Now we realized it wasn't quite so. Now, how much "so" was there?

That very night I had been assigned to a two-hour duty watch of "launch readiness," meaning I would sit and wait in one of our night fighter Hellcats on the catapult, machine guns loaded, engine warmed up and ready for almost instant launch if a suspicious blip appeared on the ship's powerful radar. There was an obvious worry that Japanese bombers, out for retaliation, would be searching for us. This readiness duty was rotated; my time was midnight to 2:00 A.M. and was the reason I missed being in on the first big naval carrier raid on Japan itself. Not being a gum chewer by custom, I was nervous enough that night to decide I should do something (chew gum) to alleviate my anxiety as I sat in complete darkness on the catapult, cockpit hood cranked shut, waiting to see if I would be sent off and hoping I wouldn't. Just how interested were the task force admirals in me? I now had a new apprehension—not very. On top of all the apprehension of knowing that when I went off I'd be all alone (we usually flew at least in pairs) was the fact that it was now beginning to snow hard and the wind was blowing, so hard that at times, the carrier dipped into an oncoming wave. Heavy spray would come over the bow and drench the plane; I'd not only have to launch but also land in such weather. Not the nice weather I wanted for being shot off the catapult, and certainly not the kind of weather I had ever, ever, landed in. My hope was that the Japanese felt likewise about the weather and were staying home. So, chewing my gum, every 20 minutes I'd start the engine briefly to keep it warmed up and to warm myself using the cockpit heater.

Now, here I was at 20,000 feet. I throttled back to standard cruise settings for the engine which immediately quieted the blasting roar of the unmuffled 18-cylinder 2,200-horsepower plant. Still chewing my gum, I went into orbit and called in for the vector. Just as I was given a direction toward Japan, I noticed I had an engine surge, adding immensely to my nervousness, drying my mouth further and increasing my pulse. Though the engine tachometer on the instrument panel seemed steady at 2,200 RPMs the surge was definitely there, so I nervously requested time to investigate. An impatient C-I-C voice acquiesced. The surge then suddenly disappeared as I concentrated intently on turning to my exact heading. I was relieved by the surge's disappearance, as I had great fear that my motor might be about to fail me. My fertile mind quickly made up the scenario that I'd have to glide down in the snow and dark and then either attempt a water landing next to a radar blip (that I'd hope was a rescue destroyer) or parachute down and land in the ocean with my one-man raft and tiny flashlight—I had little enthusiasm for either! I was just about to call in and say I was on the heading when again the engine surge came back. Perplexed as to what it was I went back into orbit, but then I stopped chewing gum to listen more attentively, and the surge went away. Then, alternately chewing or not chewing, I realized that, as I chewed, my headphones in my soft leather helmet were rocking on the muscles of my jaw with each nervous muscular chew, and the engine noise would get louder and quieter with each chew, hence the apparent surge! Embarrassed (what kind of a dauntless and intrepid hero was I?), I radioed that I'd figured out the problem (not telling them what it was) and went out on the vector at top speed some 80 miles, firing my six wing guns briefly to make sure they were working. Though not appreciated by me at the time, it was a beautiful night, the almost full moon shining on the tops of the puffy white clouds below. When I got out 80 miles I found only an especially large cloud (probably the cause of the ship's radar blip); no hostile aircraft could be seen as I circled and probed up and down in the cloud with my plane's radar. Reporting in, I was told to start back.

I now began concentrating on the next problem, which had been in the back of my mind as soon as I'd been catapulted; would I have enough gas left to stay airborne so I could land on the carrier after dawn and maybe be able to see a little something? I called in for the most economical engine settings for my Pratt & Whitney engine followed by the key question, "Do I have enough gas to stay airborne 'til dawn?" I almost knew what the answer was going to be, and didn't want to hear it. The answer soon came back, "No." I'd never have enough gas. Chewing a new pack of gum, I started for the carrier with thoughts of having to land on it in the night and snow, and again about Doty. How did I stack up in the captain's equation?

Over the many months of training to be carrier night fighters we had developed conceptually a carrier landing plan in case of bad weather and darkness, but we'd never had to carry it out, since we had never been sent off in such weather. The conceptual plan depended largely on timed straightaways and careful standardized turns—all on instruments only—incorporating as best we could the biggest variable, wind speed over the deck of the carrier. All of my previous night landings had occurred with at least a little light from the stars or moon filtering through the clouds, and never in the rain and certainly not snow. When close enough to the carriers we could always make out the faint darker shadow of the carrier on the water and always see which was sky and which

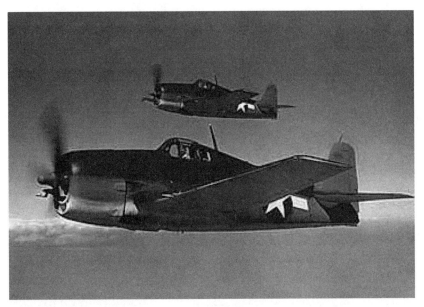

Type of plane flown by Will Cochran. The Hellcat was the Navy's dominant plane in the second part of World War II, helping the United States secure air superiority over the Pacific. (*Wikipedia*)

was water. Now, with no visibility whatsoever, I would be carrying out a landing approach pattern entirely on instruments. We'd all thought through just how many minutes and seconds—mostly seconds—(and at what speed) we'd fly each arm of the pattern before making the various left-hand turns—and at what steepness, much depending again on the wind speed over the deck. The whole idea was to enable our approach to the rear of the flight deck to be made while still in a left turn, so that, with the plane propped up in a nose-high just-above-stalling-speed attitude, we could, while still turning, look out the left side of the cockpit and see, standing on the port rear corner of the flight deck, the landing signal officer, unobscured by our huge engine bulking in front of us. (Looking straight ahead, especially when in such a nose-high landing mode, vision straight ahead was totally obscured by the huge engine.) We always struggled, mostly unsuccessfully, to be still in a left-hand turn just before landing, giving us an unobscured view. It wasn't easy to orchestrate even in good weather, night or day. On a clear night though, with our night vision at its peak, at least we could always dimly see the darkened carrier, even with its lights off, throughout most of the nearer finer approach. This time there would be no shadowy carrier to use as a guide.

Getting set to start this rectangular landing pattern, and helped in orienting myself by the *Saratoga's* C-I-C radar following my every move, I made the first upwind pass at an altitude of about 200 feet, with flaps and wheels down, over what I thought was our carrier, as I saw its big blip moving down my little 5-mile radar screen. The carrier, now headed straight upwind, always shone a narrow core of very bright light straight up from the island superstructure, so as you flew over its flash of light you could start your timing clock accurately. The first pass I saw no such light so I called in to be sure they had the light on. I was assured they did. Coming around again I dropped down to just over 150 feet, and coming upwind this time over the carrier I could see a dim glow in the snow. My pulse climbing and my chewing more vigorous, I punched my timing clock and started the computed straightaway and turns I predicted necessary for the wind speed over the deck. (I was told the wind speed over the deck was considerably faster than usual because of the intensifying storm. It usually is around 30 knots; now it was close to, or even over, 40.) After going upwind a few seconds longer than average, I turned 90 degrees to the left and quickly another 90 degrees, now going downwind and lateral to, but in the opposite direction of, the carrier. A carrier-based narrow-beam radar now picked up the plane as I flew past it downwind. This carrier radar not only determined how far lateral to the carrier I was but pinpointed my position as I passed the downwind end of the flight deck. This announcement plus the wind speed over the deck helped me decide how quickly and steeply I should make my looping turn toward the carrier. I had hit the lateral distance about right (1,200 yards), but because of the higher wind speed I knew I'd have to turn quickly and more steeply toward the carrier than the standard, thus adding a new variable.

Starting this calculated turn toward the carrier, I locked my shoulder harness tight and opened my cockpit hood. Now the accompanying louder roar of the engine and the blast of the wind stream intensified my already tensed muscles. My super reliable radio altimeter was reading a height between 50 and 100 feet off the rough ocean surface so I wasn't quite sure how high I really was, not wanting to be too high and certainly not wanting to run into the stern of the carrier if too low. I was aiming for just over 80 feet. Every time I put my goggled head out to take a better look ahead I got snow mixed with rain in my face, so I had to keep my face just inside the wind stream. As an aid to our beloved landing signal officer I had turned on all my lights, navigation ones but also, importantly for him, the specially designed three different colored lights sequenced longitudinally on the belly fuselage of the plane. Seeing how these lined up, the landing signal officer could see, by the spacing between them and their alignment, whether I was coming straight at him or not, whether I was going too fast (the plane flattened out) or too slowly (too cocked up). My red lit instruments I'd dimmed as much as I dared so that I could just see them. With wheels down and flaps fully extended to maintain a flying speed just above stalling I was using considerable power. Relying totally on instruments for an actual carrier landing like this I had never done, nor had I heard about someone else having done it from any of our more senior pilots. (Whenever any new, sometimes tragic, experience happened to some pilot who had gone through an unexpected flying emergency, we other pilots would all listen carefully to the details, and now, each thinking ahead, plan how we might respond if we ever got in a similar jam. Now I was in that new experience and I was nervous!) If you can visualize it, one is making a turn to line up behind the carrier deck and at the very, very end of the turn to be coming straight at this rear deck. I had no idea whether I was lining correctly or was I to the right or left of the carrier's deck.

As I turned more and more toward the carrier's heading into what is euphemistically known to pilots as "the groove" where one is by now easily able to see, even at night, not only the landing signal officer and his signals (either you're OK or slow down, speed up, drop lower, climb higher, turn this way or that) but also see the hooded deck lights. Nothing but darkness and snowflakes, lit up by my wing lights. Always, as one approaches the carrier, even if everything is going correctly, one begins, at first faintly, to smell diesel exhaust of the carrier's engines as well as feel the air turbulence caused by the carrier's island superstructure as, passing through the air, it disturbs it. I began to smell diesel smoke and feel this increased roughness in the air but had no idea whether it meant everything was still OK or was I just about to run into some part of the carrier. Looking alternately ahead into the snow and darkness and back at my instruments as quickly as I could, and feeling the plane increasingly wobble through what seemed to be more and more turbulent air, the diesel smell increasing, I was just about to abort this particular landing attempt, put on full power and go around and try again. Suddenly, as I looked out to the left once more, there, seemingly suspended in darkness and "standing in the air" was the landing signal officer! He was already holding his signal paddles in what is known as the "cut" position, the signal to cut power, drop the nose briefly then pull it up to land hook first. I had not seen the signal given. (He later told me he could hear me coming but could see nothing until my plane suddenly popped out of the snow, close to the right landing position—pure lovely luck!!) At night the landing signal officer wore a fluorescent striped jumpsuit, lit by a Wood's light. Lighted up, the stripes appear greenish, somewhat like a Halloween skeleton. His signaling paddles, one in each hand, were similarly striped. What I first saw was just the fluorescing part of his suit and paddles. Rote training does have its payoff.

One of the "absolute rules" of all carrier landings is, if you don't see the cut given by the landing signal officer—a former carrier pilot himself—don't take it. Add full power, go around and try again. The concern is if you haven't actually seen the cut given you may now have progressed too far up the deck and might land against the cable barrier erected halfway up the deck to prevent you from smashing into the planes parked forward, or even worse, land on the parked planes. We had all seen training movies of all these scenarios. Though I hadn't seen the cut given, flashing through my mind was the realization that, even if so, thinking back to all my previous landings, the landing signal officer wasn't that far beyond his usual position where one does see the cut given. Also, suddenly looming big on my mind was the fact that, by God, I was almost there. And, since there was more wind speed over the deck, I wouldn't be advancing up the deck so fast. What's more, I wasn't at all sure how long the captain would be willing to steam into the wind while I might have to make attempt after attempt to land (I remembered Doty's fate with those damned admirals in charge). All the time, heading into the wind, the carrier was getting more and more out of its central position in the huge task force. To this day I praise the human brain which can compute so many facts so fast—give each one a relative weight—that variable not easily available to a computer—and then include fear in the equation.

I took the cut, dropped to the deck and immediately felt the hook catch. The weather had worsened and the carrier was rolling as well as pitching, so my plane veered off to starboard. So close, and now I'm going over the side, I thought. Just then the landing cable snubbed up tight and my plane came to rest ten feet from the edge of the deck, the top of the propeller spinning just below the muzzle of a 5-inch antiaircraft gun. I then noticed that all the lights, deck and island, were on bright!! The captain had dared to light up the carrier as best he could.

"Red," my plane captain, slithering across almost an inch of wet snow on the deck, jumped up on the wing to help me out saying, "Christ, Cochran, I never thought I'd see you again." I vociferously agreed, but then a strange thing happened. I got such a severe case of the jitters I couldn't undo my seat belt and harness, couldn't release the hook of my one-man life raft attached to my Mae West, couldn't disconnect my radio ear phone plug, let alone climb out of the cockpit. I couldn't even talk coherently, I was so tensed up and jumpy. I couldn't even chew my gum. With

Red's help I finally did get out of the plane and laughing nervously (some might say hysterically), walked jerkily with his help to the pilot's ready room, while the plane handlers secured the plane to the slightly rolling and pitching deck. I thought maybe if I had a cigarette it might calm me down, so Red lit one but I couldn't hold it between my lips or in my shaking hand.

I decided I needed our flight surgeon's help. Art Hill was called and came in to the ready room, saw my condition and took me to his stateroom. There he plied me with "medicinal" liquor for an hour or two, telling me that I was "just so full of nervous adrenaline" I'd have to let my body burn it off. After an hour or so of drinking, laughing, talking and smoking, I finally calmed down and went to bed. I still rarely chew gum.

Cliff Larson

Born 1920 · Waltham, Massachusetts

Second lieutenant Cliff Larson during World War II.

Cliff (Clifton Colby) Larson was born in Waltham, Massachusetts, and graduated from Waltham High School. He enlisted in the United States Army Signal Corps in 1943 and spent ten months training to become a radio technician. He then enlisted with the Army Air Corps Cadet program and was sent to Navigation School in Honda, Texas, becoming a second lieutenant navigator. He was assigned to the crew of a B-29 bomber and was sent to Saipan, where he flew many missions over Japan. After his discharge in 1946, he returned to Waltham where he founded a company, Graphic Microfilm of New England. He retired from Graphic Microfilm in 1985. He married Doris M. Marshall April 18, 1948. They were married 55 years; Doris died in 2003. They had one son, James, and two grandsons. Cliff moved to Brookhaven in January 2007. Cliff was a member and a past president of Woodland Golf Club, Newton, Massachusetts, and a past president of the New England Senior Golfers Association. He was a lifelong member of the First Lutheran Church in Waltham.

Twenty-Five Bombing Missions Over the Japanese Homeland

By Cliff Larson

> "[As a second lieutenant navigator] my next assignment
> was to a crew of a B-29 bomber....I flew 25 missions
> against the Japanese homeland....The crew that dropped
> the atom bomb...was part of our group...."

I WAS BORN in Waltham, Massachusetts, and graduated from Waltham High School. Except for my years of military service, I spent all of my life in the Waltham/Lexington area.

I enlisted in the Army Signal Corps in October 1943. My first ten months in the Army were spent in school learning to be a radio technician. When I finished my Signal Corps schooling, I had the opportunity to enlist in the Army Air Force Cadet program. After seven months of training, I graduated from the Honda, Texas, navigation school as a second lieutenant navigator.

My next assignment was to a crew of a B-29 bomber. Our crew spent three months training in Victorville, California. We were then ordered to report to the 882 Bombardment Squadron stationed on the Pacific islands known as the Marianas.

The B-29 had a flight range up to 31,850 feet at speeds up to 350 miles per hour. Late in 1943, the U.S. Army Air Force had decided to commit the B-29 Superfortress to Asia since its long range was good for over-water flights to China and Japan. The first B-29s began flying from India and China to targets in the Pacific. In June 1944 B-29s, flying from China, struck Yawata, Japan, the first raid on the Japanese homeland since Doolittle's raid in 1942.

B-29 Superfortress. Fourteen B-29s flew the first combat mission in the Pacific in October 1944. The first raid on Tokyo, where Cliff Larson flew, was November 24, 1944, when 111 B-29s bombed Tokyo. (*Wikipedia*)

By the end of 1944, B-29s flew regularly over Japan from the islands of Saipan, Guam and Tinian. There were as many as 1,000 B-29 raids a day bombing Tokyo. Although it was designed to be a high-altitude daytime bomber, the B-29 actually flew more low-altitude nighttime incendiary bombing missions.

After a lengthy flight from California with one stop in Hawaii and a second on an isolated island in the Pacific (the name of this island escapes me), we arrived at the island of Saipan. While stationed on Saipan I flew 25 B-29 bombing missions against the Japanese homeland. The B-29 had a flight range up to 31,850 feet at speeds up to 350 miles per hour. Although it was designed to be a high altitude daytime bomber, it actually flew more low-altitude nighttime incendiary bombing missions.

After the war ended I flew a number of support missions to provide the prisoner-of-war camps with much-needed supplies. The crew that dropped the atom bomb (a B-29, the *Enola Gay*) was part our group, although they flew that mission from the island of Tinian.

I was discharged from active service on December 9, 1944 and shortly thereafter, along with an associate, started a business to provide microfilming services and equipment. This company was called Graphic Microfilm of New England and was located at the corner of Trapelo Road and Route 128 in Massachusetts. I retired as president of the company in 1985.

The *Enola Gay*, B-29 Superfortress landing after delivering the "Little Boy" atomic bomb over Hiroshima, August 1945 in the Mariana Islands. The B-29 Superfortress was the plane in which Cliff Larson flew 25 missions over Japan. (*Wikipedia*)

Richard L. Gardner

Born 1923 · Norwood, Massachusetts

Lieutenant, junior grade Richard L. Gardner, United States Navy, 1943.

Richard Lewis Gardner "Dick" grew up in Massachusetts and attended Wellesley, Massachusetts, public schools, Noble and Greenough School, Massachusetts (1941), Harvard College, BA 1945, U.S. Navy and Harvard Business School, 1948. He was born June 11, 1923, to Louis and Elizabeth Gardner. He served as an ensign in the Navy 1944–1945, then married Pauline "Polly" Gardner in 1948. He was president of General Heat and Appliance Co, vice-president of Trinity Oil Corporation and president of General Chemical Corporation. He and his wife moved to Brookhaven in 2004; he died in 2008,

The Big Picture

By Richard L. Gardner

> "My thought was to find a superior officer who could tell me what had happened and what to do next. There were a number of dead bodies and parts of corpses on the deck as I made my way forward. I met no officer, but when I got to the middle of the ship I discovered what had happened. The entire forward section of the ship was missing. It had been blown to bits."

ONE OF THE skills we were supposed to learn in business school was that of looking at the "Big Picture." Nowadays, in the era when business education has become very academic, they probably call it "strategic planning." Even before I went to B-school, I had the habit of putting life's situations in a broad context. On the occasion I am telling about, this practice of mine could have had very unfortunate consequences. Instead, it resulted in my surviving the war and adding at least 50 years to my life. Incidentally, when people of my age refer to "the war," they mean World War II, also known as "the good war."

I reported for duty aboard the USS *Halligan* (DD584) in the spring of 1944, at Pearl Harbor. I was a complete rookie in spite of the ensign commission bestowed on me in acknowledgment of my successful completion of four courses of naval science in addition to the regular requirements for a Harvard BA. Although those of us in the naval ROTC put in a respectable amount of time on the course, the subject matter we studied had very little to do with the real world of the U.S. Navy in wartime. We learned close-order drill, the details of an obsolescent 4-inch gun and naval nomenclature, so that we wouldn't commit the unpardonable sins of calling the overhead a ceiling or going downstairs instead of below.

"5" guns of a United States Navy destroyer in action.

We were given careful instruction on protocol, being assured that there was nothing wrong with officers receiving all sorts of special treatment and benefits far beyond anything due because of ability or experience, RHIP (Rank Has Its Privileges).

In a sense the *Halligan* was also a rookie, having never faced a gun fired in anger. A Fletcher class 2,100-ton destroyer, she had been built in Boston at the South Boston naval shipyard facility. Her captain was an extremely able Annapolis graduate, Cmdr. Clarence E. Cortner. He was a career officer who had endured the low pay and generally low public esteem of the peacetime Navy so that when the nation found itself forced into war he was ready to fill the breach with his expertise and his leadership ability. The officers and crew were mostly reservists like me who were there for the war only. There were three Annapolis graduates besides the captain, and three mustangs (Navy slang for officers not Academy trained, who had risen on merit from the ranks of enlisted men). Add to this a selection of officers with special training such as the doctor, the supply officer and a radar officer. There was also a cadre of experienced chief petty officers.

With 30-some officers and over 300 enlisted men, the captain had a big task to accomplish getting the *Halligan* ready for combat. My job was complicated by the nature of the mission of destroyers. 'Tin cans," as they were affectionately known, were the all-purpose gofers of the navy. The *Halligan* was assigned to the fleets, and our primary mission was to support amphibious landings as the Army, Navy and Marine Corps went island-hopping toward Japan. This was not the glamorous world of the Fast Carrier Task Forces under Admirals Halsey and Spruance, which received most of the press attention. While they cruised around at flank speed, searching for the Japanese fleet, we performed the more pedestrian tasks of getting the troops on the ground, at which point the infantry took over and did all the heavy lifting. One day we might be using our five S guns to supply fire support for an amphibious landing, and the next day we might use the same guns to shoot down an enemy plane while we were on escort duty for a group of small aircraft carriers. Some other "missions" we ran were rescuing pilots whose planes malfunctioned during takeoff, transporting a deck load of missiles from one ship to another and acting as escort for various groups of vessels such as aircraft carriers, ISTs, LCIs, superannuated battleships, and miscellaneous supply ships.

The first time the *Halligan* encountered the enemy was in October 1944 at Leyte, the first of the Philippine islands to be recaptured after we lost them in 1942. We were part of the fire support group, in effect acting as gunnery for the Army troops who made the actual landing. We were assigned a section of the beach, which we kept under fire from our S guns as we lay about a half mile offshore.

My battle station was on the flying bridge, a sort of platform above and just aft of the main bridge from which the captain ran the ship. I was in direct communication through sound-powered phones with the batteries of 40-mm and 20-mm guns around the ship. My job was to be alert to any enemy threat, either in the air or on water, particularly while our principal armament, the five 5-inch guns, were occupied with shelling the beach. When I spotted such a target I was supposed to give the orders to the guns under my control to fire on the target. ("Commence firing to port," for example.) The view from the flying bridge was breathtaking. There seemed to be hundreds of ships and boats of all sizes, each with an assigned task, all directed to a great master plan. In fact, I had seen the plan itself. It was a thick book approaching the size of a metropolitan phone directory. It listed detailed instructions for every one of these units, all of which I could see spread out before me. I felt as if I had a box seat to history in the making.

There was one notable omission from the picture. Where was the enemy? I could see no sign of any activity on Leyte, an island of peaceful green hills sloping down to the water. Of course, the enemy was there. Else why were we, this powerful armada, shooting tons of explosives, to be followed by thousands of fighting men, at this harmless-appearing island?

Flying low over the green hills a Piper Cub appeared. Of course I now know it probably was not a Piper Cub, but over the years I've always thought of it that way. It was a small single-engine monoplane, with fixed landing gear. It certainly bore no resemblance to any of the silhouettes of Japanese planes that we had studied. As it continued to approach us, various thoughts passed through my mind trying to explain this incongruous phenomenon. Could it be an artillery spotting plane belonging to our side? The general rule was that if an unknown aircraft approached the ship you should shoot first and ask questions later. I should be saying, "Bogey on the port beam; commence firing!" In the event, not a word left my mouth. I have thought many times about my silence on this occasion and the best explanation (excuse?) I can offer is that I was so impressed by the panoramic sweep of the "Big Picture," that I forgot my immediate responsibilities.

Meanwhile, the Piper Cub continued straight over our ship at a very low altitude. As it passed over something dropped from it and fell harmlessly into the water a few hundred feet away from the ship. The plane continued on to seaward and as far as I know was never heard from again. This whole incident lasted only a couple of minutes and seemed afterwards to have consumed only a few seconds. Needless to say, the captain was livid. The enemy had appeared, threatened his ship and not a shot had been fired in our defense. That no harm came to us was pure luck. When confronted with my dereliction, I could offer no explanation or excuse. Although he took no punitive action against me, he did try to correct the obvious chink in our armor. My battle station was changed to a less sensitive place at the after 40-mm battery where all I had to do was protect our rear. The post atop the flying bridge with the view of the Big Picture was assigned to a lieutenant with considerably more combat experience.

Six months and three amphibious landings later the *Halligan* was patrolling the waters just off Naha, the principal city of Okinawa. The landing on the island was supposed to be the last stepping-stone before the invasion of the homeland of Japan itself and was scheduled for April 1, six days hence. Putting myself in the minds of the planners of this operation, I assumed that date was chosen because it was Easter Sunday, and it was hoped the enemy would assume we would never launch an attack on such a holy day. On the other hand it was also April Fools' Day.

The *Halligan* had a new captain who had taken command of the ship about a week earlier. Captain Cortner had moved on, having received a well-deserved promotion making him too senior to command a destroyer. His successor was a young Annapolis graduate who had been executive officer of another destroyer like the *Halligan*.

Morale aboard was good. There was a feeling that our ship had performed her many duties competently at Leyte, Lingayan Gulf and Iwo Jima. Now we were anxious to show our new skipper that he had a first-class ship under his command. Of course he had some big shoes to fill, but we were anxious for his success. Our current job was to guard a number of mine sweepers from attacks from the enemy while they carried out their job of clearing mines from the area.

It was late in the day and we had been at General Quarters for several hours, as was always the case when enemy action was likely. This was also called Condition One, which meant we were all manning battle stations, ready to fight. There had been no sign of the enemy, and before the sun went down the captain ordered what we called Condition One Easy. Battle stations were maintained continuously, but arrangements were made for the crew to take turns eating a cold supper. In my turn I walked forward to the wardroom and had a ham sandwich. There were several other officers there and I made some small talk with them, not knowing that this was the last time I would see them alive.

Back at my station my only view was aft. I could not see the Big Picture, so I did what I was supposed to and concentrated on being alert for any enemy activity that might come into my view. Thus I was unable to see what happened next, but I certainly heard it. There was a series of very loud explosions such as when lightning strikes a tree right next to your house. My phones which I used to communicate with the bridge went dead. I looked around to see what had happened, but I couldn't tell what the trouble was. I told the men at my gun mount to stay put until I could find out what had happened. I disconnected my headphones and walked forward. My thought was to find a superior officer who could tell me what had happened and what to do next. There were a number of dead bodies and parts of corpses on the deck as I made my way forward. I met no officer, but when I got to the middle of the ship I discovered what had happened. The entire forward section of the ship was missing. It had been blown to bits.

I had seen this kind of destruction before, although at considerably more distance. We had been at the same anchorage as an ammunition ship when it was blown up. We were anchored about a mile away and were unharmed, although we were hit by some falling debris. Some ships who were closer sustained damage and casualties. We dispatched a medical party to assist. As far as I know no survivors of the ammunition ship were ever found.

That was almost true of the forward part of the *Halligan*. There was one lucky signalman who was blown off the bridge and landed almost on the torpedo tubes amidships. Those missing in action and presumed dead included all the officers, except an assistant engineering officer and myself, and about 150 enlisted men. The other officer was Ben Jameson, who had been in the Navy even a shorter time than I. His battle station was in the after engine room. He had sustained a broken arm and consequently he was shipped home by another route from Leyte. We still exchange Christmas cards but otherwise we have not kept in touch. As the senior surviving officer it fell to me to give the official order to abandon ship. This was accomplished by stepping from our deck to the deck of one of the two minesweepers that had come alongside to give assistance. I had learned enough naval protocol to know that I had to be the last man off.

The perversity of fate had decreed that I should survive and a large number of my shipmates did not, merely because my failure to react quickly at Leyte caused me to be reassigned to the after part of the ship during General Quarters. Is there a lesson here? The only one I can think of is that it is better to be lucky than to be smart.

Richard Gilbert

Born 1925 · Brookline, Massachusetts

Richard and Joy Gilbert celebrating their 50th wedding anniversary in 1999.

Richard Gilbert graduated from Brookline High School in Massachusetts and enlisted in the Army in 1943. After his discharge he entered Cornell University and graduated with a bachelor of civil engineering degree in 1949. He moved to Pittsburgh, Pennsylvania, in 1949 where he worked with a waterworks engineering firm. He married Joy Stern in 1949 and they raised three children. They moved to Massachusetts in 1955. After the death of his father in 1965, he took over the family real estate business which he expanded and managed until his death in 2009.

What Time Is It?

By Richard Gilbert

> "This was the first and only time I was really scared, for as we replaced the division, artillery fire started to land on our side of the hill. We took shelter in a shell crater. From the valley below us our forces were firing heavy mortars toward the unseen enemy.... On May 22 I became a private first class. I also received the best present of my entire Army career, a new wristwatch."

I ENLISTED IN the U.S. Army in May 1943. I do not remember how I got to Fort Devens, Massachusetts, on June 29, 1943, but it was probably by train. Our barracks were the standard two-story type for this period. We were given a physical examination and an intelligence test, and issued uniforms. My test scores were high enough to qualify me for officer training. We received simple marching instructions, served long hours on kitchen patrol (KP) duty and had hours and days of doing nothing. The food was decent.

On July 9, 1943, a small group from the A-12 program (for soldiers designated to take college courses) shipped out of Fort Devens on the oldest and dirtiest Pullman train imaginable. Our destination was Camp Fannin, Tyler, Texas. We were one of the first groups to arrive at Camp Fannin, which was still being built. We became part of Company C, 76th Battalion, 16th Training Regiment. The weather was extremely hot and we slept without sheets. For cool drinking water, we hung canvas bags on tripods. The water evaporation from the surface helped cool the water in the bag. Our training included close-order drill, making a field pack, firing a Garand rifle without bullets, cleaning a rifle, caring for personal belongings and other basic skills. There were not enough senior

Richard Gilbert, Asahigawa, Hokkaido, Japan, December 1945

personnel available for our Army Specialized Training Program (ASTP), so we started our basic infantry training under the direction of young officers and noncommissioned personnel.

On July 24, the 100 men in our battalion were transferred to Company C, 81st Battalion, in another part of the camp to begin our 17-week training program. Before we started, we were transferred again to Company B, 83rd Battalion, 13th Regiment.

My first wristwatch problem occurred at Camp Fannin. My watchband had broken due to the heat and I had to buy a new watch on my day off. (This was the start of a long and exciting history of ruined watches and wristbands. My watches either died or committed suicide on or off my wrist. To this day, the problem continues; I keep two or three watches on hand to ensure at least one is functional.)

We "first arrivals" repeated the first part of the training cycle for the third time. We had 56 hours of dry runs with our rifles. Fighting World War I all over again, we had physically tough bayonet drills. We also repeated the gas mask drill. Our actual training cycle began on August 16. I found the training films and the series "Why We Fight" to be very well done. We learned to shoot the M-1 Garand rifle, a carbine and the Browning automatic rifle; light a 30-caliber machine gun; throw grenades; use a bayonet; fire at airplanes; use a 60-mm mortar; protect against booby traps; dig fox holes; and fight in a village. I found the close-order drill boring and useless.

On November 11, most of the 3,000 men at Camp Fannin paraded in Tyler, Texas. To get there we arose at 3 A.M. and started marching at 8:30 A.M. It was very cold and it took until 10:30 A.M. to complete the 9-mile march into Tyler. The parade through town was a 4-mile route. The participating soldiers were young, around 20, and we had marched a total of 22 miles by the time we returned to camp.

Another old and dirty train took our group from Camp Fannin to Cincinnati, Ohio, in November 1943. Our quarters were crowded (we lived in a small former classroom) but the dining hall was large, and the food was excellent. My new watch already had a strap problem, so I had to replace it. I replaced the strap, but in January the watch stem detached and I could not set the time.

In February we learned most of the men in the ASTP would be sent into the infantry; many of them were in the Battle of the Bulge. On March 9, 1944, we were sent from Cincinnati to Camp Campbell, Kentucky, and assigned to the Provisional Headquarters Battery, 500th Armored Field Artillery Battalion, 14th Armored Division. I was later transferred out of this division, which subsequently spent 133 days of combat in Europe, suffering 4,298 casualties and a 40 percent personnel turnover.

I was assigned to Company A of the 718th Tank Battalion and in April 1944 was sent to Fort Ord, California. One of the smartest things the Army did was to turn tank and tank destroyer battalions into amphibious tank or tractor battalions. After losing many men in early amphibious assaults, especially at Tarawa where only the first wave or two of soldiers came in on amphibious vehicles, there was a great need for these units in the Pacific theatre. By taking fully organized tank battalions and retraining them, we saved time in organizing units. Motor pools with mechanics were already set up and the men had experience with tread-type vehicles.

At first, our training at Fort Ord seemed like basic training all over. We fired many types of guns and we partied. My company had a reputation for consuming hard liquor and I soon joined in. I had written to my parents asking for a new waterproof watch and on May 9, I received my new watch along with my camera. My camera was stolen when I left it in my Landing Vehicle Tracked (LVT).

We received our LVTs in May. Most of our vehicles were older versions used by previous training battalions; we learned to drive our tractors into and out of the high surf in Monterey Bay. While at Fort Ord, I was assigned to a special project and I was forbidden to write or talk about it. The assignment was to put pontoons on the front and rear of tanks and tank destroyers and a propeller for moving through the water. The pontoons could be blown off on the shore and the vehicle became a full-land vehicle. The system worked well in calm seas but not in real surf, since the pontoons turned the tanks sideways to the beach and into the waves. I don't believe these were ever used in combat.

In July we left by train for a debarkation camp near Seattle, Washington. Bound for Oahu, Hawaii, our troop ship was crowded and men were seasick or nervous. In Hawaii we lived in a tent city and continued practicing with our LVTs. Our tractor had a four-man crew; I was the tailgate man assigned to operate the rear ramp and a 30-caliber machine gun. While I was driving in the open sea, water came pouring into the open front hatch, ruining my wristwatch. We also practiced with infantry troops on board, then landed on a beach off Maui while airplanes bombed a vacant island to simulate combat conditions.

The company left Hawaii September 10, 1944, on an LST with a convoy of LSTs, landing craft infantry, minesweepers with destroyers and escort destroyers as protection. Our LST had two 40-mm antiaircraft guns at the bow and stern and several 20-mm antiaircraft guns on the sides and bridge area. I found the ship well run, although my opinion of the junior naval officers was very poor. They spent most of their time wandering around the ship without instructing or supervising the seamen. As members of the LVT crews we had little to do. We spent our time sunbathing, reading, sleeping, eating and shooting the bull.

Our first stop was Eniwetok in the Marshall Islands where the ships refueled and resupplied. We were not allowed to leave the ship. When we departed, September 26, 1944, we were told we would be invading the island of Yap in the Caroline Islands. The invasion was then cancelled and we headed for Manus Island in the Admiralty Islands

Manus had a huge lagoon where an armada of 518 ships was assembled, including 151 LSTs. Troops from the 7th Infantry Division came on board; the ships were crowded and many slept on the decks. We departed for Leyte on October 11.

The morning of October 20, at Leyte, the 7th Division infantry began loading the LVTs at 8:00 A.M. We could see Navy ships delivering the shore bombardment. Our tractors left the LST and we circled while lining up for departure to the beach. The first assault was comprised of amphibious tanks; we followed carrying soldiers. Our forces were bombarding the beach while airplanes from the carriers strafed and bombed the area. The Japanese army on our section of beach did not react. After drifting most of the day along the coast we were ordered to land on our beach and move inland about 100 yards to spend the night. The next day we walked along the beach to the main unloading area where we helped unload or guard supplies. Sometimes enemy planes tried to bomb the operation and there was a successful bomb attack on the area at night.

The weather was always very warm and the vast amounts of rain made it difficult to live, fight and build roads and airfields. We used our LVTs to haul supplies along the beach and ferry supplies across rivers. November 19 I wrote my parents to ask for a new wristwatch.

On the evening of November 26, 1944, I was on guard duty when an airplane landed north of our area. The Japanese had sent suicide squads to intercept the planes on the ground and destroy the supplies they were carrying. I volunteered to join a patrol sent out to look for these suicide squads. We were sitting near a tree when we heard rifle shots; the fellow on my right was wounded. I bandaged his shoulder before noticing my right temple was cut and bleeding; the bullet that wounded the soldier had grazed me. I was kept in the hospital because I also had dysentery. I was awarded a Purple Heart for my "Band-Aid" wound, giving me a reduction on my home real estate taxes every year.

I was then assigned to the 302nd Infantry Division of the 77th Calvary Division. We were sent to join the company at Villaba. After two months with the 77th Infantry Division I was assigned to Company A of the 302nd Combat Engineers. They needed bulldozer and grader drivers, so I was assigned to them even though I had no experience. My "bulldozer" turned out to be a hand shovel. I was then assigned to Company A of the 305th Regimental Combat

Team based on the 305th Infantry Regiment. This was my eighth and last outfit.

Our division was the first to enter the Okinawa campaign; we landed on March 26, 1945. We watched destroyers and airplanes bombard the town where we landed until I was told to enter the town to find our command post. Throughout the day we watched the infantry clear caves and tombs in the hills around our valley, often using flamethrowers.

On April 16 we arrived at Ie Shima, a small island in the Ryukyu Islands within sight of Okinawa. During the night we were part of a defense perimeter; we dug three foxholes and took turns guarding; while two men slept, the third stood guard. I was a very sound sleeper and while I slept, a suicide attack occurred about a 100 yards from my position. I never heard it. The Japanese soldiers tied satchel charges to their backs, then ran toward our line and blew themselves up trying to kill our troops. When I woke in the morning, there were body parts from these attacks only a short distance from my foxhole. The famous war correspondent Ernie Pyle, was in our area briefly that morning but was killed a day later by a Japanese sniper.

One of my jobs was to help remove traps along the invasion route. The Japanese had put airplane bombs in pits in the ground with their noses pointed up. On a square of wood over the bomb was a large rock tied to a wire which ran to a fixed location. A person or vehicle would move the wire, dropping the rock on the nose of the bomb. We used wire cutters to cut the trip wires near the bombs. We also moved small handheld bomb-shaped missiles to a stockpile for later disposal. Fellow engineers and the infantry moved to the far side of the road as we removed these explosives.

April 20 was my most climactic day. On our way to a pinnacle peak, we learned the bomb disposal squad had all been killed when their truck, loaded with removed bombs, set off a mine in the road. One of our men, three fellows ahead of me, was shot through his helmet. We climbed through narrow streets to join our infantry where there was a wounded soldier. The Japanese were rolling grenades down the hill toward us; one grenade went off near where we were putting the wounded soldier on a stretcher. Luckily, it landed in a small depression so all the force went straight up and none of us were hurt. We carried the wounded soldier over a mile down the hill to an aid station.

The next day we reached the top of the pinnacle and an American flag was put up on the highest point of the island. We left the island on April 28 after destroying more mines and bombs. We then returned to Okinawa. After a few days in a quiet area near the tombs of Okinawa our division relieved the 96th Division on the escarpment. This was the ridge where the first Japanese resistance started, not the beaches nor the airfield. This was the first and only time I was really scared, for as we replaced the division, artillery fire started to land on our side of the hill. We took shelter in a shell crater. From the valley below us our forces were firing heavy mortars toward the unseen enemy.

Our job was to keep the roads open and bring supplies to the front. Every morning we boarded a truck taking us to our roadwork not far behind the front lines. From May 8 to June 1, heavy rains made our roads a sea of mud. We brought in coral gravel and hand-dug drainage ditches to drain the roads. Bulldozers often had to pull trucks over the worst parts of the road.

One day, two of us visited the battlefield. The area looked like the western front of World War I without the barbed wire: no trees, shell holes everywhere. There was an abandoned Japanese anti-tank gun and many disabled U.S. tanks. Near the front line, a U.S. plane fired rockets at our area. We hit the ground; I looked down a well near me and saw a dead American soldier. As we returned, a sniper fired at us as we crossed between hills.

On May 22 I became a private first class. I also received the best present of my entire Army career, a new wristwatch.

We continued to improve the roads and build bridges. We left Okinawa on June 25 for Cebu to prepare for the invasion of Japan. We arrived at the division campsite at Dano, Cebu, on July 5, 1945. We set up Army tents and cots, helped build substantial mess halls and built roads and bridges. There were still Japanese soldiers encamped north of us.

After the first atomic bomb was detonated at Hiroshima on August 6, many of us felt the war would soon be over. Our division had a very low-key celebration when V-J Day was announced August 14, 1945. We were thankful that we would not have to fight the Japanese on their home islands, especially after Okinawa. A week before we left Cebu, I was made assistant company personnel clerk. Because I could type, I no longer had to perform manual labor. On September 20 we headed to the northern island of Japan, Hokkaido, which our division was to occupy. When we were issued cold-weather gear it was obvious someone had planned a winter campaign. We arrived on October 5, 1945, and found the area barely affected by the war; the harbor and trains were in good condition.

We were assigned to a former Japanese camp where the buildings were wood with double walls filled with sawdust, double windows for insulation and coal stoves for heat. We soon had hot showers and cozy living quarters. The nights grew cooler and by late November it seemed to snow constantly. I went skiing. On November 10, my promotion to technician grade V came through and I had taken the position of company clerk, replacing the clerk who had left. On December 24 a fast-burning fire destroyed the barracks next to mine, killing two soldiers. The buildings were comfortable but we knew they were firetraps. Anyone who wanted a Japanese rifle was given one; Japanese sabers were given to the few remaining combat veterans in the outfit.

I left Japan January 8, 1946, and arrived in San Diego, California, January 24. We traveled by troop train to Fort Devens, Massachusetts, where my parents picked me up after I was discharged on February 4, 1946.

Bob Rediker

Born 1924 · Brooklyn, New York

Bob Rediker, homeward bound from the Phillipines.

Robert H. Rediker was born in Brooklyn, New York, in 1924 to Estelle and Moe Rediker. Until he was 17 he lived alternately in New York and Havana, Cuba. The last five years were in Cuba, so he entered the Massachusetts Institute of Technology (MIT) as a foreign student and received his BS in electrical engineering and a PhD in physics from MIT in 1947 and 1950 respectively. His three-year "vacation" in the Army included duty in the Philippines, where his Spanish came in handy. His last assignment for the Army Signal Corps was as a technical sergeant at radio station WLVI in Batangas, Luzon. He joined the MIT Lincoln Laboratory in 1951 where he worked on semiconductor devices. He was professor of electrical engineering at MIT from 1966 to 1976, adjunct professor from 1976 to 1982, senior research scientist from 1982 to 1991 and research scientist from 1991 to 2000. From 1991 to 2000 he had a joint appointment to MIT in the Electrical Engineering and Computer Science departments and staff at Lincoln Laboratory. His work at MIT centered on optoelectronic semiconductor devices, and at Lincoln Laboratory his research focused on guided-wave optoelectronic devices. He retired in 1991. That year he joined Cynosure, Inc., as senior vice-president and head of Advanced Research and Development, where he worked on laser devices for the medical field. He retired in 2000. He married Barbara Zenn and has two sons, five grandchildren and three great-grandchildren.

Adventures in Communications

By Bob Rediker

"The war ended. I keep one souvenir on the top of my dresser. It is a small photograph of a cemetery in Batangas. On August 31, 1945, I wrote on the back of this photo, 'They won the war. It's is for us to win the peace.'"

I ENLISTED IN the Army while at Massachusetts Institute of Technology (MIT) and was called to active duty at the end of my sophomore year. My basic training was at Camp Hood, Waco, Texas. Two things I remember above all: First I was not and still am not very physically adept and needed "illegal" help from the fellow soldiers to surmount the obstacle course. Second I was one of the only soldiers to complete the ten-mile forced march in the Texas summer heat. I had been brought up in Havana, Cuba, and was very used to the heat. After basic training, I and a number of fellow students from MIT were sent to ASTP (Army Specialized Training Program) at Texas Tech in Lubbock, Texas. For two semesters at Texas Tech I was in the Electrical Engineering Department just as I had been at MIT. There were advantages of undergraduate education at Texas Tech over MIT: you had the same professor for lecture, recitation and laboratory; you got to know him and he got to know you. (When I returned to MIT after the war Professor Gray from Texas was a visiting professor and I used him as a reference for graduate school.)

After ASTP, a smaller group of us from MIT were assigned to the Signal Corps at Camp Crowder, Joplin, Missouri. There we learned about the electronic and electrical equipment in the Army and I earned my stripes (three) as a radio repairman. From there I was to be sent overseas, but it was discovered I had never had a physical, for the Army or before. They gave me a physical, which I passed, and I was assigned to the 4025th Signal Service battalion and went to San Francisco to board a Navy troopship.

The ship sailed a zigzag course to Hollandia, New Guinea, where we waited for over a week to join a convoy to Leyte in the Philippines. (This long wait earned me a battle star for the New Guinea campaign and five points toward an earlier discharge.) In Leyte, our outfit was assigned to base communications. Along the shore from the town of Tacloban, Leyte, Navy personnel were housed in Quonset huts; the Air Corps were in tents with wooden floors, the operational air base and the Army in pup tents. We slept on the ground. Next to us was a wooden sign that read "General MacArthur Returned Here."

Later the sign mysteriously disappeared and was replaced with a concrete sign. We foraged along the coast for the flotsam from ships sunk in the naval battle like cans of peaches and Coke syrup. I vividly recall a reveille when our CO advised us he was unhappy about the firing of rifles when soldiers tinkled in the ocean and made noise. He reminded us the front was just 15 miles inland and the infantry could use those who liked to fire rifles. We stopped firing rifles, worried we could be overrun by the entire Japanese army without a shot being fired!

My outfit then shipped out to Manila. We were the first ship to enter Manila Bay after it was secured. MacArthur, who was an excellent general in spite of his ego, had sent in the first cavalry (tanks) through the infantry lines to secure the Santo Tomas internment camp. My father was in the import business and knew a family in the Philippines who had been interned. I went to visit them, and the first question they asked me was why the Lucky Strike package was no longer green. They told me the Japanese commander had told them they would be liquidated before the American infantry arrived. I visited them many times and invited their son, who was my age, to my camp. I remember him in the chow line having doubles of the bully beef which I avoided and hated the smell of. I also gave him a set of my clothing. We were in a combat zone and clothing accountability was minimal. An interesting observation at this time was the order in which the ancillary support groups arrived. First the Salvation Army, next the USO (we saw Joe E. Brown in *Oklahoma* while sitting on a hillside), then the WACs and last the Red Cross.

Our group was given the assignment of setting up and running the communications for a base in Batangas, about 60 miles north of Manila. While up there, we worked about ten hours a day helping others setting up or repairing electronic equipment on our own. We arrived in Batangas ahead of the infantry and were joyously greeted by the civilian population, who fed us fried chicken and other foods. This welcome lasted about three weeks until the Filipinos seemed to decide we were just another occupation force. We were to set up three sites for radio communication with Manila: a transmitter site, a receiver site and a central site downtown where the telegraph operators were. We succeeded. Luckily, I had in my backpack a copy of the technical book *Radio Engineering* by Terman. When the officers wanted to do something I knew was wrong, I politely asked them to read the appropriate pages in this bible.

We always listened to Tokyo Rose, who read the baseball scores first. One time we moved our camp under the cover of darkness. The next morning Tokyo Rose broadcast a welcome to the 4025th in your new camp at ------. Another day she broadcast that a horrible new weapon was to be unleashed. We all put our gas masks at the ready. The new weapon was the kamikaze bombers. Batangas was the evacuation center for the invasion of Japan. As far as you could see in every direction from the road, there were hospital tents.

The Philippine landowners spoke Spanish as well as their native tongue. With my Cuban background, I became friendly with a nearby landowner. With an election coming up, he asked me for which candidate should he instruct his peasants to vote. The Philippines are now one of the poorest countries in the region. They have very large families and their main export is their young women and

American Army Cemetery, Batangas, Luzon, Philippine Islands. Robert Rediker wrote on the back 8/31/45: "They won the war. It's for us to win the peace." He has kept this framed photo with him to view ever since.

men to be servants throughout Asia and Europe. America's nation-building is flawed.

The war ended. I keep one souvenir on the top of my dresser. It is a small photograph of the Army cemetery in Batangas. On August 31, 1945, I wrote on the back of this photo, "They won the war. It's for us to win the peace." Now that the war was over, I wrote in detail the wiring diagram for our site for my replacement. In fact, our radio sites were closed. WLVI Batangas was no more. I was sent for a short period to a microwave site. The regulations required that one telephone channel be monitored. The 4025th controlled the switchboard and that was the channel for the conversations between the hospital staff still in Batangas and those on leave in Manila. It was dubbed the "sex channel."

I became the NCO in charge of receiving the Signal Corps equipment from outfits returning to the U.S. We had a huge warehouse with a conveyor belt running from the receiving area to the other end of the warehouse. I remember one lieutenant who, seeing our system of putting each item on the conveyor belt as it came in, told us that he was in a rush and would dump everything on the ground, thus fouling up our system of unloading equipment to the proper place in the warehouse. He dumped everything and we started to count the items before signing off on the delivery. He went to see the captain in charge of the warehouse. I advised the captain that the inspector general had visited last week and emphasized accountability, but if he would give me a direct order I would sign off on the delivery. He didn't, and we continued counting and putting the items on the conveyor belt. Our contingent of college students were regularly called "college f....rs."

It then was my turn to return to the United States on a very slow Liberty cargo ship. When I disembarked in San Francisco my skin disease called jungle rot had miraculously disappeared. I was discharged from the Army on Friday, February 13, 1946. When they offered to allow me to stay on and not leave on this "lucky" day, I turned down the offer. I returned to MIT, where my Cuban friends, who had rejected American citizenship and serving in the Army, were graduate students and laughed at me for being a junior. I had the last laugh because in 1960, when Castro came to power, these were the only Cubans who could not come to the United States.

Robert Coquillette

Born 1918 · Fort Wayne, Indiana

Robert Coquillette in residence at Brookhaven

Robert Coquillette was born October 31, 1918, in Fort Wayne, Indiana. He graduated from Flint Central High School in Flint, Michigan, and was awarded a Conant Fellowship to Harvard College. He received his B.S. degree magna cum laude in chemistry in 1939. He was commissioned in the U.S. Navy in 1944 and became the navigation officer on the USS *Hanson* DD832, a destroyer serving as part of the occupation force in Japan. After he left the Navy he joined the Dewey & Almy Chemical Company. When the company became part of W. R. Grace in 1955 he was appointed general manager of the Grace Overseas Chemical Division with operations in Europe, South American, Australia, New Zealand and Japan. In 1962, he became president of the Ohio Rubber Co. Division of the Eagle-Picher Company of which he was a vice president and director. He rejoined Grace in 1965 in New York City as vice president of the Corporate Administration Group. He held various positions at Grace including corporate executive vice president and sector executive of Grace's food-service businesses. From 1981 until his retirement in 1983, he was a member of Grace's Corporate Executive Office and of the Executive Committee. Following retirement, the Coquillettes resided in Mattapoisett, Massachusetts, where he was a trustee of the Old Dartmouth Historical Society, the Mattapoisett Historical Society, the Mattapoisett Land Trust and the Tri-County Music Association. He was a member of the American Chemical Society, the Harvard Club of New York City,

★ *Biography continued on page 337*

From Pearl Harbor to Tokyo Bay

By Robert Coquillette

"The battleship *Missouri* was still in Tokyo Bay when we arrived at the Yokosuka naval base. The city itself, even though only demolition and fire bombs had been used on it, was flattened so it looked like the Newark, New Jersey, dump....Later when we put into Nagasaki, I was struck that the nuclear bomb damage did not look really any different from other bombed areas."

WHEN THE PEARL Harbor attack took place in 1941 I was working for Procter & Gamble as supervisor of the process division at its Port Ivory plant on Staten Island. This was the second largest plant after Ivorydale in Cincinnati where I had started when I graduated from Harvard in 1939. The plant was put on a seven-day schedule right away as we were shipping product to the U.K. and to Russia to support their war effort. The idea was to get as much glycerin as possible for use in the manufacture of nitroglycerine, which is a key ingredient in flashless powder. Glycerin 193 is a byproduct of soap making and we were shipping it hot from the stills. This was deemed vital to the war effort and I was given a draft classification as "essential." An event early in 1942 will give an idea of the wartime mentality. A rumor spread that the Nazis were coming to bomb the big Bayway refinery near our plant. Since we would be a likely "near miss," the word came down from headquarters that all office personnel and all women in the plant were to go home, but "men in production are to stay and keep the factory running." Of course there was no air attack.

By early 1944 we were ahead of demand and I had over one million pounds of glycerin in storage in the tank field waiting for orders, so I decided I should go into the service and I chose the

Navy. I came to Boston and got a direct commission as an ensign. My wife came home to live and to take care of our first child, who was born in May. I got my orders to report to Fort Schuyler in the Bronx for indoctrination. The photo taken the day I left shows me resplendent in the new uniform with a line of diapers drying in the background!

After indoctrination, I was assigned to several training schools including subchaser training school in Miami and visual fighter director school in Brigantine, New Jersey. I was finally put in the destroyer officer pool in Norfolk, from which I was ordered to Boston as part of the complement of a new long-hull 2200 destroyer: Gearing class, the *Hanson* (DD832), built by Bath Iron Works, Bath, Maine.

After commissioning and our first shakedown cruise to Guantanamo, we were ordered back to Boston for conversion to a picket ship for antikamikaze duty. I was billeted as asst. communications officer and asst. navigator. On the first trip to Guantanamo when star sights were taken the first night, the executive officer, an An-

The USS *Hanson* DD/DR832 was a Gearing class
destroyer in the United States Navy. The ship was built
by Bath Iron Works, Bath, Maine, and commissioned
May 11, 1946. (*Wikipedia*)

napolis graduate and regular Navy, had so much trouble getting the sights and working out our position that he said to me, "Coquillette, from now on, you are the navigator."

We returned to Charlestown navy yard in Boston for conversion and then back to Guantanamo for more training. We did a couple of convoy missions and then sailed for Pearl Harbor via the Panama Canal and managed to join up with the rest of our squadron of twelve destroyers assembled at Pearl. We left for Tokyo Bay as the war ended in 1945.

During the crossing, the squadron ran into a typhoon that lasted for three days at the end of which my position report showed we had made good about 343 miles! This class of destroyer is 400 feet long and has a crew of 22 officers and about 200 enlisted men. They are not comfortable. In a station from the bridge we would look down to where the bow was and then look up to the crest of the oncoming wave. The bow would knife into the wave and rise up like an elevator until about five feet of the bow was hanging over. It would then plunge down the other side of the wave to repeat the performance. The drop of the bow was so sudden that to get any sleep at all one had to tie oneself down in the bunk; otherwise one would be left hanging in the air to come down with a terrible thump as the ship plunged over the wave. The force of the waves crushed in several of the shields around the antiaircraft guns as though they were paper. The critical roll angle on this class of destroyers is 65 degrees. If the roll exceeds that figure, the ship just keeps on going. We had a roll of 63 degrees during the storm. Earlier in the war several destroyers were lost in a typhoon.

The battleship *Missouri* was still in Tokyo Bay when we arrived at the Yokosuka naval base. The city itself, even though only demolition and fire bombs had been used on it, was flattened so it looked like the Newark, New Jersey, dump. Later when we put into Nagasaki, I was struck that the nuclear bomb damage did not look really any different from other bombed areas. We were assigned to do demilitarization in the south island, Kyushu, and took the destroyer around to Sasebo harbor, which was a major Japanese naval base. The big danger was mines that had not been swept, but we also had only Japanese charts to go by and the buoys and other aids for navigation were mostly missing. Two events of that period struck me. Nagasaki had been designated a shore leave port so everyone could see the damage from the nuclear bomb. We went in there and the crew went ashore with no restrictions. No one was apparently worried about residual radiation. As in Yokosuka, the residual population was sheltered in makeshift living spaces but were on the streets and walking around. Where the blast had been screened by hills, buildings were still standing. We went to Shimonoski, which stands at the entrance to the inland sea. Since the area had not been swept for mines at all we stopped short at a port down the coast and traveled in by jeep.

When we arrived our interpreter said, "Now I know why you won the war. You all are crazy." He was referring to the way one of our officers drove the jeep at high speed along roads which were meant for carts and people. Even at this remote place the military government people were ahead of us and had taken control of the local government so everything was peaceful. Also the cultural officers were there seeing that no damage was done to shrines and other similar cultural objects important to the people. We actually stayed in a nice country inn although it was cold! Fuel of any kind was hard to come by. In Kagoshima the officers club was called "the 40 and below club" because of the prevailing temperature in that winter. The contrast of the preparation for postwar occupation in Japan as compared to that with Iraq is really shocking. In Sasebo we never thought of any danger from the civilian population and were free to walk around the town as we wished. It was considered wise to wear sidearms, but I never heard of them being used.

We boarded all kinds of vessels to see that all guns had been destroyed and that only enough navigation equipment was on board for local trips. We threw any contraband overboard. Most of the vessels were in bad shape as a result of the war. Sasebo harbor was also a major port for repatriation of citizens and military from Korea and large numbers were being brought back.

One last story has to do with a typhus scare as a result of exposure to the returnees. Our doctor declared we should all have typhus shots and gave them to us. About three days later, we got orders from the fleet command that anyone who hadn't had a typhus shot in the last 24 hours was to have one. We all dutifully lined up for the second shot! About a week later comes an order from Pearl Harbor, anyone who has not had a typhus shot in the last 24 hours....You guessed it, we all lined up for our shots again. At least I never got typhus.

My points were up in April after we were back in Tokyo Bay. Since I was running the ship's office, I had had my orders to go back to the States typed up and had put them with other orders for the captain to sign about a week before I was due to leave the ship. When I came in to say goodbye to the captain on the appropriate day, he said, "You can't go. We will not have enough qualified officers to get the ship underway." I said, "You have signed my orders, Captain, and it's now the Navy's problem to fill the complement." I got back to Pearl Harbor and then got transport to San Diego on a jeep carrier. I was discharged in San Diego in May of 1946.

★ *Biography continued from page 332*

the New York Yacht Club, the Mattapoisett Yacht Club, the Mattapoisett Casino and the Chemical Management & Resources Association, of which he was recipient of the 1977 Award for Executive Excellence. He was a member of the Permanent Class Committee of the Harvard College Class of 1939. Mr. Coquillette was married for 66 years to Dagmar Bistrup. The couple had two sons, seven grandchildren and ten great-grandchildren.

Benjamin T. Wright

Born 1922 · Berkley, California

Ben Wright and his late wife Mary Louise taken during the 1994 Olympic Winter Games in Hamar, Norway. Mary Louise died before Ben moved to Brookhaven, but this picture reflects their long-time partnership in skating. Mary Louise was a skating world judge for many years.

Ben Tappan Wright was born in 1922 to Prof. Austin Tappan Wright and Margaret Garrad Stone. He graduated from Governor Dummer Academy, earned a BS from Harvard University and a JD from Boston University. He married Mary Louise Premer. He served in the U.S. Army from 1940 to 1965, retiring as a lieutenant colonel AUS. From 1951 to 1987 he worked at Badger Company, Inc. retiring as a senior vice president and general counsel. He is a past president (1973–1976) of the United States Figure Skating Association and previously served as vice president (1970–1973) and secretary (1966–1969) for that organization. He was chairman of the ISU Figure Skating Technical Committee (1988–1992); World Championship Referee in Figure Skating (1970–1993); National Referee and Judge in Figure Skating (1970–present). He is an honorary member of the International Skating Union, the United States Figure Skating Association and the Skating Club of Boston and a member of the World Figure Skating Hall of Fame.

A Military Tourist in the Pacific: 1940–1965

By Benjamin T. Wright

> "I am proud to have been a part of it [the 136th Field Division Battalion of the 37th Infantry 'Buckeye' division formerly of the Ohio National Guard]. The veteran division had five Medal of Honor winners among its troops."

MY MILITARY CAREER started in the fall of 1940 when I arrived at Harvard as a freshman in the Class of 1944 and signed up for the Army ROTC unit, which was for the field artillery in those days.

With the entry of the United States into World War II in 1941, the active ROTC cadets were all enlisted as privates in the Enlisted Reserve Corps (ERC) in 1942. Because we were already enlisted, we were never included in the draft.

Being in the ROTC resulted in our remaining in college until graduation a year early in May of 1943. We had regular classrooms for the class work and down on Soldiers Field there were stables, as we had horses to pull the guns we were issued (French 75s from World War I). We used to ride the horses around the perimeter of the field to exercise them. Needless to say, we never fired the guns.

One highlight of our ROTC activity was that all the units then at Harvard in the fall of 1942 were called upon to march into Harvard Stadium before the Army–Harvard football game of that year (Harvard lost the game 0–14), in replacement of the West Point Corps of Cadets, which due to the war did not come that year.

I was able to graduate in 1943 due to the addition of a full semester in the summer of 1942, regular classes for the first time, which, incidentally, included the ladies from Radcliffe College in the regular classes for the first time. We attended commencement in uniform, following which I went into the basement of University Hall to find my diploma in a big series of cardboard boxes in the basement. My class had no class book, but only a listing in the back of the book for the Class of 1943.

Two weeks later, I reported to Fort Devens in Ayer, Massachusetts, where, to my surprise, one of the NCOs processing my entry to active duty happened to be Richard L. Hapgood, Harvard Class of 1927, who had been the manager of the Skating Club of Boston until his enlistment. Dick was one of my mentors in skating and turned me in the direction of becoming a judge instead of a competitor, telling me that I "would never make it as a skater, so go take down numbers." I became a skating judge in 1942 and still am today.

The graduating seniors were scheduled to go to the Officer Candidate School (OCS) at Fort Sill, Oklahoma, our "reward" for three years of work. It should be noted, however, that we received course credit toward our degrees for our ROTC courses, which is not true today.

Had we graduated a year earlier, in 1942, we would have gone to the ROTC summer camp Fort Ethan Allen in Colchester, Vermont, and been subsequently commissioned second lieutenants in the field artillery following its completion. But that camp was cancelled in 1943, so all we got was a ticket to OCS instead.

We had to wait for a class to open at Fort Sill, so the group of about 50 of us were shipped off to a camp in Putnam, Connecticut, to a military police battalion (the 709th), where we were armed with shotguns and drilled while we waited for the trip to Fort Sill. The trip itself was by troop train and there was a little misbehavior on the trip, so when we got to the OCS we were presented to the commanding colonel and informed that we were restricted to quarters for one month. The Princeton ROTC unit was in Class No. 86, we (Harvard) were in Class No. 88 and the Yale unit was in Class No. 89. Since one had to be an NCO to attend OCS, we were all promoted to corporal upon arrival at Fort Sill.

During our stay at Fort Sill, a touch football game was organized between the Harvard and Yale cadets. Somehow, our team had "acquired" a Texas A&M cadet (the Texas A&M cadets were in Class No. 84), who had been what would be a wide receiver today. We eked out a win, which got written up at home at Harvard as the only athletic contest between Harvard and Yale that year!

In the end, the group all got through OCS, received their gold bars as second lieutenants in the field artillery and went their separate ways. I had trouble with gunnery and was saved by my college roommate Bill Slichter and by our instructor, Bob Hackford, who happened to be a Harvard ROTC graduate from the class of 1943. Bill had been our leader and the cadet colonel in Cambridge.

I was assigned after graduation from Fort Sill in November 1943 to go to Fort Bragg in Fayetteville, North Carolina, to the Field Artillery Replacement Training Center (FARTC), known, of course, as the "Fart" Center. There we were often out in the field in the area of Southern Pines, which is near Pinehurst, a famous golf resort.

After a six-month period of training in relative peace and quiet at Fort Bragg in the middle of the war, I was finally sent to Camp Gruber, near Muskogee, Oklahoma, as a replacement officer to Battery B of the 542nd Field Artillery Battalion of the 42nd "Rainbow" Division of the New York National Guard, with which I fully expected to ultimately head for Europe. The 542nd was a "light" artillery battalion with 105-mm howitzers.

However, I was not there for long, as I was soon sent back to Fort Sill to attend the Officers Communication Course. I was later pulled out of the school and returned to the 542nd in anticipation of deployment, but this did not happen, and I then transferred to the 534th Field Artillery Battalion at Gruber, which was a "heavy" artillery unit with 8-inch guns, which were then new in the Army.

As I look back on it, I regret that I did not stay with the 534th, as the 8-inch howitzer was one of the finest pieces of ordinance ever created, with a high degree of accuracy and enormous fire power with a 200-pound shell. You could drop it in a barrel at 25 miles!

But it was not to be. I was returned to Fort Sill to finish the Communications course. From there it was on to Fort Ord, California, as a casual, to wait for transportation to the Pacific. After waiting almost a month, I was finally off in March 1945 to San Francisco and a military transport for a 31-day trip to Manila, in the Philippines, with stops in Finschhaven and Hollandia, New Guinea along the way.

After arrival in May 1945 I was soon sent from the replacement depot in Paranaque outside Manila up to Balete Pass, the "entrance" to the Cagayan Valley in the northern island of Luzon to join the Headquarters Battery of the 136th Field Artillery Battalion of the 37th Infantry "Buckeye" Division, formerly of the Ohio National Guard and originally from Toledo, to serve as an assistant communications officer (ACO).

The division, which had been in the Pacific since 1942, was part of the Fourteenth Corps of the Sixth Army. Its commanding general, Robert Beightler, had been in command since the beginning of its overseas deployment. It was truly a veteran outfit, with combat experience in Bougainville and New Georgia before Luzon in the Philipines, where it had landed at Lingayen Gulf early in 1945. I am proud to have been a part of it, even if it was just at the end of the war in the Pacific. The division already had five Medal of Honor winners among its troops.

The mission of the division, which had been in the Pacific since 1942, was to clear the Cagayan Valley in northern Luzon of the remaining military forces of the Japanese Imperial Army, which had retreated into the valley following the recapture of Manila. It was a swift and fast-moving campaign of almost 300 miles, with considerable resistance still being encountered from the Japanese armed forces. It took two months for the division to finally reach Aparri, the small city and port at the "top" of Luzon.

In September 1945, I received my first promotion, to first lieutenant. With the campaign ending I was transferred to the position of personnel officer, in which I served until I was transferred out of the division. As the division prepared to return home, I was sent to the 465th Field Artillery Battalion at a camp near San Marcelino, which is north of Bataan and not far from the naval base at Subic Bay.

Several more transfers occurred as units were sent home after the war in the Pacific ended in the summer of 1945, including the 145th AAA Operations Detachment and the 70th AAA Group.

Finally, in July 1946, my turn came to return home. After returning to the replacement depot in Paranaque, where I ran into my college roommate and fellow ROTC graduate Bill Slichter, I was sent to Hawaii to be relieved from active duty. I chose Hawaii because my older brother, Lieutenant Commander William Wright of the U.S. Navy, was stationed there at the time and I was able to choose that location accordingly.

It was a long trip across the Pacific, this time by air in military air transports, four-engine C-54s with bucket seats (no jets then). First we flew eight hours to Guam, where we had to wait a week due to the atom bomb tests at Bikini Atoll. Then, it was another eight hours to Kwajalein Atoll; another eight hours on to Johnston Island; and finally four hours to Hickam Field on Oahu.

On Oahu, I was processed out of active duty at Schofield Barracks and at the same time assigned to the U.S. Army Reserve (USAR), in which I would remain until 1965. I spent my terminal leave of 50 days with my brother and his family at Aiea Heights in Honolulu overlooking Pearl Harbor.

In the fall of 1946, I finally returned to Boston. I had arranged my military orders for military transport from Hawaii to Boston, traveling in a Constellation across the United States, returning to my home in Cambridge, Massachusetts. Not long after my return, I began to suffer from malaria, apparently acquired in the Philippines, which became active after the artificial quinine (Atabrine) we all took in the Pacific theater wore off. Fortunately, a sister, who lived in New York City, looked after me while the disease ran its course, but the effect was that my entry into the job market or to graduate school was delayed until 1947.

By 1948 I was assigned to my first Army Reserve unit, the 420th Field Artillery Group, which trained at the old South Boston Army Base (now Black Falcon Terminal), with 15-day tours of duty each summer at a variety of locations, including Camp (later Fort) Drum, New York.

By 1950, the 420th had been converted into the 302nd Logistical Command. When the Korean War started in 1950 there was the real possibility of the 302nd being activated to serve in South Korea as the port command at Pusan, but another unit from New Jersey was designated instead. While with the 302nd I was also promoted to captain in 1952. During my tour of duty in the 302nd I went to Fort Drum five straight years!

In 1955, I was transferred out of the Logistical Command to a small "mobilization designation" unit of just 14 officers, called the Boston Team for National Postal and Travelers Censorship (NPTC). The team was part of a joint program with the U.S. Air Force for the operation of postal and travelers censorship in wartime. I remained there until my retirement in 1965. I became a major in 1958 and a lieutenant colonel in 1962.

The required 15 days of active duty for training for the NPTC, as it was called, was held alternatively at Army posts and Air Force bases, starting in 1956 with Kessler Air Force Base in Biloxi, Mississippi; followed by Fort Sheridan, Illinois; Wright-Patterson Air Force Base, Ohio; Fort Lee, Virginia; Lowry Air Force Base, Colorado; Fort Meade, Maryland; Maxwell Air Force Base, Alabama; and Fort Devens, Massachusetts. It was a unique opportunity to be at some of the oldest and most famous military bases in the country.

Finally, in 1965, after 20-plus years in the Army Reserve and 25 years of service overall, it was time to retire. I was over age for my grade as a lieutenant colonel. I was not a "hero," holding no combat decorations, having been in actual combat only for a few months in the Philippines. However, I do hold a collection of service medals, including the American Campaign Medal, Asia Pacific Campaign Medal with battle star, Philippine Liberation medal with battle star, Philippine Distinguished Unit Citation, Philippine Independence Medal (for being in the islands on July 1, 1946!), World War II Victory Medal and Armed Forces Reserve Medal with hourglass device for a second ten years of service.

I am proud to have served in the military for as long as I did, and I am especially grateful for the benefits that I have received, not only retirement (after age 60), but also health care benefits in the form of TRICARE for Life, which includes Medicare supplementary insurance and full drug coverage, which were finally authorized for retired veterans by Congress in 2000.

John C. Simons

Born 1920 · Philadelphia, Pennsylvania

A smiling John Simons, wearing his shiny new gold dolphins, shortly after earning Qualification in the Submarine Corps, October, 1944.

John C. Simons was born in 1920 in Philadelphia to John and Geraldine Nice Simons. He graduated from Frankfort High School and from Drexel Institute of Technology in 1942. He began work for Atlas Powder Company. He joined the Navy in November 1942. Commissioned as a first lieutenant, he volunteered for the submarine service and was assigned to the newly commissioned submarine *Pilotfish*. After the service he earned a PhD in physics from MIT in 1946. He married Hildred Dodge in 1948; they have three children. He subsequently worked for Westinghouse on the design of a nuclear power plant for the first "atomic" submarine, USS *Nautilus*.

Beneath the Sea

A World War II Submarine Odyssey

By John C. Simons

> "The wolfpack mission was to coordinate both search and attack, with short-range radio communications between the subs using a very limited two-letter code."

A SUBMARINE IS primarily a naval weapons platform, a means to surreptitiously observe enemy vessels and, if desired, to destroy them. The evolution of the submarine is a long story, but it was not until World War I and the introduction of aircraft to warfare that the submarine matured to usefulness as a combat tool. Submarines were an important part of the arsenal for World War II.

World War II submarines could stay submerged (and undetected) for 16 to 24 hours. They then had to resurface and charge their batteries, usually at night, taking about six hours. On the surface, the submarines were powered by diesel fuel from four diesel fuel engines at a top speed of 20 knots. They carried enough fuel to cruise over 11,000 miles and stay at sea 75 days. Submerged speed was only 3 knots using two immense batteries. A World War II submarine was about 308 feet long with a 27-foot beam.

As World War II approached, the U.S. submarine service had totally unrealistic training and doctrines. During this time, German submarines had already sunk 1,500 British ships in the Mediterranean and the Atlantic. On December 6, 1941, the U.S. submarine force consisted of 111 units, including 31 boats from just after World War I and number of "experimental" submarines. By the end of the war 204 new submarines had been commissioned.

There were five submarines at Pearl Harbor, but the Japanese attack plan did not target the submarines or the submarine base repair facilities. On December 7, 1941, the chief of naval operations issued a directive, "Execute unrestricted air and submarine warfare against Japan." Because of lack of training in the submarine force, the early days of the war were very difficult. Not only was the lack of training a major problem, but also the submarine's offensive weapon, the torpedo, was not reliable. They would detonate prematurely or not detonate at all.

As the submarine crews gained experience and overcame the problems with the torpedoes, submarines became an important part of the war in the Pacific. At the Battle of Midway, June 1942, there were 26 submarines in the area, and the submarine *Nautilus* sank the Japanese carrier *Soryu*. But the problem of so many "dud" torpedoes was not solved until October, 1943.

I enlisted in the Navy's V-7 program as an apprentice seaman in November 1942 and was commissioned as ensign in June 1943. I volunteered for submarine school and subsequently reported to the Portsmouth, New Hampshire, navy yard assigned to the USS *Pilotfish,* which was under construction. Our ship was commissioned December 16, 1943, and we immediately began sea trials. We reported to Newport, Rhode Island, for test torpedo firing, then to New London, Connecticut, for additional training and from there through the Panama Canal to Pearl Harbor. It was June 1944.

A typical war patrol departed from a sub base, travelled two or three weeks to a patrol area, mostly on the surface for training dives and drills. We typically spent 30 days in the operating area submerged during the day and surfacing at night to charge batteries and change position. Our mission was to attack targets of opportunity but there were also many special missions for gathering intelligence.

Our first patrol was in a wolfpack with submarines *Pintado* and *Shark*. The wolfpack mission was to coordinate both search and attack, with short-range radio communications between the subs using a very limited two-letter code. We were allowed in the

Saipan area for a week and were then to clear out to the Luzon Straits before the landings on Saipan began June 19. In those seven days we encountered five Japanese convoys; we were at battle stations 60 percent of the time.

Pilotfish had not fired a single torpedo. As we got into position to fire, the convoy would suddenly change course. It seemed as though the enemy knew right where we were. It wasn't until later that we learned our gears were unusually noisy, making it easy to detect us. Our contribution was to drive the convoy ships toward other wolfpack subs so they were able to attack and sink the ships that changed their course to avoid us.

On this first patrol, we saw enough action for a whole war in just 23 days. Half of our crew had never seen combat duty before, and for many it was their first time at sea and their first cruise on a submarine. We had tracked five convoys and sunk nine ships totaling 50,000 tons of shipping. Almost half of a Japanese division were drowned and those who did reach shore were without guns and battle gear.

Our subsequent patrols were, after the fact, rather boring. We were assigned lifeguard duty for various carrier-based aircraft during air raids on the Bonin Islands, Volcano Islands and Iwo Jima. We were then assigned to Guam for a "refit." While we were there the squadron commander collected submarine personnel who could be spared from the refit crews and anyone who could speak Japanese, and they sailed on the submarine tender *Proteus* to an undisclosed destination.

Japan started the war with 6,000,000 tons of merchant shipping, with 3,000,000 of this needed for Japanese civilians. At the end of the war Japan had 300,000 tons of shipping. U.S. submarines sank over 5,000,000 tons of merchant shipping, 1,178 vessels. They also sank 214 naval vessels (580,000 additional tons), including 23 submarines. These losses of oil, strategic materials and food supplies essentially starved Japan into submission. It took B-29's and two atom bombs to convince the emperor and the Imperial War Cabinet to capitulate.

There was a steep price for America's submarine force. Of 288 American submarines, 52 were lost in the war; 48 of these were lost in combat. The toll of lives was severe; personnel strength of the submarine force averaged 14,750 officers and men; 3,131 men and 374 officers died.

August 8: The base's daily newspaper was headlined, "Atom Bomb Dropped on Japan." Who knew what an atom bomb was? On August 9, we set out on our sixth patrol assigned to lifeguard duty close to the Japanese mainland. We watched as B-29s came over by the dozens at night with all their running lights lit, since the danger of colliding with each other was greater than the risk of Japanese AA fire. What a sight! Three days later came the news that Japan had surrendered. We were then ordered into Tokyo Bay where we tied up alongside the submarine tender *Proteus* (along with eleven other submarines).

On September 1, I had liberty ashore. As we walked around the village, the Japanese people ignored us, looking right through as if we weren't there. On September 2, on the battleship *Missouri*, the Japanese government formally surrendered. Our admiral, Charles Lockwood, represented the submarine force on the *Missouri*. After the signing, the admiral threw a cocktail party for the submariners.

We returned to Pearl Harbor and then to San Francisco. *Pilotfish* had 18 months of duty covering 75,000 miles, 313 days of war patrols and over 1,000 dives. We were submerged over 3,000 hours.

The *Pilotfish* returned to Pearl Harbor and was preparing to leave for Bikini Island to the atomic bomb tests. I wanted to go back to school and left the ship before it got to Bikini. The *Pilotfish* was part of the underwater detonated atom bomb tests and today is on the ocean floor in Bikini's nuclear graveyard.

Ed Gilfix

Born 1923 · Dorchester, Massachusetts

Ed Gilfix at the entrance to the tomb of Sun Yat-sen, founder and first president of the republic of China. Nanking, China, 1945.

Edward Gilfix grew up in Dorchester, Massachusetts, where he was born in 1923. He graduated from Dorchester High School and was drafted into the U.S. Army Signal Corps. During World War II he served in the CBI (China, Burma and India) theater, where he served with the Chinese Combat Command. After his discharge he attended the University of Massachusetts with a BS in electrical engineering and then received a MS in electrical engineering from the University of Michigan. He is a member of Tau Beta Phi and was a licensed professional engineer in the state of Massachusetts. Early in his professional career he worked on computer applications for Chrysler Corporation and the DATAmatic Corporation. Subsequently he worked at Mitre Corporation concentrating on critical areas in command and control of tactical forces involving the U.S. Strike Command and the U.S. Tactical Air Command. He retired as a principal engineer at Raytheon's Missile Systems Division where he was engaged in analysis and design of information systems for command and control, and multiuser information storage and retrieval applications.

A G.I. in the CBI

By Ed Gilfix

> "'All the Japanese forces hereby surrendered will
> cease hostilities.... They are now noncombatant troops.'
> The Japanese then rose and departed. The surrender
> ceremony was complete."

WHEN WORLD WAR II ended in 1945, there were over eight million people, usually referred to as G.I.s, in the U.S. armed forces. They were scattered in regional areas (referred to as the Mediterranean theater, the European theater and the Pacific theater). There were also about 60,000 military personnel assigned to China, Burma and India—a remote area referred to as the CBI theater. I was one of those 60,000.

I entered Calcutta, India, moved through that country to Ledo, India and then proceeded along the Ledo Road to its intersection with the Burma Road, stopping intermittently for extended stays in small villages (Lasio, Bhamo) and finally arrived in China. I had become a member of the Chinese Combat Command. In performing my military duties, I travelled to and enjoyed the uniqueness of a number of Chinese cities—including Kunming, Hangchow and Chickiang before being assigned to Nanking. I finally arrived at Shanghai, my last location. The city was a source of considerable cultural stimulation and my experiences there remain vivid to this day.

The war officially ended on the battleship *Missouri* in Tokyo Harbor, September 2, 1945. However, a large and hostile Japanese army, numbering over 1,300,000, was still on the Chinese mainland. Chiang Kai-shek planned an official ceremony for the surrender of these forces, to be held in the auditorium of the Central

Chinese General Ho and senior military officers representing allied forces rise to leave the formal Japanese surrender activities. The surrender ceremony has been completed. September 9, 1945.

Military Academy in Nanking. I was able to attend and photograph the event. Two long tables, facing each other, were positioned on the floor of the auditorium. General Ho Ying-Chin, commander in chief of the Chinese army, was seated at the center of one of the tables flanked by military officers representing other allied forces involved in China. After a short wait, the Japanese, led by Okamura Yasutsugu, commander of the Japanese forces in central China, arrived. His group positioned themselves at the other table facing the Chinese. As with General Ho, General Okamura was also in the center of his table with his military personnel on either side. Standing at their table, the Japanese all bowed to General Ho and waited. After a long pause General Ho flicked his head and the Japanese returned to a full standing position and then seated themselves.

First, there was a series of document exchanges between the two generals, specifying the details of the surrender. All the documents were then signed and verified by the two generals. The details specified that the emperor of Japan and the Japanese government direct that the senior commanders of ground, sea, air and auxiliary forces within China should surrender to General Chiang Kai-shek. I quote: "All the Japanese forces hereby surrendered will cease hostilities....They are now noncombatant troops." The Japanese then rose and departed. The surrender ceremony was complete.

The number 9 is associated with this ceremony and must be significant to the Chinese. The surrender ceremony took place in 1945 at 9:00 o'clock on the ninth day of the ninth month, September. The 4 and 5 in 1945 also add up to nine. For the Chinese, World War II was officially ended.

After many years, a new mystery related to my tour of duty in the CBI theater has developed. I received a phone call from someone in Indiana who claimed to be a photojournalist. He had purchased from E-bay some old negative film of pictures that he thought had been taken during the Vietnam War. Among the films, he found my name. I was mystified when he asked me to help him identify the pictures. When I reviewed them, I realized they were not pictures of the Vietnam War but MY pictures taken during my travels while I was serving in the CBI theater. When I told him the pictures included the surrender ceremonies in Nanking, he expressed an interest in creating a document of my travels in World War II.

At first I was concerned the phone call might be the beginning of a scam. I could not understand how my negative film ended up on E-bay to be purchased by a photojournalist in Indiana. (I presume that it could have been inadvertently discarded with other household items during the downsizing process preliminary to our move to Brookhaven and retrieved by an E-bay participant. A relative who had worked with my caller as a photographer at the *Ann Arbor News* reassured me he was credible. Since then I have cooperated with him in his efforts to utilize these pictures. So, 67 years later, I am once again focusing on my travels and experiences during my time as a soldier of the United States Army.

Part Eight

Still Preparing for War

AFTER THE ARMISTICES with Germany and Japan were signed, the war was over and everyone looked forward to peace and settled lives. Back to where they had been when war so rudely interrupted.

But it didn't happen. Servicemen did come home and restarted their lives, peace returned in many aspects. Sadly the war also left any number of issues that would cloud the future of the world. Instead of an active fighting war, a cold war had begun and an arms race followed. The shadow of war hung over the country and the business of war continued. Korea, Vietnam, Iraq and Afghanistan have disturbed our peace since then. Our armed forces have continued training for war.

Tom Sheridan

Born 1929 · Cincinnati, Ohio

Tom Sheridan. Air Force Aeromedical Laboratory, Wright-Patterson Air Force Base, Dayton, Ohio.

Tom Sheridan grew up in Cincinnati, Ohio, where he graduated from Walnut Hills High School. Born in 1929, he was the son of Esther and Mahlon Sheridan. He graduated from Purdue University, Indiana, in 1951 and entered the Air Force, becoming a first lieutenant. He was assigned to the Air Force Aeromedical Laboratory in Dayton, Ohio, where he did experimental research in the physiology and psychology of human performance. He met his wife Rachel in Dayton, Ohio, and they were married in 1953. He then earned a master's degree at UCLA in California and a PhD at MIT in Massachusetts. As a teacher at MIT he was the Ford Professor of Engineering and Applied Psychology in the Mechanical Engineering and Aeronautics/Astronautics Departments and directed the Human-Machine Systems Lab. He was awarded an honorary doctorate from Delft University in the Netherlands and is a member of the National Academy of Engineering.

Testing Survival Equipment for Air Force Test Pilots

By Tom Sheridan

"I was 'volunteered' to be a test subject in various experiments...[riding] an ejection seat test track, where a rocket kicked you in the butt...[ejected] 60 feet up in the air...swimming around in ice water wearing a rubber suit with a thermocouple inserted in my rear end to test how quickly I got cold...trying to fly a B-24 while lying in the prone position in the bombardier station in the nose of the airplane..."

ALTHOUGH I NEVER was involved in actual battle, I did see action of a different sort, by serving as a junior officer (first lieutenant) in the Air Force during the Korean War.

Right out of college ROTC I was assigned to the Air Force Aeromedical Laboratory at Wright-Patterson Air Force Base in Dayton, Ohio, to serve as the assistant to a test pilot who at the time held the world speed and altitude records for ejection seat bailout tests in fighter aircraft. We were testing all kinds of survival equipment: ejection seats, parachutes, G suits, pressure suits and so on.

Being young and unmarried I was "volunteered" to be a test subject in various experiments. So I got to ride an ejection seat test track, where a rocket kicked you in the butt and you suddenly found yourself 60 feet up in the air. And I got to go through the Army paratrooper jump school at Fort Benning, Georgia, just to learn what parachute jumping was all about. The officers always enjoyed being first out of the airplane. I also recall swimming around in ice water wearing a rubber suit with a thermocouple inserted in my rear end to test how quickly I got cold. And trying to fly a B-24 while lying in the prone position in the bombardier station in the nose of the airplane, with a real pilot in the usual location ready to take over. The most vivid memory is of being strapped at the end of a 30-foot arm of a centrifuge whirling around to create high G forces on the body. I got up to ten times gravity for two minutes in the prone position before the forces on the chest muscles were such that it was impossible to breathe.

Being a research unit of the Air Force, the Aeromed Lab had a very informal atmosphere. I worked with one ophthalmologist who was drafted and really did not care for the military. He declared that he never would clean or press his uniform the whole two years he was in the service. As I recall, he carried out his wish.

One day my brother, a "spit and polish" Marine captain at the time, paid us a visit. As he entered our office my boss and I were sitting with our feet up on our desks. Because my boss was a major my brother stiffened to attention and saluted. I recall how awkward and, in retrospect, how funny the moment was.

During this period I also met a young teacher in Dayton who was doing her very first teaching stint in an inner-city school with 50 interracial kids in her class, taking bullets and knives away from boys twice her size. I admired her bravery and eventually married her. Those were memorable times for both of us.

William F. Pounds

Born 1928 · Fayette County, Pennsylvania

William Pounds with his Grumman Cougar (F9F8), 1953, Oceana, Virginia.

William Pounds was born January 9, 1928, on a farm in Fayette County, Pennsylvania. He was delivered by the same doctor who had delivered his mother, Helen Pounds. His father was Joseph Frank Pounds. He graduated from the Wilkinsburg, Pennsylvania, high school and attended Carnegie Mellon University, Pennsylvania, to study chemical engineering. He graduated in 1950 and worked at the Kodak Company until he entered the service the next year. After flight training in Pensacola, Florida, he was assigned to a fighter squadron at Quonset Point, Rhode Island, and then to the carrier USS *Bennington*. He left the service in 1955 and returned to work for Kodak. He then returned to graduate school at Carnegie Mellon to study mathematical economics. He was working for Pittsburgh Plate Glass when he was asked to join the faculty at MIT. He then completed his PhD studies in industrial administration at Carnegie Mellon. In 1966 he became dean of the Sloan School of Business Management at MIT, where he remained until 1980 when he stepped down to work as a senior administrator to the Rockefeller family until 1991. He returned to MIT as a professor of business management in 1991, officially retiring in 1998. In 1993 he was chairman of the board for the Boston Museum of Fine Arts. He married his wife Helen Means in 1954, and they have a son and a daughter.

Will I Be Able to Land?

By William F. Pounds

"While circling in the fog I resolved that, if I survived, I would not go up again."

THE KOREAN CONFLICT ended with an armistice in July of 1953 but the Cold War remained in full swing. In order to test the organization and effectiveness of NATO naval forces, a vast exercise was undertaken in mid-September that involved hundreds of ships arranged in two large task forces that were to simulate a battle in the North Atlantic. I was a minor participant in Operation Mariner—a young pilot in VF-74, a fighter squadron flying F4U Corsairs from the USS *Bennington*, an old Essex class aircraft carrier.

On September 23, the *Bennington* was one of three carriers, two American and one Canadian, at the center of a task force moving northeast across the North Atlantic looking for an "enemy" task force thought to be moving westward. In the early afternoon, combat air patrols—groups of aircraft to be stationed at altitude forward of the fleet to seek contact with the "enemy"—were to be launched from all three carriers. I was assigned to fly one of four planes ordered to hold over a destroyer located well ahead of our main task force.

At the time of takeoff the sky was clear, cool and sunny with only a bit of low cloud on the horizon. The wind was 42 knots and the seas were very rough. As the ship turned into the wind to launch aircraft, it began to pitch—rising on one wave and plunging into the next—such that green salt water was occasionally thrown onto the flight deck, normally 60 feet above the waterline. Planes were launched on the upswing.

The three carriers launched a total of 52 aircraft uneventfully. I joined our formation of four planes and we proceeded to our assigned station 10,000 feet above the destroyer that would direct our movement by radio. Shortly after takeoff, I noticed that we were flying over a solid layer of cloud far below us.

We circled easily in the bright sunshine for over half an hour with no word from our controlling ship. Finally our leader called the ship to be sure we were still in contact. We all heard the reply. "Oh, you're still there? Haven't you heard? All planes have been recalled to their ships." We were then given a course and the distance to the *Bennington*. We headed back expecting to see our ship in a half hour or so.

After 45 minutes all we had seen was the top of the cloud far below us that extended as far as we could see. Our leader called the *Bennington* and we all heard that only 10 of the 52 aircraft had been able to land before a dense fog had enveloped the entire task force. Like us, 42 aircraft were still aloft. We were further advised that there was no land that any of us could reach with our remaining fuel. We joined all the others in circling in the clear but darkening air.

Knowing that fuel would be important, I adjusted my engine to a mixture so lean that every time I adjusted my throttle my engine coughed, paused and then restarted. There was nothing else to do. We circled and waited.

Several attempts were made to direct a plane to a ship by radar but each time it was waved off at the last minute when the pilot could not see the ship and there was a risk of his simply crashing into it. I later learned that at this time it was impossible to see across a flight deck.

A plane with radar searched for a hole in the fog over a wide area and could find none.

As it got darker I remembered I still had my sunglasses on and thought I won't need these any more and tossed them into to the bottom of the cockpit. There was a lot of time to think.

Finally orders came. We were all to proceed 100 miles downwind, there to rendezvous with the USS *Red Fin*, a submarine that reported good ceiling and visibility at its location, and there (Lat. 53-38.5N—Long. 41-20W) to ditch in the sea to be picked up by the sub (in the dark). The prospect did not seem promising.

When flying a prop plane it is impossible to see straight down. There is too much engine and wing. But when I banked to turn to the specified course I looked straight down my wing and saw a destroyer through the cloud. I immediately asked permission to ditch by it and was told to wait. The hole in the fog quickly closed.

But there was hope that the visibility was improving. The order to go to the submarine was cancelled. The task force was rearranged so that the three carriers were sailing a mile apart, abreast and in parallel. All the other ships were far astern. Floating flares were dropped in a line behind each of the carriers. Individual planes were directed on diagonal paths just above the waves to intercept the lines of flares. Someone reported seeing a flare and turned to follow it. He reported seeing a carrier looming high above him. He proceeded to fly upwind, circled and landed.

I was flying in the number two slot in my formation, on the wing of the leader. We were directed down as a group and I could soon feel the effect of the waves under my wings—we were flying very low and very close together so that we could see each other. An order came for our group to turn toward me and I knew I had to pull up because there was nowhere else to go. I could not go any lower. I soon found myself back on top of the fog alone in the clear night air. I think the moon was shining.

In time I was directed down, found the flares and landed. Everyone got back. Two hours later the thick fog descended again and it was like that for several days. Some called the brief clearing luck. Some called it a patch of warm water. Some called it a miracle.

I have considered every day of my life since that day to be pure profit.

Epilogue

Several days later I found my sunglasses in the bottom of my airplane.

Three planes from the *Bennington* landed on the Canadian carrier *Magnificent*, where much celebratory alcohol was available, a tradition handed down from the British navy. Those of us who returned to the *Bennington* made do with tiny bottles of medicinal brandy, a long-standing rule in the U.S. Navy. When the fog cleared and the hangovers faded, those three planes were flown back to the *Bennington* and we discovered that the U.S. insignias on their wings and fuselages had been painted out and replaced with bright red Canadian maple leaves. They remained that way for the rest of the cruise.

I visited the *Red Fin* at a port in the Mediterranean and reminisced with several of the crew about the evening of September 23. They knew we were coming and were on the surface waiting. But all their hatches were closed and green water was going over their entire ship including their conning tower with each passing wave. Several officers and men were on the tower with lights but could see almost nothing in the heavy seas and darkness. They were not optimistic that they could have found anyone.

The senior pilot flying with us on the 23rd had been a young pilot during the war in the Pacific. He had flown in an attack on a distant Japanese fleet known to be so far away that no plane could make it back to its carrier. After the attack he ditched in the sea and was rescued by submarine.

While circling above the fog I resolved that, if I survived, I would not go up again. As the cruise continued and we entered the Mediterranean the plane ahead of me for takeoff went into the sea because the ship was not quite up to speed. The pilot was recovered, the ship sped up and off I went.

Norine Casey

Born 1928 · Arlington, Massachusetts

"Young Norine," Miami Beach, 1954.

I was born in Arlington, Massachusetts, the youngest of four children. In 1933, my dad, a structural engineer, almost lost a leg while helping someone change a tire. Despite treatment he had great pain and was unable to work. Needing income to help support the family, my mother, who had been a teacher in Boston before her marriage, opened a first grade in the living room of our house. I was a student in her first class of the Bartlett School which grew in size and reputation over the years. I graduated from Wellesley College on a scholarship and earned an MA in teaching at Radcliffe. After a year as a research and teaching assistant in biology at Wellesley, I joined the Bartlett School working with my mom. In 1978, I moved the Bartlett School to a public school building I had leased and ran the school there for 22 years until I retired. Both of my brothers were in the service. After World War II my brother John worked for airlines and became president of Braniff Airlines. My brother Al attended Harvard Business School on the G.I. Bill and became the president of the *Los Angeles Times*, then president of American Airlines. My brother-in-law, Dave Carey, often visited his buddies from the Battle of the Bulge. He was a CPA and ran several businesses. I do miss visiting with my brothers John and Al, and Dave, now all deceased.

Snapshots of World War II and Vietnam

By Norine Casey

> "What we didn't know was that John was assigned to the very secret atomic bomb project in Los Alamos. In April of 1945, he called home to say, 'I can't tell you how or why, but the war will be over soon.' When the two bombs were dropped on Japan, my parents knew that this had been John's project."

MY DAD WAS a World War II warden on our street '41–'45, and I remember him walking our street after dark to be certain that everyone had blackened the windows. I was in high school and I remember Mom lovingly placing a two-star flag in our window. My older brother John attended MIT and thought he'd be in structural engineering, as my dad was. However, when the Army Air Force recruited John, he joined up. For a while he designed airplanes at Curtiss-Wright in Buffalo, where he met his wife. He got his pilot's license and occasionally flew low over our house. He and June were assigned to live in Wendover, Utah. Mom and Dad were upset with him for not calling home often. What we didn't know was that John was assigned to the very secret atomic bomb project in Los Alamos. In April of 1945, he called home to say, "I can't tell you how or why, but the war will be over soon." When the two bombs were dropped on Japan, my parents knew that this had been John's project. He was Chuck Sweeney's copilot when the bomb was lifted to the plane on Tinian. If there had been a third bomb, John would have piloted the plane—thank goodness the dropping of the second bomb caused the Japanese to admit defeat.

My brother Al, who graduated from Harvard, didn't go overseas. He was assigned to the Signal Corps and of course his work

John, brother of Norine Casey, during military training, Greenwood, Mississippi, 1944.

Al Casey, brother of Norine Casey, 1944.

was secret. He also learned Italian to supervise Italian prisoners of war.

My brother-in-law, Dave Carey, was a senior at Boston College in 1944 under an Officer Training Program. Instead of studying to become an officer, Dave was sent directly into the terrible Battle of the Bulge, where Americans were surrounded on three sides by Germans. Dave was wounded and sent to an Army hospital. For a while his family heard that he was "missing in action," but after some time they learned that he was recovering from his wounds. Dave received the Purple Heart award for his fighting. For many years after the war Dave could never talk about this terrible time with his buddies. They had annual reunions all around the US, and in 2002, the year before Dave died, the buddies from the Battle of the Bulge arranged to have a van drive them around the area where they fought so bravely.

I was a peace advocate all through the Vietnam years, frustrated that so many lives were lost there in the jungles. I organized with Peg Spengler of Brookhaven a group called the "Tom Dooley Youth League." Dr. Tom Dooley was a U.S. naval officer in earlier days when many families were allowed to relocate from North Vietnam to South Vietnam. He started an orphanage in Saigon with the help of Mme. Ngai.

Peg and I invited Arlington High School students to help fund this orphanage by volunteering on Saturdays to cut lawns, remove snow, paint, etc. The Arlington families paid the students and they gave all their money to the orphanage. They were wonderful boys and girls. In 1968, I decided to fly to Saigon to meet with Mme. Ngai and see the orphanage Dr. Dooley had opened. When I walked in, I saw several buildings with Vietnamese titles, and one said in English, "This building was erected by the Arlington Massachusetts High School students." I was very proud and loved playing with the orphan children there.

Part Nine

War Is Hell

AT LAST, WHAT is there to say? WAR IS HELL! 72 million people died in World War II. We continue to watch men (and women) die in the service of their country. Here are testimonials about how wars have imprinted survivors.

Ed Townsley

Born 1927 · Charleston, South Carolina

Ed Townsley at Brookhaven.

Ed Townsley was born in 1927 in Charleston, South Carolina. His father was in the regular Army and the family lived in several places. He graduated from Exeter Academy in Massachusetts in 1944. He graduated from West Point in 1949. During his army career he served in Korea, 1950–51, and in Vietnam, 1967–68. Between wars, he attended Army schools (Engineer School, Parachute School, Ranger School, Command and General Staff College, National War College) and civilian schools (Harvard Littauer MPA, University of Illinois civil engineering PhD) and had a variety of duty assignments, both in the United States and overseas (Germany, Okinawa). His assignments included research and development (nuclear weapons effects, night vision, etc.) and engineering and construction (military housing, hospitals, airfields, hydropower, navigation, flood control). He retired as a colonel from the Army in 1978. He was then executive director, Building Research Advisory Board, National Research Council; and project management, Fluor Corporation. He was also deputy director, Science and Technology, Institute for Defense Analyses. Retired in 1997.

The Ordeals of a Conscientious Objector

By Ed Townsley

"A problem we Americans have often seemed to have: an excessive and false patriotism leading to what can clearly be termed unwarranted persecution."

THIS IS NOT my story but a brief story about my wife's first cousin, who was a conscientious objector in World War II. I think it is important because it highlights a problem we Americans have often seemed to have: an excessive and false patriotism leading to what can clearly be termed unwarranted persecution.

Allen, a kind and gentle soul, was a conscientious objector during World War II. Like other COs he was rounded up and sent to a work camp in Montana where he and others were used to fight forest fires—a task he enjoyed and found personally rewarding. However, the forest fires petered out and the camp inmates were idled. Allen repeatedly asked the camp staff to give him something to do. For whatever reason, they did not. So he walked out of camp, eventually to find work as an orderly in a hospital in Chicago.

Government authorities tracked him down, stripped him of his citizenship and sent him to prison for five years.

Well after the war was over, he was released and, as a CO, felon and noncitizen, he had considerable difficulty in finding work. Eventually he was able to support himself and his family as a skilled carpenter and cabinetmaker for barter—which enabled him to earn a living without having to pay taxes to a government that had treated him with such unnecessary harshness.

Fortunately, after several years, his citizenship was restored and his life returned to normal. It was an experience that would have forever seared a less understanding, forgiving, and generous person—someone more like me than Allen.

Thorne Griscom

Born 1931 · Philadelphia, Pennsylvania

Thorne Griscom in 2012.

I was born in 1931 in Philadelphia, Pennsylvania. I was raised on a farm in southern New Jersey. After receiving an AB from Wesleyan University in 1952, I received an MD from the University of Rochester in 1956. I trained in pediatrics and radiology at Massachusetts General Hospital, 1956–1958 and 1960–1963, then became a professor of radiology at Harvard Medical School and Boston Children's Hospital, about 1984–2012. I am a former president, Society for Pediatric Radiology and the New England Roentgen Ray Society. My stepwise retirement from Harvard Medical School and Boston Children's Hospital was completed in 2012. I was married to Joanna Starr in 1955, and we had four children, Elizabeth (died in 2002), Daniel, Elinor and Mathew. I moved into Brookhaven in 2012, shortly before my beloved wife died of metastatic cancer.

Where Was I and What Was I Doing When Pearl Harbor Was Bombed?

By Thorne Griscom

> "Would one or all of us three boys choose to be a
> conscientious objector, never an easy or automatic position
> to take? (Peace came, hurried by the bombs at Hiroshima
> and Nagasaki, before we reached draft age. We therefore
> no longer had to consider the excruciating decision that we
> were conscientiously opposed to any war, however just,
> whether or not our nation was attacked first.)"

THE JAPANESE GOVERNMENT had concluded that war with the United States was inevitable. President Roosevelt and his advisors believed war was likely sooner or later. Japan's preemptive strike fell on the great naval base at Pearl Harbor just before 8 A.M. Hawaii time on Sunday morning, December 7, 1941.

The East Coast of the United States is five time zones ahead of Hawaii. My parents, my two brothers and I had gone to First Day (Sunday) School and then to meeting at the Friends' meeting-house in Moorestown, New Jersey. If things went according to custom, the hour-long meeting was spent in silent meditation, quite hard on young boys, interrupted by short messages from members of meeting as the spirit moved them to rise and speak. Grandfather Thorne sat on the men's facing bench and had probably spoken, as usual. Grandmother Griscom sat on the women's facing bench but had not spoken; she never did. The elders sitting on the facing benches shook hands to break meeting at about noon, as was usual.

After meeting we went to Grandfather Thorne's nearby house for dinner, always a fairly formal occasion. Then we all moved to the living room. The adults talked while we three boys (age elev-

Thorne Griscom (eight: born June 21, 1931) and his brothers Dick (four: born May 14, 1935) and Sam (nine: born March 24, 1930) in front of the fireplace on the farm, Marlton, New Jersey.

en, ten and six) maneuvered blocks of varying sizes and shapes, seeing how tall we could tower them before they all collapsed; more age-appropriate diversions were not available. Our all-time record precollapse height was about five feet.

Then we noticed that the adults were quietly upset. Someone had phoned Grandfather to tell him about the attack on Pearl Harbor. The radio—this was long before television—confirmed the news, but details were scanty and contradictory. No one knew the implications. Were the bombers just a rogue segment of the Japanese navy? Was the bombing the prelude to an invasion of Hawaii, which was not yet a state but nevertheless part of the United States? Would mainland U.S.A. then be invaded? Would millions of young American men be drafted, and how many would die? (Answer: yes; 405,000 would die.) Would we lose the war? What did all this mean for convinced pacifists? Was it all President Roosevelt's fault? (Grandfather was active in county politics and, as a staunch Republican, would have been inclined to blame it all on FDR.) Would the war last for years, and would we three boys be among those drafted and possibly killed? (For the United States, the war lasted almost four years; for many Europeans, it was six years.) Would one or all of us three boys choose to be a conscientious objector, never an easy or automatic position to take? (Peace came, hurried by the bombs at Hiroshima and Nagasaki, before we reached draft age. We therefore no longer had to consider the excruciating decision that we were conscientiously opposed to any war, however just, whether or not our nation was attacked first.)

The Griscom family drove the five miles home to our farm in our 1940 Ford, greatly upset by all these questions. The world had turned upside down. The adults were distressed. We three boys were deeply confused. But, compared to others around the world, we, and most other Americans, were spared the worst horrors of war.

Ed Townsley

Born 1927 · Charleston, South Carolina

Ed Townsley at Brookhaven.

Ed Townsley was born in 1927 in Charleston, South Carolina. His father was in the regular Army and the family lived in several places. He graduated from Exeter Academy in Massachusetts in 1944. He graduated from West Point in 1949. During his army career he served in Korea, 1950–51, and in Vietnam, 1967–68. Between wars, he attended Army schools (Engineer School, Parachute School, Ranger School, Command and General Staff College, National War College) and civilian schools (Harvard Littauer MPA, University of Illinois civil engineering PhD) and had a variety of duty assignments, both in the United States and overseas (Germany, Okinawa). His assignments included research and development (nuclear weapons effects, night vision, etc.) and engineering and construction (military housing, hospitals, airfields, hydropower, navigation, flood control). He retired as a colonel from the Army in 1978. He was then executive director, Building Research Advisory Board, National Research Council; and project management, Fluor Corporation. He was also deputy director, Science and Technology, Institute for Defense Analyses. Retired in 1997.

War Is Hell—War Is Real

By Ed Townsley

> "That war was pure hell for me. I only wish that it be as real and hellish for the president who wants war, the congressman who votes for war, and the lapel-pin patriot citizens, who root for the war."

WAR HAS CHANGED: students of war used to focus on Hannibal at the battle of Cannae, 216 BC; Caesar in Gaul; Ghengis Khan; Gustavus Adolphus, Thirty Years' War, 1618–1648; Frederick the Great, Seven Years' War, 1756–1763; Napoleon; the Civil War. In all those wars, fighting troops were grouped together on isolated single battlefields—that is the kind of war about which Clausewitz and Sun Tzu wrote.

But, World War I, World War II and Korea were linear wars. The battle line ran continuously from the Channel/North Sea to Switzerland on the North European Plain, from coast to coast in Italy and Korea. Essentially, *the enemy was always right there in front of you*. Now we are back to the old-style war with combat raging in widely isolated battlegrounds. *The enemy may be anywhere.*

The Academy Award-winning movie *The Hurt Locker* showed me how the wars in Iraq and Afghanistan compare with war as I knew it. In the film, war in Iraq is a spectator sport with literally hundreds of people watching from their balconies or windows—reminiscent of the First Battle of Bull Run when residents of Washington, D.C., took carriages out to watch the action. The presence of spectators might seem a trivial difference, but for me the battlefield had always seemed empty—no civilians were to be expected, few or no soldiers was a surprise at first, a surprise until one realizes that to be seen on the battlefield is to become a target. The soldiers were there, just not readily visible, not anxious to be targets.

There is one other very important thing: the war in Iraq is also a war with IED, Improvised Explosive Devices, remotely controlled most probably by one of the spectators.

The enemy could be anybody.

For the soldier in battle, that is a whole different concept. One always faces the fact that one might be killed in battle, but generally that is a matter of fate. In previous wars, lots of soldiers shooting lots of weapons against all sorts of targets—*but* rarely a specific individual soldier—that is, nobody is aiming specifically at ME. With an IED, the device is in place, the man who will detonate it is also in place—hiding, concealed and/or disguised where he can see and choose when to detonate the weapon. It is specifically HIM—unseen, unknown—against ME.

Actually the roadside improvised explosive device was very much used in Vietnam. Unexploded dud artillery rounds, wired fuses, remotely detonated…Deadly.

I'm sure you have all heard the expression "War is real" or "War is hell," perhaps you've even had occasion to say it yourself. Those abbreviated expressions hide much more than they reveal.

What makes WAR real? One American general, Maxwell Taylor, I believe, has said that war is glamorous and exciting right up 'til the time you first get shot at. I've been in two wars—Korea and Vietnam. I was shot at in both. I was hit in Korea. But it was the war in Vietnam that was, for me, a very real and present HELL.

In Korea, I was a young subaltern in the combat engineers—I went where I was told to go and did what I was told to do. And it could get pretty exciting. (I was wounded behind enemy lines. That is a story in itself about how the Army's battlefield medical system is designed to provide the best and timeliest care possible, TV show *M.A.S.H.* notwithstanding. Yes, I've been in a M.A.S.H.—Mobile Army Surgical Hospital.)

In Vietnam I was a battalion commander. I told people where to go and what to do. I was there during the Tet Offensive, in the First Cavalry Airmobile Division. We had just been sent north to get the Marines out of Khe Sanh. Tet occurred before we had completed our move north. We were bivouacked in the coastal plain between Hue in the south and Quang Tri in the north we were cut off both north and south. After the initial shock of the attack we quickly stabilized the situation, fighting our way into Hue from the north and Quang Tri from the south. But the roads we needed to use were still not open. One of my battalion's jobs was to clear those roads of obstacles and mines every day both north and south—roads that the North Vietnam Army (NVA) would mine again every night.

Some of those mines were made of dud artillery rounds buried in or alongside the road and command-detonated with an electric fuse, which was controlled by an enemy soldier hiding and watching from some safe place—somewhere close enough that he could watch over the mine and could see the mine-sweeping team approach the mine, detect the mine, then prepare to disarm the mine, all the while waiting for the right time to set the mine off. We were losing one, two or three men every day. Those men were men I was responsible for, men I had, so to speak, broken bread with. They were there because of my orders. And I was there with them... watching. We were losing men every day. I watched, I saw....

Since we were working both south and north, I alternated— one day with the teams going south, the next day with the teams going north. My jeep, with me in it, was the first vehicle following the sweeping teams. A jeep is relatively small and light and less likely to set a mine off. A fully loaded five-ton dump truck followed me, backing up so that the more heavily loaded wheels would go over the mine before the driver, who was partially shielded by the heavy steel dump bed in the rear of the truck.

But all that only after the team had slowly and carefully, AND IN PLAIN SIGHT, worked their way up the road—first the two-man sweep and mark team, then some distance behind them (because too many together make a target) the survey and assessment team, and finally the disposal team, the men who would have to spend some time working on the IED itself. These were the guys most at risk. These were the guys I spent the most time with. These were the guys who were taking the most casualties. Only after they had finished would I call my jeep forward.

But what was worse for me, not only did I watch and see this every day, every night I had to go back to my command post and order more men, some the same, to go out the next day and do the same thing, to face the same end*....

That war was very real to me. That war was pure hell for me. I only wish that it be as real and hellish for the president who wants war, the congressman who votes for war, and the lapel-pin patriot citizens, who root for the war.

---

*I have been asked about letters to the family: I had four companies, each with its own commander, in my battalion. My policy was:

   1. I would write letters to the families of any and all officers who became casualties.

   2. The company commanders were responsible to either write a letter or make sure their platoon leaders wrote letters to the families of any and all men under their command who became casualties.

   3. If the company commander had any reason to want me to write to the families of his NCO leaders (first sergeant, platoon sergeants, squad leaders) who became casualties, I would be glad to do so.

We did not lose any officers during Tet. We did lose several crackerjack NCOs.

Lilly Wolffers Szonyi

Born 1924 · St. Gallen, Switzerland

For Europeans the war is finally over. Lilly Szonyi got married, 1945, Zurich, Switzerland.

Lilly Wolffers Szonyi was born April 25, 1924, in St. Gallen, Switzerland, the youngest of three children (her brother Hans was nine years older, her brother Artur ten years older). Her family moved to Berlin in 1927 and thought about applying for German citizenship but because of her brother Artur's strenuous objections did not do so. On August 1, 1939, the family moved to Zurich. There Lilly worked for the Swiss Refugee Assistance organization and a number of other jobs in her late teens and early twenties. She met her husband, Geza Szonyi, a Hungarian-Jewish graduate student at the University of Zurich in 1942. They married in 1945 and had a daughter, Petra, and a son, David. In 1952 the family moved to Canada and came to the United States in 1953. After receiving an MSW from the University of Pennsylvania in 1960 she worked as a clinical social worker and later was in private practice. She moved with her husband Geza to Brookhaven in 2001. He died in 2009.

School Days and Life in Nazi Germany (1927–1939)

My Childhood in Berlin

By Lilly Wolffers Szonyi

> "Jewish Pig! And there I stood, twelve years old, surrounded by enemies who were my own schoolmates.... Nobody came even close to me....I cannot remember how I walked home that day or how I survived it all."

I WAS BORN in St. Gallen, Switzerland. When I was three years old—that was in 1927—the Great Depression hit Switzerland in a big way. My father worked for the embroidery industry for which Switzerland, especially St. Gallen was famous. He lost his job and was unable to support our family. My brothers were nine and ten years older than I, and they must have worried a lot. I was too young to understand what was going on. My father was a Swiss citizen. My mother had lived in the Rhineland, the daughter of German Jews who lived in a small village and were observant. Her older brother, Joseph, had become a very well-to-do fur merchant in Berlin, and he promised to help my father start a new life in Berlin. My mother had become a Swiss citizen through marriage, and, of course, my brothers and I were Swiss too. Nobody could even imagine what a blessing this would turn out to be.

It is amazing what impressions a three-year-old can retain. My most vivid memories are of homeless, hungry beggars who lined the street where my father's business was. I remember seeing a beggar collapse as I entered the bakery next to our business with my mother to buy some sweets—I have never forgotten that scene!

What I saw was a microcosm of what was happening in Germany in the years 1927–1933. There was much hunger, unemployment and despair all over the country, but especially in Berlin. My father was selling inexpensive rabbit fur coats to those who had jobs and needed to protect themselves from the harsh winters in Berlin.

I entered first grade in 1930 and life seemed pretty normal seen through the eyes of a six-year-old. Gradually, the name of Adolf Hitler penetrated my consciousness. Again, an early memory stands out; it was New Year's Eve in 1933. My parents had invited some relatives and I was supposed to be sleeping—but I was not. I heard them talk about the elections, and then I heard them say: Hitler was elected—but it wouldn't last long—it couldn't last! Nobody took him seriously. It was anything but a lively party in my parents' apartment. I could feel the gloom, even if I had no idea what this was all about.

But life went on. After four years of elementary school I entered the Goethe Lyceum in Berlin-Lichterfelde, which was about a 45-minute walk from our apartment to the school.

I loved school and was a good student. To get into a Lyceum or Gymnasium (girls' or boys' high school) you had to be a good student. It was the first step in a selective educational system, very different from our system here. My schoolmates were mostly from middle-class families; many fathers were doctors and lawyers. My father, being a businessman, always sounded a little inferior.

In other ways, too, I began to feel inferior. Everybody knew that I was Jewish, the only one in my class, and thus I was excluded from talks about events in the BDM—Bund Deutscher Mädel, a circle of German girls, a nationwide organization which together with the Hitler Jugend, the boys' group, represented an ever-growing arm of the Nazis, well organized to include all Germans. My only consolation was my girlfriend Hannelore who waited for me every morning at a certain crossing so that we could walk to school together.

It was now 1936, the year of the Olympic Games in Berlin, and I was twelve years old. Friendships are very important at that age. One particular day, my friend Hannelore was not at our regular meeting place. I waited a while, but then decided to go ahead, in order not to be late for school. I walked fast and suddenly saw my friend with other schoolmates ahead of me. I caught up with them and said "hello," but there was no response. I was stunned—what had I done? We reached the school and as I entered the classroom I was surrounded by icy silence.

It was eerie and terrible, and I couldn't understand what had happened. Our first break came. I got my lunch out of my school-bag and went down the stairs to the schoolyard.

Nobody came even close to me. I was totally alone in a big crown of students—isolated!

Some of that day's events remain foggy for me, but even today, 64 years later, I see a long row of students, a human chain forming a circle around me. They chanted: Jewish Pig!

Jewish Pig! And there I stood, twelve years old. Surrounded by enemies who were my own schoolmates. I cannot remember how I walked home that day or how I survived it all.

My mother knew immediately that something was terribly wrong, but I refused to tell her what had happened. Towards evening I finally broke down. All she said was: "You are not going back to that school." But I simply insisted that I was not a coward and that I wanted to go back. My mother talked to me with her usual gentleness and good common sense, and she also explained that as a Jew I was no longer wanted there. As young as I was I understood completely.

My cousins who lived in a different part of Berlin were enrolled at a private Jewish day school, and my well-to-do uncle saw to it that I could go there too. It was not a school that offered a religious education, but rather a broad curriculum including modern Hebrew and modern Jewish history.

This wonderful school was like an oasis in a world gone crazy. In spite of the terrible times and the ever intensifying anti-Semitism, my school friends and I felt safe in a beautiful setting in the famous "Grunewald" (Green Woods) in Berlin. We had our own outdoor swimming pool, which was very rare in 1936.

Our peaceful existence was shattered in November 1938. You've heard about Kristallnacht? The Night of Broken Glass. It happened on the 10th of November. All Jewish stores were attacked by Nazi gangs, shop windows were broken, furniture was smashed and graffiti was painted on walls with slogans: Jews Get Out!

However, the worst was the knock on the door at night: the Secret Police came to pick up Jewish men to take them away to concentration camps. There were not yet extermination camps, but they were brutal and horrible in their own way.

My own father was spared such a terrible fate. The Nazis knew that we were Swiss and for some reason they respected the Swiss consul's request not to touch Swiss citizens. My father's business was not destroyed, although he had to close it soon afterward.

My friends' fathers were not so lucky. Many disappeared on November 10. Some came back after a few months, some did not. The same applied to our beloved teachers at the school. Most of them were young, not even 40 yet, but also some of the older teachers were arrested. Our most popular teacher never returned. This was the beginning of the end for the Jews in Berlin and all over Germany.

Although we were young teenagers at the time, we became adults overnight. Nobody could hide the terrible truth from us. Any family or individual who was unable to leave Germany would be doomed. No other country was eager to offer us refuge and that included the United States. Everyone wanted to go to America but only those who had relatives there and could provide an affidavit had a chance. The only hope for children whose parents could not get out was to join a "Kindertransport" to England or to Palestine—and many did. They left without their parents. Before and after Kristallnacht we had clung to each other as friends do when in danger.

Many years after the war when we had a wonderful reunion in New York, we realized that all of us who had survived would be friends for the rest of our lives. But, of course, many had died.

Again, my own family, protected by our Swiss citizenship, had a place to go: back to Switzerland.

We stayed in Berlin until the end of July 1939. The reason was that my uncle, who helped my father in 1927 to come to Berlin, was now hiding in our apartment. He had not been arrested on Kristallnacht, but now the Gestapo was after him.

The dreaded knock during the night never came to our apartment, and my uncle was able to flee to Holland and from there to England.

In looking back, it is hard to grasp that we lived in Berlin during these terrible times and found our way back to Switzerland where we were safe during World War II and were able to start life anew.

David Gil

Born 1924 · Vienna, Austria

David Gill, 2010, Lexington, MA.

Born in Vienna in 1924, David Gil fled to Sweden and to Palestine after Hitler occupied Austria in 1938. He attended Allenta High School in Vienna. When he visited Vienna in 2013, there was a tablet on the wall of the school commemorating the children and teachers who had been forced out of the school in 1938 when Hitler occupied Vienna. In Palestine, he was employed in a home for neglected children and later on as a youth probation officer with the governments of Palestine and Israel. In 1947, he married Eva, a colleague at work, with whom he had twin sons. In 1953, he received a United Nations Scholarship to study at the University of Pennsylvania, School of Social Work. After graduating, he returned to Israel where he became deputy director of the Youth Probation Service and also studied sociology and education at the Hebrew University in Jerusalem. The family immigrated to the United States and settled in Philadelphia in 1957, where David worked in social services and studied for his doctorate at the University of Pennsylvania. After graduating in 1963, he conducted research for the Massachusetts Society for the Prevention of Cruelty to Children (MSPCC). In 1964, he joined the faculty of the Heller Graduate School of Brandeis University to develop a child welfare training program, funded by the U.S. Children's Bureau. He taught social policy and published scholarly books and papers until retiring in 2010. While teaching at Brandeis, he traveled to Africa and Asia, visiting students and lecturing at universities. He and his wife moved to Brookhaven in Lexington in 2007.

My War Expriences:
World War II and Israel-Arab Wars

By David Gil

> "Gradually, an issue took hold of my mind that eventually became a key motive of my life and work: How can the painful experiences of my family, and many others, be prevented in the future? Struggling with this issue, I concluded that violent retribution against Germany would not prevent vicious cycles of mutual destruction. "

I WAS NEARLY 14 years old when Vienna, the city of my childhood, was occupied by Hitler's Germany, in March 1938. My father was soon interned in a concentration camp and his business, our livelihood, was expropriated. It was also the end of my formal education. My mother succeeded to arrange for my escape to Sweden with a group of refugee children. We lived in a children's home in a rural area north of Malmö, and each boy was assigned to a farm, to be trained in agricultural work. My main job on the farm was to take care of a herd of cows. I felt sad and unhappy, being separated from my family, worrying about them and not knowing whether I would ever see them again.

Working with the cows had also positive aspects. Cows are pleasant and peaceful animals. The setting was quiet and I could lose myself in thoughts. Gradually, an issue took hold of my mind that eventually became a key motive of my life and work: How can the painful experiences of my family, and many others, be prevented in the future? Struggling with this issue, I concluded that violent retribution against Germany would not prevent vicious cycles of mutual destruction. Subjecting German people and their children to destructive experiences would be as tragic as my and my family's situation and would solve nothing. It would not liberate humanity from perpetual mutual destruction.

While searching for constructive answers, I happened to read a biography of Mahatma Gandhi. Gandhi's philosophy of active nonviolence offered an alternative approach to deal with the curse of perpetual conflicts and warfare, and I became an adherent of Gandhi's teachings just as Germany started World War II in September 1939. I joined the War Resisters' International and became a conscientious objector.

Early during the war, in 1940, I immigrated to Palestine. That country was then governed by Great Britain with the conflicting goals and promises to establish a Jewish national home and an independent Arab country. The Jews in Palestine joined with Great Britain in the war and mobilized their young men into Jewish armed forces or the British army. When I refused to join the Jewish underground forces or the British army, I was unable to get civilian employment but was able to work as a volunteer in a home for neglected children.

As the conflict between Jews and Arabs intensified throughout and after World War II, I joined a peace movement around the Hebrew University philosopher Martin Buber. Our movement opposed the division of Palestine into separate Jewish and Arab countries. We urged Great Britain and the United Nations to establish a binational Jewish/Arab Commonwealth. Our proposal failed to gain adequate support from Jews and Arabs, and on May 14, 1948, Palestine was divided by the United Nations into Israel and an Arab country. The establishment of Israel was immediately followed by the first of several wars between Jews and Arabs.

Israel mobilized its armed forces to defend its newly won statehood. All men had to serve in the army, and when I refused to be drafted as a CO, I was briefly imprisoned. Eventually, I was permitted to do alternative service as a social worker for soldiers' families. I left Israel for the United States in the 1950s because of opposition to the politics of Israel and the occupation of the Palestinian territories and the domination of their people. I continue

A Memory

For Charles

By Florence Wallach Freed

In memory of My Dear Husband, Charles Freed (1926–2010), who managed to survive World War II. Charles eventually became a senior scientist at MIT's Lincoln Lab, where he did award-winning research on the development of lasers.

This photograph of my husband, Charles Freed, was taken in 1999 when Charles was 53 years old. He was senior research scientist at MIT's Lincoln Laboratory at Hanscom Field, Bedford, Massachusetts. That year he received an award from the Institute of Electrical and Electronic Engineers (IEEE) for his "pioneering development of ultrastable lasers." He built and did research on lasers for almost his entire career. He loved America very much after all he had suffered in Hungary and Russia.

You're a curious boy
taking clocks apart
building bridges and cranes
with your cherished Erector set—
kicking the soccer ball
diving from the high-board
with your arms spread out
like an eagle's wings—
getting excellent grades—

munching cherry pastries.....
But, on your eighteenth birthday
March 21, 1944,
the Nazis invade Hungary—
enter Miskolc, your town,
where you are wearing
a yellow star which
your mother, Ernestine,
sewed with shaking fingers
onto your woolen jacket.....
Eichmann's hornets swarm
stinging the life
out of the Jews—
almost a half million
stuffed into ghettos
tortured in jails
shot into the Danube
frozen in forced labor
transported to Auschwitz
in filthy cattle cars.....
You are captured
first by the Nazis,
next by the Communists
advancing from the East
and forced to march
to a Russian Prison Camp
in Zaporozhya where
you starve and freeze
for three and a half years
dragging away bombed out

war rubble.....
The best meal you ever get
consists of roasted crows
which your ragged guards
shoot out of the trees—
usually you get watery beet soup,
a raw onion, a hunk of bread—
you shrink down to sixty-six pounds—
lying on the dirt floor
picking off the crawling lice
you imagine running into
the electric fence.....
Your father, Ernest, perishes there—
is buried under the snow
without prayers or tombstone—
you and your brother, George,
manage to survive and are
returned to Hungary in 1947
in a prisoners-of-war deal—
you learn that your Mother,
Grandparents, Aunts, Uncles and
all the Little Cousins were
part of Hitler's final solution—
gassed in Auschwitz.....
Now the Fascists are out
but the Communists are in—
you escape illegally to Vienna
and contact your Uncle
your Mother's Brother,
Dr. Leo Duschnitz, in Manhattan

who gets the necessary papers—
and finally, you arrive, finally—
in America, America, in 1949.....
Over forty years later
missing faces flicker
in the glowing candles
Ernest...Ernestine...
and all The Others
snuffed out too soon—
your seven-layered
chocolate birthday cake
can never really
taste sweet.....

Kathryn McCarthy

Born 1924 · Andover, Massachusetts

Kathryn McCarthy, newly appointed provost of Tufts University, fall 1971 in front of Ballon Hall, Tufts University, Medford, Massachusetts.

Kathryn McCarthy was born in 1924 in Andover, Massachusetts. Her parents were Joseph and Catherine McCarthy. She grew up in Andover and graduated from Punchaid High School (later Andover High School). She then enrolled in Jackson College (then the women's college at Tufts University, Medford, Massachusetts), majoring in math. She worked at Baird Atomic as a mathematician from 1946 to 1953. While at Baird, she fell in love with physics and left Baird to study applied physics at Tufts University, earning a master's degree. She received her PhD in applied engineering and physics from Harvard University in 1957. Her fields of research were light transmitting and sound transmitting. To participate in the Harvard Graduate Program, she was required to register at Radcliffe. From Harvard she went to Tufts University as an associate professor of physics. She was dean of the graduate school at Tufts for two years, then in 1970 she was named provost for Tufts University and became a senior vice president of Tufts for eight years. She retired in 1999.

War

By Kathryn McCarthy

> "We taught these students knowing they were going
> to war. Maybe war would go away....One of my Navy
> mathstudents died in the North Atlantic....A second
> student was killed in the South Pacific....A third [who chose
> to remain in the service] died in Vietnam."

MUCH OF MY professional career was spent at Tufts University, Medford, Massachusetts. During World War II the University had 2,000 U.S. Navy ROTC (Reserve Army Training Corps) students (some V-12) on the Medford campus. There were many students who had been English literature and humanities majors but needed good grades in mathematics in order to be commissioned. I was a laboratory assistant at the time, and the Navy needed tutors for those who could not pass the navy arithmetic requirements. I was asked by Tufts to tutor one group of these students. There were about 15 in the group.

Teaching them was like teaching sophomore and junior students. Have you ever taught? When you teach in college the freshman are not yet focused on what they are doing and the seniors are thinking beyond graduation. When students are eager to be taught, as sophomores and juniors are, there is a kind of a love and eagerness on their part—they want to be taught—and you want to be a good teacher. These Navy men were that kind; their majors were humanities and they wanted to learn.

We taught these students knowing they were going to war. Maybe war would go away? Not so quickly! As we were moving toward the end of the war and my students had been commissioned, would the war be over before they could come to harm?

Kathryn A. McCarthy, June 1930, at home in Andover, Massacusetts.

In one of the summers during the Korean War, I was hired by a company in Cambridge, Massachusetts, to work on optic physics problems. The results of our work were war connected. Optical sites on rifles were developed so that our troops could put light on the enemy, but the enemy did not know there was a light on them. Again, I realized my work was supporting military efforts and contributing to a war.

Later on, as the United States moved to the war in Vietnam, we knew Russian rifles used by the Vietnamese had the same optical devices so that their rifles were as good as the American rifles in their sighting capabilities, letting soldiers on both sides kill each other more effectively. After World War II the United States became a world superpower. With such efficient weapons American leaders had come to believe war was the answer for settling disputes and no longer depended on diplomacy.

During the most of the Vietnam War, I was not in war work and was back on the campus at Tufts. During those years the American public seriously divided about the decisions for war our leaders were making. Students on campus could not understand why their government was involved in this war, and began to speak. They stopped going to classes and barely thought about their studies. Many students used campus unrest as a chance to completely neglect their studies. SDS (Students for a Democratic Society) became the largest "fraternity" on U.S. campuses. Many people remember the riots on campuses that threatened the basic purposes of a university. The front pages of American newspapers reported student unrest across the county. There was great anger across the country. By going to college, students learned more about their country's inability to settle disputes peacefully than they learned about academic subjects.

When the Vietnam War was over in the mid '70s, the Tufts president unveiled a plaque listing students who had died in World War II, Korea and Vietnam. One of my Navy math students died in the North Atlantic when his ship was attacked. A second student was killed in the South Pacific. A third Navy alumnus of my group chose to be a career Marine Corps officer. He died in Vietnam. When I read their names on the plaque, I thought, they wouldn't have been there without the wars.

World War II Timeline

1933   Hitler takes power and begins to expand his German Empire in Europe. Persecution of Jews begins.

1937   Japan invades China.

1938   *September*—Germany demands the Sudetenland, a part of Czechoslovakia.

Neville Chamberlain travels to Germany attempting to appease Hitler.

November—"Kristallnacht," Night of Broken Glass; 1,350 Jewish synagogues burned, 97 Jews killed.

30,000 Jews put into concentration camps; 70,000 Jewish businesses destroyed.

1939   *September*—Germany invades Poland.

September—Great Britain and France declare war on Germany, followed by Australia, Canada and most of the British Commonwealth countries.

United States declares its neutrality.

1939–40   "Blitzkriegs" (lightning wars) enable Hitler to overcome Belgium, Denmark, France, Holland, and Norway.

Finland falls to the Soviet Union, along with Latvia, Lithuania and Estonia.

1940   Germany bombs industrial and civilian targets in Britain.

1941   *December 7*—Japan bombs Pearl Harbor, destroying much of the United States Pacific fleet.

December 8—The United States declares war on Japan.

December 11—The United States declares war on Germany, Italy and other Axis countries.

1942 The United States mobilizes for war, converting factories to build planes and ships, drafts men into the service, organizes auxiliary services for women.

Japan attacks U.S. ships and Pacific islands.

Nazis begin mass extermination of Jews at death camps.

March—Internment of Japanese Americans begins.

June 4–6—Battle of Midway; U.S. Navy defeats Japanese navy.

August 7—Marine invasion of Guadalcanal.

United States bombers attack Japanese-occupied territory, flying the Hump over the Himalayas from India.

Fall—British and American victories in North Africa.

1943 Allied forces invade Sicily, southern Italy; Italy surrenders.

1944 *June 6*—D-Day. Allies begin major invasion of France at Normandy.

United States invades Guam and the Philippines.

August 25—Paris is liberated.

December 16—German counter-offensive "Battle of the Bulge" begins in Ardennes Forest near German-Belgian border.

1945 United States forces invade Iwo Jima (February); Okinawa (April).

April 30—Hitler commits suicide.

May 8—V–E Day. War in Europe ends; Germany unconditionally surrenders.

August—The United States drops nuclear bombs on the Japanese cities of Hiroshima (August 6) and Nagasaki (August 9).

August 14—V-J Day. Japan surrenders. World War II ends.

Acknowledgements

SO MANY PEOPLE contributed to this book—their memories, their ideas and their steady belief that Brookhaven residents have something to say about World War II. It was truly a team effort.

Following a suggestion from Heidi White, Joan Keenan and Kathryn McCarthy decided to explore the idea of publishing a book of residents' memories of World War Two. They organized a team to begin working on the idea including George Hanford, Bob Kingston, Margo Lindsay, Dick McAdoo, Lynne Romboli, Ben Wright, Nancy Hubert, and themselves. This team worked on locating articles and deciding on length and formatting. They also did early proofreading and fact checking. Diana Bailey helped enter stories into the computer. Vivian Berman helped with suggestions for the cover design. Bob Kingston was our computer "guru." He turned our computer documents into publications format, scanned documents and pictures, and tracked our stories as we gathered biographies, pictures and updated versions of orginal stories. Many others at Brookhaven helped in various ways. We especially thank all the residents who contributed stories.

The staff at Brookhaven has been patient and always helpful. Jim Freehling, CEO/President at Brookhaven applied to the Dana Home Foundation for the very welcome monetary award the Brookhaven book project received. He has taken the lead in helping with the project in so many ways. Sue Kirkpatrick, EVP/COO for Brookhaven helped locate essential data, collected permissions from contributors to the book and dealt with contract issues. Laura Anderson, Director of Community Living, probably did more than her fair share as she helped assemble biographies, pictures and other data for the book. She came late to our project but was quickly up to speed and so helpful.

We also had lots of help from people outside Brookhaven. The monetary award from the Dana Home Foundation was invaluable and Brookhaven is especially grateful to them for their help and belief in our project.

Last, but certainly not least, Brookhaven is forever indebted to Michael Bentley and his company Bentley Publishers. Michael donated the services of his company and his employees who helped us get the book together. Michael's advice about the ins and outs of publishing, titles, formatting and other book details were helpful and valuable. Janet Barnes, Director of Publishing, and Andrea Corbin, Production Coordinator were knowledgeable, easy to work with, and made our job much easier. Many thanks to all three of them.

Nancy L. Hubert, Editor

Index

List of Contributors

Alphabetical by last name

———

Cover photographs:

1. 1945. **Philip Lane**, third from the left, with members of the 10th Armored Division, on occupation in the Garmish-Partenkirchen area. (Ellie Lane, page 60)

2. **Liz Toupin** in her senior prom dress, 1943, Hawaii. (Liz Toupin, page 262)

3. Officers of **Jack Roberts**' WWII plane: from left to right: Joe Buehler, navigator; Roger Weum, copilot; Jack Roberts, bombardier; Ray Armour, pilot. Photo taken in London, England. (John R. Roberts Jr., page 90)

4. **Miriam McCue** in her Navy uniform ready to ride in the 50th Anniversary of World War II parade in Lexington, Massachusetts, 1994. (Miriam McCue, page 152)

5. Cologne, Germany, Cathedral in ruins. (Heidi White, page 14)

6. **Susan Haller** with two girl scout friends, "Sojo," "Gipsy," and "Loyos," taken on an outing in Switzerland in 1941. (Susan Haller, page 30)

7. **William Pounds** with his Grumman Cougar (F9F8), 1953, Oceana, Virginia. (William Pounds, page 362)

8. In the winter of 1945–46 **Mary Stewart** and U.S.M.A. cadet Frederick L. Hafer were beginning to think seriously about marriage. (Mary Hafer, page 198)

9. **Samuel Berman** in a B-25 airplane. Taken by the Army for hometown newspaper. (Samuel Berman, page 94)